IN THE COURTS OF THE LORD

IN THE COURTS OF THE LORD

JAMES FERRY

FOREWORD BY THE RT. REV. JOHN S. SPONG,
BISHOP OF NEWARK, NEW JERSEY

KEY PORTER·BOOKS

Canadian Cataloguing Publishing Data
Ferry, James
In the courts of the Lord: a gay minister's story

ISBN 1-55013-472-8 hardcover
        1-55013-494-9 paperback

1. Ferry, James. 2. Anglican Church of Canada - Clergy - Biography.
3. Gay clergy - Ontario - Unionville - Biography. 4. Anglican Church of
Canada - Discipline. 5. Homosexuality - Religious aspects - Anglican
Church of Canada. I. Title.
BX5620.F47A3 1993   283'.092   C92-095705-6

Key Porter Books Limited
70 The Esplanade
Toronto, Ontario
Canada M5E 1R2

The publisher gratefully acknowledges the assistance of the Canada
Council and the Ontario Arts Council.

Printed and bound in Canada

93 94 95 96 97 6 5 4 3 2 1

CONTENTS

TO MY BELOVED AHMAD

Psalm 84

How dear to me is your dwelling, O Lord of hosts!
  My soul has a desire and longing for the courts of the Lord;
  my heart and my flesh rejoice in the living God.
The sparrow has found her a house
and the swallow a nest where she may lay her young;
  by the side of your altars, O Lord of hosts,
  my King and my God.
Happy are they who dwell in your house!
  they will always be praising you.
Happy are the people whose strength is in you!
  whose hearts are set on the pilgrims' way.
Those who go through the desolate valley will find it a place of springs,
  for the early rains have covered it with pools of water.
They will climb from height to height,
  and the God of gods will reveal himself in Zion.
Lord God of hosts, hear my prayer;
  hearken, O God of Jacob.
Behold our defender, O God;
  and look upon the face of your anointed.
For one day in your courts is better than a thousand in my own room,
  and to stand at the threshold of the house of my God
  than to dwell in the tents of the wicked.
For the Lord God is both sun and shield;
  he will give grace and glory;
No good thing will the Lord withhold
  from those who walk with integrity.
O Lord of hosts,
  happy are they who put their trust in you!

From the Book of Common Prayer 1975 of the Episcopal Church of the United States of America

FOREWORD

THIS BOOK BECAME POSSIBLE when representatives of the Christian Church determined that being honest and loving another human being were not virtues that the Church was willing to support. Such a strange twist on the traditional religious understandings could only occur where prejudice was operating so deeply as to distort rationality.

No prejudice is more alive and well in Christian circles today than the prejudice against gay and lesbian persons. In the service of that prejudice within the Church, honesty is frequently punished and dishonesty is clearly rewarded; stable, loving relationships are rejected and, unwittingly, furtive and promiscuous relationships are thereby encouraged. It is a picture of the Christian Church at its worst, being confused, distorted, and unreal, but it is nonetheless a picture that emerges when the issue of homosexuality confronts an institution in which that particular prejudice is still in power.

James Ferry was and is a competent and loving priest. He is also deeply committed to Jesus as both Lord and Christ. He has, in his priestly career, demonstrated substantial skills. He has shown the power to energize congregations, to inject hope, to provide loving and life-giving pastoral care, and even to be loyal to and supportive of the ecclesiastical hierarchy of the Church he served.

Yet during his eleven years of effective service to the Church as an ordained person, James Ferry was struggling in loneliness to come to a level of self-acceptance in regard to his own sexual orientation. The Church received willingly and even joyfully his talents, but he knew even then that the Church did not and would not accept his being. Both his Church and the society in which he lived proclaimed by word and deed that to be what he knew himself to be was evil, sick, and depraved. He tried to be faithful even to that judgement by denying his own being. He prayed for God to change him or cure him. He repressed his own desires. He even got married, in order to prove to himself and to others that he was "normal and straight."

When these mighty efforts failed him, James Ferry began the slow and tortuous task of "coming out"—first just to himself alone. He sought to find his own identity. He began to allow himself to feel and experience things he had always before denied. He read both the findings of the scientific community and the personal stories of those who, like himself, had experienced an awakening to the discovery of their own homosexuality. Slowly, painfully, he began to allow himself to follow his heart and dare to love those to whom his deepest affections were directed.

But this honesty brought him into direct confrontation with the Church that had ordained him and in whose service his life was dedicated. Conflicts which once had been limited to his own interior life began to move outward into his external world. The more honest James Ferry became about himself, the more dishonest he found the Christian Church and its leadership to be. Some ecclesiastical figures, he discovered, winked knowingly at his reality and stated through their deeds the values by which they had learned to live: "It is okay to be a homosexual person privately, as long as you do not admit it or express it publicly." This was and is the long-standing ecclesiastical position that has been enshrined as the standard of ethics that guides at least a part of the Church's leadership.

Other ecclesiastical figures, including some in high places who were themselves gay, tried to use their positions of power to force their sexual attentions onto this priest. They could have been charged with sexual harassment but the price to the one bringing such a charge simply would have been too high. Still others in the hierarchy resorted to a form of blackmail—playing on the high level of public prejudice against homosexual persons to expose and ruin the professional career of this priest, if he dared to be himself. This was especially true when this priest sought to express his wholeness and love in the same way that heterosexual people do—namely by living faithfully with the one mutually chosen to be his life partner. No one in Church leadership seemed willing to accept this priest's very being as a gay man who wanted to be honest and who did not believe that he was called to the loneliness of celibacy. His vocation as a priest and the natural homosexual desires of his life were thought by his Church to be completely incompatible.

Finally, unable to resolve this conflict by himself, this priest decided to trust his bishop by sharing with him the truth of his life. The result was a tragic commentary on ecclesiastical integrity. The bishop, feeling the need to uphold the good order of the Church and to abide by recommendations that he interpreted as binding rules, then acted to dismiss this priest from his position and inhibited him from practising his priesthood. Finally, the bishop put him on trial for "disobeying his bishop." It was a technically correct charge, for the bishop had ordered him to leave his partner or the priesthood. This priest refused to do either. It was, however, a charge that in no way spoke to the profound issues that this priest's life raised for the Church.

The ecclesiastical hierarchy gathered around the offending bishop to protect the institutional needs of the Church from the erosion of public confidence. Not one Canadian Anglican bishop would testify on James Ferry's behalf — not even those who themselves had knowingly ordained gay candidates to the priesthood. Insight into the way institutional religion functions became blatantly apparent. In the Church bishops and priests who are homosexual and dishonest continue to serve, while those who are homosexual and honest are removed. Bishops and priests whose capacity to be righteous and judgemental far exceeds their capacity to be loving and life-giving achieve high position and public honour, while loving, whole life-giving gay priests are dismissed. Prejudice is an enormously powerful emotion. Even within Church circles prejudice creates the capacity to proclaim that honesty and love are vices that must be punished in order to save institutional prejudice, institutional power, and institutional good order.

James Ferry tells his story gently and cogently. He is remarkably free of anger, despite the abuse he has absorbed. He loves his Christ and the Church and he yearns to serve both with the passion of his commitment and the integrity of his being. He asks only that his Church might bless him, accepting him as one created in God's image, loved infinitely by Christ, and called into the fullness of life by God's Holy Spirit. James Ferry knows that gay and lesbian clergy serve every part of the Christian Church in significant number. He knows that some of those clergy protect their closets by vicious public attacks on the "evils of homosexuality." He believes that honesty and a love that is faithful and committed must be held up as virtues in the life of the Church in both homosexual and heterosexual worlds.

So here we have James Ferry's story. It is simple yet powerful. It is both profound and moving, honest and loving. Like the patriarch Jacob of old, James Ferry will not let go of the divine power that the Church represents and with which he wrestles until and unless it blesses him—and bless him the Church ultimately will do. When the history of the Anglican Church of Canada is written, James Ferry will be a chapter where grace is celebrated, and his accusers and judges will be minor footnotes unworthy of much time or space. They will be seen as people who had a chance to make a difference in their generation but who ducked the opportunity in order to preserve their position and prestige.

I did not know James Ferry until the day he called to ask me if I, as an American Anglican bishop, would testify at his trial. "How can I testify on behalf of one I have never met?" I asked. "I am not the issue," he reminded me. "I am just a symbol of the issue. You can share your experience of gay and lesbian clergy who have, within the atmosphere you have helped to create in your diocese, been able to live openly as Christian priests and still to serve effectively." It is, in fact, an experience that I do possess and of which I am enormously proud. Ten of the priests in the Diocese of Newark are openly gay or lesbian. They are fully out of the closet. Most live in covenanted relationships and they all serve with competence and rare integrity.

So I accepted his invitation, flew to Toronto, and testified. In that way I became part of James Ferry's story and my life has been blessed by his friendship. He stands as a beacon of light, asking the

Church to live out what the Church says it believes. He speaks as a representative for gay and lesbian clergy and laity in every Christian tradition who serve the Church faithfully and well, but who cannot and will not be honest about who they are. James Ferry has given a voice to these voiceless ones and is himself a visible incarnation of their invisible presence.

Perhaps this book will call the Church to reach out to its gay and lesbian sons and daughters, to confess our role in their oppression, and to open wide the doors of our ecclesiastical welcome. We Christians do continue to call ourselves the "body of Christ." As the body of Christ it is our vocation to live out the life of Christ, to embrace all whom Christ would embrace. When we fail to do that the body of Christ is wounded. If that failure is not addressed, the body of Christ dies. James Ferry places the choice of life or death before the Church and pleads with that sometimes battered but occasionally noble institution to choose life.

Pray God that we will hear this message and make that choice and, in the process, recover our integrity and our ability to be the body of Christ at the dawn of the twenty-first century.

The Rt. Rev. John S. Spong,
Bishop of Newark, New Jersey

PREFACE

W OULDN'T GIVE UP GAY LOVER, PRIEST FIRED. GAY REV. GIVES UP
CHURCH FOR LOVER. Until the story hit the media, I was just
another Anglican minister, doing the enjoyable and challenging work
in the Church he loved. I was also a gay man, trying to remain both
in a loving relationship with a man and in the Church.

When I refused, in July 1991, to choose between the two loves
of my life, I found myself thrust onto the international stage by a
bizarre sequence of events. After firing me for refusing to give up
the man I loved, the Bishop of Toronto issued a press release, without telling me, that bared my private life to the media.

Caught up in a web of political intrigue, I found myself at the
centre of a series of chain-reactions, culminating in my public trial in
a Bishop's Court in February 1992 for refusing to obey my bishop's
instructions to give up my relationship.

In the end, in a bizarre twist, the Bishop's Court found me not
guilty of disobedience since the bishop had never in fact instructed
me to give up my relationship, but guilty of wrongdoing for refusing
to give it up. The bishop issued a severe sentence, stripping me of
my licence to function as a priest. Unemployed, and effectively barred
from employment anywhere in the Church, I have become a very public person. In the process, I lost the man I loved.

◆

When I first decided to write this book, it was going to be about
gays in the Church, with a large section detailing my trial in Bishop's
Court. The story of Jim Ferry was to serve as a paradigm of how the
Church treats its gay and lesbian members, cloaking our existence in
a painful conspiracy of silence. My editors wanted more than that: they
thought the public should know about the person behind the issue.
As I began to write, the book evolved into a very personal story, more
personal than I had originally intended. But the treatment of gays

and lesbians in the Church and in society is not just an abstract issue, it is about real flesh-and-blood, people like me.

I have written about my early life not because I think it unusual or interesting, but precisely because it is not. My story is, I think, typical of those of many millions of gays and lesbians around the world. We are born into ordinary families, and lead normal lives, except in one respect: as we grow up we discover we are gay, not straight. The story of my struggle to learn to accept and love myself as a gay man is, in a sense, the story of every gay person. It is my hope that in coming to know a little about one gay man, readers will be more open to the gays and lesbians in their own lives. We are not wild, exotic, or dangerous creatures — I hope the ordinary goodness of most of our lives is self-evident.

My love for the Church family will, I hope, also become apparent. I wanted to write about daily life in the Church, in good times and in bad; what it's like for any minister, gay or straight, to strive and assist others to strive to find ways to live with "a love that knows no boundaries." That central message has been a healing and energizing force in my life, and often, in spite of the Church's failings, has had a powerful effect on the lives of countless others.

Inherited prejudices of ancient societies have been successfully challenged by the Church in recent years; barriers of prejudice against women, divorced persons, and people of colour have been broken down. But one barrier remains: prejudice against gays. My Church claims as its mission "to embody — in word and action — God's reconciling love, justice, compassion and liberation" and "to respect the dignity of every human being," all the while denying gay people the joy of love and intimacy with one special other.

The Church's adherence to this sexual double standard must come to an end if it is to have anything at all to say to society at large. In this book — as in my initial refusal to resign or to give up the person I loved, followed by my decision to submit to a public trial in a Bishop's Court — I have one paramount purpose: to hold the Church accountable to its own message.

The letters I have received from around the world indicate that many people have been moved by my struggle. It is the struggle of every gay man and lesbian for equal dignity and treatment, but, more than that, it is the universal struggle of all human beings who long to be loved and accepted as they are.

A NOTE TO THE READER

Many, but not all, of the events in this book are a matter of public record. I have changed the names and circumstances of some persons to protect their privacy.

ACKNOWLEDGEMENTS

I AM DEEPLY INDEBTED TO the many hundreds of people who wrote and telephoned, offering their support, after I was fired by my bishop. It was their overwhelming concern that moved me beyond my personal suffering to a recognition of the historic moment in which I was caught up, and gave me courage for the long and public struggle this book recounts.

I never dreamed of writing a book, but when Garry Lovatt, a friend and former publisher, first raised the idea, I knew I had to do it. Then came the additional encouragement of John Shelby Spong, Bishop of Newark and author of many books, who offered to read and make comments on the manuscript. I greatly appreciate the friendship and support of these two remarkable people who came into my life in the months following July 1991. Of course, without the vision of the people at Key Porter Books who took the risk of signing up an untested, first-time author, this book would never have come to fruition. My thanks go out to them; to my agent, Lee Davis Creal; and to my editor, David Kilgour, who kept me on track.

There are too many people deserving of thanks for their loving support in the past year and a half to mention all of them: friends old and new; parishioners from St. Saviour's, Toronto, and St. Philip's on-the-hill, Unionville; my friends at Integrity Toronto, Kingston, and Vancouver, as well as Integrity U.S.; my friends at Kirkridge Retreat Center in Pennsylvania, and John McNeill and Virginia Mollenkott, who lead the annual retreat for lesbian and gay Christians there; the support group that quickly formed to give me moral and practical support; my friends at Metropolitan Community Church of Toronto and Christos M.C.C.; my hard-working fundraising committee; the more than six hundred people who generously donated to my defence fund; the justice-seeking people of the Church of the Holy Trinity, Toronto; and the congregation of Church of the

Redeemer, Toronto, who made a welcome space for me.

My family has been unflagging in their love and support: my father, Victor; my brother Tom; and my sister, Jill, along with her husband, Steve. Bless you.

I thank my witnesses in Bishop's Court for a job well done, sometimes at considerable personal risk: James Reed, Cyril Powles, Bradley Lennon, Douglas Fox, Rosemary Barnes, Walter Stewart, Darrell Briggs, Jack Fricker, David Norgard, John Whittall, and John Spong. They helped provoke the conscience of a Church and a nation.

Finally, I give my deepest thanks to my lawyer Valerie Edwards, and her assistants Paula Dadd and Cathy Milne; their efforts on my behalf far surpassed the requirements of a solicitor/client relationship. Through those efforts, the day when there is no prejudice against gays and lesbians will come sooner.

CHAPTER 1

MY FAITH AND MY SEXUALITY both go back as far as I can remember. I grew up in a working-class neighbourhood of strawberry-box bungalows in Agincourt, a suburb of Toronto. Born in 1952, I was part of an ideal 1950s family: a father who worked long hours (as a technical producer at a TV station); a mother who stayed home; two older brothers, Ric and Tom; and a younger sister, Jill. We were a typical suburban WASP family — a little strict, perhaps, and uncommunicative, but loving.

Like many gays, I felt different from the beginning. It wasn't just a matter of being unathletic and bookish; it went far deeper. Looking back, years later, I might identify it as my gay temperament, something I was aware of but couldn't describe, a different way of relating to the world and to people. The other children sensed that I was different too, intuiting in a way that disappears with adulthood, as individuals learn to guard more carefully their inner thought-world. A gentle, sensitive boy, I was teased mercilessly by the school bullies, who had a field-day with my differentness. My family name didn't help. "Tinkerbell!" "Fairy godmother!" "Ferryboat, toot, toot!" "Pansy!" — the permutations seemed endless. Ignorant of the sexual connotations of the slurs, I still knew that I was different. Unable to form important friendships with my peers for most of my childhood, I related to the adult world instead. I became very good at pleasing my teachers.

In early childhood I discovered one place where I felt really loved and accepted: the Church. The pre-kindergarten room in the local United church my family attended was bright and filled with music. The big windows at ground level looked out on an old cemetery, a vision of green trees and grass, set against a blue sky. My most vivid memory is of spring. As the teacher played, we sat around the piano, singing:

1

God sees the little sparrow fall
it meets his tender view;
If God so loves the little birds
I know he loves me too.

Simple children's hymns had a profound impact on me. I felt safe and secure with a God who loved even the little birds outside the window. Although the neighbourhood children seemed to dislike me, throughout my childhood I sensed that God was there for me. I loved singing hymns and hearing stories of Jesus. They formed a tightly woven fabric of love for me.

It was not until I reached puberty at age eleven that I began to realize just how I was different. While the other boys were talking about girls and sex, I was thinking about *them* and sex. It was a deep, dark secret that drove me even farther into the private world of my own thoughts and feelings. I thought that I was all alone, that I was the only one with these shameful sexual urges. When I began to realize the meaning of "faggot" and "queer," it only increased my sense of isolation. Nowhere did I see anything but standard nuclear-family models for life and sexuality: a mom and a dad with three or four kids. While my parents' relationship may not have been ideal, it conformed to the general image of what was "normal." With a life image deeply ingrained in me by both family and cultural stereotypes, as a child I had expected that, in the normal course of things, I would fall in love with a woman, get married, have children, and form the only kind of family I had ever known.

With the onset of puberty I began a painful spiral of denial, repression, secrecy, efforts to change, failures, anger, depression, bargaining with God or science, self-hate, and mourning, with occasional glimpses of acceptance. Coming to terms with being gay is like dealing with death or dying — in fact, the grieving process can be much longer and more painful because of the ambiguity of sexual issues. While death is inevitable for everyone, and must sooner or later be grieved by every human being, the gay child, taught to believe that everyone is made to be "normal," is the odd one out. The grief of that loss of identity and future must be endured in secret and solitude, for the gay child believes that no one could possibly understand. To give up the life image so deeply ingrained in childhood is more threatening than death itself for some gay teenagers, with the result that suicide is far more common among them than among heterosexual teens.

Death of the ideal self, the life image we are taught to treasure, involved many years of torment for me. I went through, again and again, all the stages of grief that Elisabeth Kübler-Ross described in her book *On Death and Dying*.

Because it became more and more important for me to conceal my real sexual feelings during my teen years, I outwardly played it "straight." I hoped that my gay feelings were just a passing adolescent phase. Nowhere back then, in the mid-1960s, could I see any adults or other teenagers who were gay. There were simply no positive role models for me to identify with. The occasional references to gay men made in the media or by the kids at school were accompanied by snickers or outright contempt. No way did I want to become one of *them*. And so I was torn with longing and dread, all the while trying to deny my true sexual feelings.

At the same time, my adolescence was a rich, sometimes very happy time for me. I enjoyed high school. New faces, new teachers, new activities, and no bullies: it was a whole new life. I discovered that my intellectual and musical abilities had a valued place in the classroom, and in the band and choir. For five years, my world expanded as I took part in concerts, school dances, musicals, and other activities, and made top grades. A part-time job at the local gas station gave me a measure of financial independence, and boosted my self-esteem. I learned to drive trucks and perform minor auto repairs. Since I was a bona fide grease monkey, my peers had no questions about my manliness.

At the age of sixteen, in a pique of teenage rebellion, I stopped attending church and youth group. The church was full of hypocrites, I thought. When they fired the beloved old minister I had grown up with, ostensibly because he was too old to relate to the young members of the congregation, it was the last straw. For a couple of years I took part in my friends' parties, experimenting occasionally with marijuana and alcohol.

In grade thirteen I discovered that my best friend was having the same sexual problem I was, only he didn't see it as a problem. There's a whole gay world out there, he assured me, and he was going to find it when he went off to university. He lent me the first gay magazines I saw, full of beautiful men in posing straps and bathing suits, and my heart pounded with desire. That had certainly not been my reaction when I leafed through my older brother's *Playboy* magazines.

Until that point I had managed to repress my gay feelings, and had briefly dated a girl. But I had always been attracted to the other boys at school, which carried with it a terrible sense of being all alone. It seemed that all the other boys had turned out "normal" and I thought it was only me who was different. I wanted to be like my peers, to fit in, to be accepted by society, but I felt I was a failure. It was with tremendous relief that my friend and I could share our secret, and know that we were not entirely alone. Still, I didn't act on my sexual urges.

My dream was to enter medical school, and with that in mind I began studies in sciences at the Scarborough campus of the University of Toronto. I had selected the suburban campus deliberately to avoid the gay life that I had heard was a part of the downtown campus. I was still too fearful of my secret self. With a summer job at a local tractor dealership, and living at home with my parents, I could pay my own way at university, buy my own clothes, and not be a burden on the family.

Try as I might to avoid my sexual reality, I couldn't. It seemed that all my college mates were pairing off in heterosexual couples, and I was more alone than ever. One day, in my introductory psychology course, the topic of homosexuality came up. Two young men from a gay organization came to speak to the class about being gay. Heart racing, I lingered after class, but I couldn't get up the nerve to speak to these exotic creatures, afraid that someone might think I, too, was gay. But it was the impetus I needed to make a decision: I called my high school friend and asked if he would take me to a place where I could meet some gay men.

My friend took me to a gay bar, where I met David. He was twenty-one; I was eighteen. We danced, my heart pounding to conflicting rhythms of fear and longing, and arranged to meet the following Saturday.

The date was a disaster. I'd had one thought in mind: to make love for the first time in my life. Never having experienced desire for a woman, yet fearing my attraction for men, I desperately wanted to know the truth about myself. David was sweet and thoughtful, but my anxiety was an impenetrable wall. What would my parents think? Would they be ashamed of their son? Would everyone think I was a pervert? When I left David that evening, my virginity was intact, but my heart was in torment.

◆

My first adventure in the gay world precipitated a crisis like none I had ever experienced. The conflict I was going through was making me physically ill. I wanted desperately to be straight, but no matter how much my culture, peers, family, and mind told me I should be attracted to women, I was still drawn to men. I made a conscious decision to deny my homosexual feelings, and that reduced the pain and anxiety for a while, but my heart was still in a state of siege. I hated myself, and wanted desperately to change, but realized I was powerless to do so.

It was in this besieged state that I had a spiritual awakening. An old friend who had been a classmate all through public school had become a Christian. Day after day she quietly shared her faith with me and a few others, and I became intrigued. She knew a singing group that played in local coffeehouses, and had fallen in love with one of the men. Would I like to go with her to a performance? With some nervousness I agreed.

It's hard to describe what happened that night in November 1971, but I know it was real. In the midst of my pain and self-hate I heard, as though for the first time, that there was one who loved me, completely and unconditionally. As simple as that revelation was, it reoriented my whole life. I became involved in a youth group in Agincourt with others who had also discovered the love of God. We studied the Bible voraciously, prayed together, and developed a wonderful sense of loving community unlike anything I had experienced. We agreed the members of the early Christian Church must have felt that same love.

As tremendous a formative experience as this newfound "church" was, it was, nonetheless, hostile to gay sexuality. God doesn't make anyone homosexual, I was told, and will cure anyone of those feelings if they love him. I swallowed it. I wanted to believe that God could fix me. I longed to be free of the feelings that made me so different, so lonely. For a time my denial worked. For half a year I dated a girl from my high school class. Our families wanted us to get married, but, despite this beautiful woman's physical charms and her sweet, caring, and passionate personality, I could not break free from the overwhelming physical attraction I felt to men. Maggie said she didn't care if I had a "problem," she loved me.

I wanted to give my whole self to this woman I loved, but I knew I couldn't. I was unable to live with myself, so how could I expect her to live with my secret? In tears, I broke off the relationship.

Attempting to bury the pain and self-loathing, I kept very busy with my university courses, and with the gospel group my Christian friends and I had formed. At church-basement coffeehouses, schools, and church services, we sang of the love and healing power of Jesus. But why wasn't Jesus healing me?

After a while, I broke down and shared my struggle with my mother. When she recovered from the initial shock and stopped crying, she told me that her best friend had recommended a pastor at a Baptist church who was a great counsellor. Why not see if he could help?

The pastor turned out to be very kind. He assured me that he knew all sorts of men who had been healed of homosexual urges. All I needed was prayer and a good attractive woman. I wanted to believe him so badly that I turned my problems over to God on the spot. After kneeling with me for prayer, he assured me that God was healing me, and that I would soon find the woman God had planned for me. I left his office with a tremendous sense of relief and hopefulness. Each Sunday morning for the next two years I would return to worship in my new pastor's church.

◆

My university courses in biology and psychology were, all the while, giving me fresh insights into the physical and mental make-up of human beings. Sexuality was a key component. I learned of the disagreement in the scientific world about the relative impacts of heredity and environment, about which had the most influence on human behaviour. The "biology" school would have me believe that genes play the major role in determining how people think and behave, whereas the "psychology" school said that it was mostly a matter of programming, dependent on the environment and an individual's experiences. Nature versus nurture.

As a young man with gay feelings in a straight world, I had a particular stake in the nature/nurture controversy. If my sexual orientation was genetically determined, then I might as well get used to being gay. If it was just a matter of programming, there was hope that I could change, given the right environment and experiences.

Same-gender sexual orientation is like left-handedness in the biological model. Both are innate, built into the genetic code of each newborn baby. At birth, it is not obvious whether a child is right- or left-handed, but as the weeks and months go by, and the baby begins to reach out to explore the world within arm's length, it becomes obvious which hand the child will use. Nature consigns a minority of people to left-handedness.

The environment model suggests that training and experience are the major determining factors: with proper conditioning, people can be trained to use their right hands. Rewards for using the right hand and punishment for using the left should suffice to produce right-handed humans.

The argument is similar for sexual orientation. The nature school would have me believe that being gay or straight is predetermined by an individual's genes, while the nurture school would say it's all a matter of programming and that, with appropriate rewards and punishments, the entire human race could turn out to be straight.

For a growing child, however, expressing who you are is not an issue for academic debate. Doing what seems to come naturally poses real problems for the left-handed child. The world is set up by and for right-handed people, and left-handed children learn that they are "different," that there is something "not right" about them. Even language is subtly against them, as they learn the difference between *right* and wrong, and learn that evil-minded people are *sinister* — the Latin word for "left." This attaching of moral value to simple human behaviours can have devastating consequences. At one time, it was common practice in our society to train left-handed children to use their right hands instead. In some cultures, left hands were tied down to force conformity, and in others you were considered jinxed if someone used his or her left hand in your presence.

Could it be the same with sexuality? I wondered. When I was born, my parents could not tell whether I would be gay or straight. Looking at me, they knew only that I was a baby. They assumed that I would grow up to be "normal" and someday produce grandchildren for their old age. According to the *nurture* model, the overwhelmingly heterosexual environment I grew up in, completely lacking in gay role models (let alone positive ones), should have ensured that I grew up straight. According to the *nature* model, sexual orientation was a given predisposition, so I might as well get used to being gay. My fundamentalist friends assured me that, by choosing God's way, I could be cured, healed, or reprogrammed and become a true, happy heterosexual. Through self-acceptance, the psychologists told me, I could become a happy, healthy gay man.

The decision of the American Psychiatric Association to remove homosexuality from its list of psychiatric disorders in 1972, in the midst of my studies, only added to my confusion. But I discovered one scientific model that helped mitigate the nature/nurture controversy:

the rubber-band theory. According to this theory, genes provide the basic substance of the rubber band, but upbringing provides the "stretch." The tendency to left-handedness or homosexual orientation might be innate, but environment, training, or reprogramming might change a person. I hoped desperately that there was enough "stretch" in my sexuality that, with lots of prayer and help from God, I could become heterosexual. The tremendous pressure of parental expectations, straight role models, peer pressure, and the boy-meets-girl culture that surrounded me had not yet effected a transformation, but perhaps a deliberate attempt on my part would make the difference. I waited in hope and fear for what the future might bring.

It wasn't long before I met Marion. A bright, outgoing, and very attractive bible-college graduate whom I had met at the Baptist church, she had grown up in a strict Baptist family. Drawn by her deep faith and commitment to Jesus, I began dating her, and before long we started thinking of marriage. She made it all seem so simple: trust in God and anything is possible — even my sexual "problem," which I told her about not long after we met, could be healed.

Convinced that God had brought us together, we announced to our families our intention to marry. Neither her parents nor mine were without reservations. To Marion's father, I was a new Christian from a heathen family, and had a lot to learn about the faith; my father thought her family uptight fundamentalists.

Despite our families' reservations, we visited the Baptist pastor to book a wedding a few months hence, and to ask for premarital counselling. "You don't need counselling," he said. "You've got the Lord." He had confidence that two good young people whom God had drawn together, walking in the will of God, would be able to build a wonderful relationship through faith and prayer. Marion's mother, who, like her daughter and me, had had a very brief courtship, said that ours would be a fine marriage since God was in our relationship. The Lord would provide.

Instead of finding all this certainty on the part of the pastor and my future in-laws unsettling, I found it inspiring. I wanted desperately to believe that God had a detailed plan for my life, and that I could experience it fully by aligning my will with his. A month after I graduated from university, we were married.

◆

On the sunny June day of our wedding, Marion and I drove north to her parents' cottage, where we were to spend our honeymoon. Confident that God had brought us to this moment in his gracious plan, we lit a fire, opened a small bottle of champagne, cuddled up on the old sofa, and enjoyed what we thought was the normal romantic prelude to sexual bliss. In reality, these two virgins knew little of what was entailed in a man and a woman coming together. When we finally went to bed it was a disaster.

After a few days of frustration and anxiety we abandoned the honeymoon cottage and returned to Toronto so that we could visit the family doctor. He assured us that everything was quite normal, that all we needed was time. But as the weeks and months slowly passed in frustration, our love life improved little. Gradually I became aware of the terrible psychological damage that had been done to Marion by her strict fundamentalist upbringing.

Her naïvety about sex was just one of many prison bars that a dysfunctional religious system had used to trap her, denying her the usual adolescent exploration of life. In a devout Baptist home where Father always knew best, made the important decisions, and had the final word, Marion had been carefully protected from the realities of a complex, challenging, and often ambiguous world. As a dutiful and loving daughter, Marion had been complicit. With faith, everything was simple. One didn't entertain doubts because that was to give in to the devil. With Father, everything was clear, secure, and unambiguous, and, in marriage, Marion's childlike trust and obedience were to be simply transferred from her father to her husband.

I was not willing or able to become a stern patriarch, and, deep down, Marion knew she didn't want me to either. The constant tension among the patriarchal model, my repressed homosexuality, and the union of equals we both really desired provoked many arguments.

"Till death do us part" — a lifelong commitment was something irrevocable to Marion and me. With faith and determination we believed, or hoped, that we could work out the problems in our marriage, and yet crisis followed crisis as unrelentingly as the tides. When we married, we planned that I would attend Ontario Bible College, Marion's alma mater, to prepare for my ordination to the ministry. Marion found a job at a mission in Toronto to support us while I began studies, even though it chafed her that a wife should have to support her husband. Looking back, I'm amazed at how much we gave each other, how we tried again and again to make the marriage work, even though I now believe it was doomed from the beginning.

In that first autumn of our marriage, the prison bars of my own fundamentalism began to shake. Increasingly I became aware that I did not fit in at Ontario Bible College. The narrow, rigid orthodoxy banned too many people from the arena of the "saved" for me to feel I really belonged. At the same time, the pastor at the downtown Toronto Baptist church where we had started attending membership classes was making it increasingly clear that he believed most people who called themselves Christians were damned and going to hell. His definition of Christianity was so limited that it seemed to bar most people from heaven, perhaps even my wife and me. We began to long for a church where we could feel truly welcomed, where there was an all-inclusive, non-judgemental spirit. The first Sunday morning we sat in the Church of the Resurrection, the Anglican church across the street from our apartment in Toronto's east end, we knew we had found such a place.

I had had a moving experience in the Anglican Church during my time at university, when I attended Midnight Mass on Christmas Eve with Paul and his fiancée, Betty, who were quickly becoming my best friends, at the Anglican church in Agincourt where Paul's father was rector. The powerful liturgy had stirred in me a sense of God's love for humanity, and for me in particular. The beauty of Anglican worship, and the sense of reverence at the communion, formed a strong memory, and it drew me to the Church of the Resurrection.

There, the rector, a gentle and loving man, welcomed Marion and me to what I came to see as a remarkably open, diverse, and inclusive church. Catholics and Protestants, conservatives and liberals, ritualists and evangelicals, fundamentalists and social-gospel folk — all were drawn together in a remarkable synthesis that respected the dignity of each. I learned that "unity in the midst of diversity" was the hallmark of the Anglican Church. This was, indeed, a place where Marion and I could feel welcome. More than that, it was a safe environment in which my wife and I could begin to examine and break out of the confinement of our fundamentalism.

With relief, I quit Ontario Bible College after the fall term, and went to work driving a bus for the physically challenged. Driving for Wheel Trans was a dose of reality for me. In the daily rounds of transporting people to and from work in the morning and evening rush hours, and to medical appointments in between, I was in the company of people of remarkable courage and depth. Some of my passengers were in wheelchairs; others walked with great difficulty. While a few were angry at their lot in life and were bitter or downright miserable, others were a real inspiration. I had worked as a hospital orderly for several summers when I was at school and I was not unfamiliar with people in health crisis, but the daily rounds on Wheel Trans provided me the opportunity to develop ongoing friendships with people with chronic physical limitations. Most of my passengers held down jobs against considerable odds. Getting to work on time was a problem, as the Wheel Trans buses were not always on schedule. Few employers were willing to install the necessary ramps, doors, and washroom facilities for wheelchair access. Frequent medical appointments could interrupt a regular work schedule.

I also learned of the daily discrimination most of my passengers endured. People would stand by while they struggled with doors. Store clerks would ignore the person in the wheelchair and speak to the accompanying "walker," asking, "What size does she take?" Some said they were ridiculed because of speech impediments. I learned that it took heroic efforts by many of my passengers just to do ordinary things and lead the sort of life that most people take for granted.

Jack and Bonnie, for instance, wanted to get married. For months I listened intently to their laboured conversation, and gained skill in deciphering the slurred speech that is often symptomatic of those with cerebral palsy. I discovered that many people ignorantly interpret slurred speech to mean dull minds. During our frequent trips to their workplace and church, our friendship grew, and Jack and Bonnie shared their dreams and frustrations with me. Having fallen in love in the institution they shared with others with their condition, they wanted to move out and begin a life together. Everything seemed to be against them. Romances were not encouraged in the institution, so they couldn't live together there. Social services could not provide the level of assistance that they would need in an apartment. People told them it wasn't "appropriate" for them to have physical relations. Even their church refused to bless their marriage because it was assumed that they could not fulfil the main purpose of marriage: procreation.

With shame I realized my own prejudice. I, too, was uncomfortable imagining these two people in bed with each other. With that realization came some deep self-examination. Were these people somehow incomplete? Were they less human than me? Did I, society, or their church have the right to deny them the human intimacy that most of us take for granted as a God-given right? Was there something wrong with me because I couldn't see their full humanity? What did God see when he looked at them?

If only we could see with God's eyes, I thought, we could recognize the full humanity of every person. Who was I to invade the privacy of my friends' intimate moments in my imagination, and then condemn them? God had given them a precious gift: the capacity to love and be loved, and to express that intimately. What right did I or anyone else have to deny them that gift? How easily we assault the dignity of other human beings by focusing on one aspect of them that is outside the "norm." Prejudice against others who are somehow different, I realized, was a pervasive part of human society and coloured my perceptions as well.

Jack and Bonnie's struggle came to an end when Jack died suddenly of natural causes, but it marked a turning-point in my assumptions about who and what is normal. I began to think of my high school friend who had embraced a gay life. Could my newfound openness be extended to include him? No. Not yet. I was too afraid of myself and what I might do if I allowed for the dignity of homosexual love. I could keep myself in check only by labelling my friend and his life, along with my own gay impulses, as perverted sexual acts. Nonetheless, the long process of coming to terms with my sexuality had begun.

◆

In the fall of 1976, Marion and I both started attending classes at Wycliffe College; I drove a Wheel Trans bus part-time to make ends meet. Although Wycliffe, an Anglican theological college affiliated with the University of Toronto, was conservative, it was by no means fundamentalist, so it provided us with an environment that encouraged real liberation. Because we could take half our courses at other member colleges in the Toronto School of Theology (TST), it was possible to challenge rigid perspectives with much more liberal scholarship. Some of my fellow Wycliffe students nicknamed the TST introductory New Testament course "New Testament Heresies" because of the modern scholarship taught there. One professor was fond of telling new students that "we must leave our Sunday school mentality behind." Even Wycliffe's arch-conservative Old Testament professor did not hold the view that the Bible was dictated by God to Moses. It was all intensely exciting for both Marion and me, and in spite of hard times — Marion had a miscarriage that year — we managed to keep going.

As we entered our second year of studies, however, our marriage was becoming increasingly strained. Marion began to find the intellectual stimulation that she craved, which I often felt I couldn't give her, in other students, and she began developing platonic crushes on some of the men at school. After months of successfully excluding homosexual thoughts from my mind, my fantasy world began to be filled with men. No matter how hard we worked at our sex life, it was never satisfying. Poles apart intellectually, emotionally, and sexually, we had little left to give a marriage that had begun in a fundamentalist haze. The evening a handsome man tried to pick me up in the Hart House gym at the university, I knew I was in serious trouble: my natural urges had not disappeared, even though I had never acted on them. But in spite of my wife's attraction to other men, my aching for intimacy with men, and nothing but conflict and frustration in the marital bed, we nonetheless felt locked into a lifelong commitment.

In the spring of the third year of our marriage, and our second year of studies, we paid a visit to Archbishop Lewis Garnsworthy, Anglican Bishop of Toronto. I had gotten to know him in the previous year as I took turns with my fellow students, chauffeuring him around on Sundays to various churches in the diocese. An imposing man in the pulpit or at church meetings, he was regarded by many as cool and aloof. In my experience he was a man of few words when it came to relationships, but with a genuine pastoral heart. The archbishop listened carefully as we explained our situation, and the terrible pain we were both suffering at being locked into a disintegrating, impossible marriage, and then said tersely, with a cocked eyebrow, "You know, sometimes there is something worse than divorce. If something is dead, you bury it. But make sure it's dead first." I don't recall him saying any more than that, but those few words breathed life into what seemed a hopeless situation.

A tremendous burden had been lifted in the archbishop's office. Permission had been given to us to exercise our consciences for the first time in deciding the fate of our marriage. Even so, we both felt a dreadful sense of failure, and a loss of our hopes and dreams. For me it meant giving up the certainty and security of knowing God's will. Hadn't I been sure that God wanted me to marry this woman, and that God would provide and protect the marriage bond? It was with despair that I began to admit that even in that most devout moment almost three years earlier I had made a mistake. I could no longer be certain about God's will for my life.

For a few more months Marion and I struggled along, as the marriage became more and more untenable. Finally I stopped approaching her to make love, because it only heightened my sense of inadequacy and rejection. I was powerless to affect the struggle for freedom going on in Marion's psyche, and now, although I had resisted it, I ached for freedom too. During my summer placement as a student minister at Fenelon Falls our best friends, Paul and Betty, dropped by on the way to their cottage. When they saw the terrible state we were in, they urged us to make the decision to separate, a decision we had both long avoided. We knew the marriage was dead, and living with the corpse was making both of us so sick that it was apparent to our best friends. That night we made the difficult decision.

The day after Marion and I agreed to get a divorce, a dramatic transformation took place. When I arrived home for lunch, Marion was in the sunporch of the house that had been provided to us for my summer placement. The sun and the wind were streaming into the porch as Marion stood by an easel, wearing an old shirt splotched with paint, paintbrush in hand, glowing with excitement.

"Look, Jamie! What do you think?" The canvas was brilliant with colour. In this stylized self-portrait, Marion's beaming face was surrounded by what looked like butterfly wings. It was like a physical blow.

"What's the matter? Don't you like it?" she asked, with a look of concern. Finally, like a butterfly bursting its cocoon, Marion was free. I could see it clearly. In my pain I thought bitterly that, despite my best efforts and patience, our marriage had been nothing more than a prison cell for my wife. Now, the captive was free at last. Her sense of elation only intensified the pain that had been building inside me. I couldn't see that my own prison bars had started to come down.

◆

"Just remember, Jim, after death comes resurrection. It may seem dark now, but there is that light at the end of the tunnel." The words of Dr. Reginald Stackhouse, principal of Wycliffe College, brought a tremendous sense of relief. I knew when Marion and I separated that my future as an Anglican minister could be jeopardized. The college might forbid me to return for my third and final year, and so might my bishop, who had sponsored my theological studies. Instead, the principal offered healing words. He wanted me to return in September, and move into a room in residence. The college bursary fund could provide the costs of room and board, as well as my tuition. Not only was I not to be made an outcast, but I was to be welcomed back and cared for. My faith in the Christian community was not just verified, but strengthened. My wife would be able to finish her studies the following year, after I had graduated. The college faculty decided it would be best for all involved if we did not both return at the same time.

I left Fenelon Falls a few weeks later to visit my bishop with a lot of anxiety. The postulancy process towards ordination had involved many interviews with individuals and assessment panels, but I had not yet become a full candidate for holy orders. As far as I knew, no candidate for the ministry had ever been ordained in the midst of a separation and divorce. I was aware of at least one priest who had been divorced and remarried some years after ordination who was still functioning as a rector in a big parish, and quite successfully. But this was different. Why should the Church take a chance on me? It was only twelve years earlier, after half a century of acrimonious debate, that the Anglican Church of Canada had decided it would perform second marriages for the divorced. Extending that privilege to clergy had been a divisive issue. Would Toronto's Archbishop Garnsworthy take the politically safe route?

A few days later, I was seated nervously in the diocesan office; the archbishop leaned back in his chair, feet on his desk, and puffed on his ever-present cigarette.

"You'll need to take a year off after you graduate, Jim." I heaved a sigh of relief. No guarantees of ordination, but I was being told to wait, to take some time to work things through in my personal life. Postponement, not rejection, was the chief pastor's response. He was willing to take a chance on me, and give me some time to heal after the trauma of a broken marriage. "You'll need to see a lawyer to work out a separation agreement when you get back in the fall. Give the chancellor a call, and he'll direct you to someone."

I returned to Fenelon Falls with a heavy heart, but encouraged that the principal and the bishop had both responded to me in what seemed to be the spirit of love. The remaining weeks in Fenelon Falls were made bearable — and, even more than that, fruitful — by my placement supervisor, Dick Downey. A good priest and an excellent supervisor in the parish training program, he wouldn't allow me to become too morose for long. We began each day with morning prayer and a supervisory session in which I might share with Dick an encounter with a parishioner, reflect with him on an issue that had come up during the week, or receive from him some practical instruction, followed by a more personal conversation about what I was going through. His laughter was contagious and cathartic. With the laughter, weekly invitations to dinner with his wife and young children, and the steady challenge to reflect theologically on my experiences and beliefs, Dick nurtured me through a difficult summer.

Half-jokingly, Dick would tell me that I must have been a priest in a previous life. The affirmation was heartening. Parishioners, bishops, supervisors, peers — all seemed to affirm my vocation to ordained ministry, and seemed willing to walk with me, sometimes supporting me, through those terrible days.

During the summer, the parish of Fenelon Falls grew from four little church congregations to five, with the addition of St. John's Rosedale. In alternation with Dick Downey and a lay reader, I preached and took services at two of the churches each Sunday morning. St. John's Rosedale was the most intimidating, not because it was jam-packed each time with a hundred summer cottagers, but because my professor of preaching sat in the back pew each week, assessing my sermons. Leonard Griffith, who was a renowned preacher and thus a bit frightening to a novice, attended while he was on vacation at his cottage nearby. I was delighted at the end of the summer when he asked me to be the first one to preach in homiletics class; he said he knew I had a good sermon prepared.

◆

The difficult transition to single college life that fall was eased by the loving non-judgementalism of the faculty and my fellow students. Most had watched my marital struggles over the previous two years and were not very surprised when I returned to Wycliffe alone. The college arranged for Marion and me to see a top-notch psychiatrist at the Clarke Institute, so that we could have the benefit of marriage counselling, and the college could have an independent assurance that we had, in fact, done everything we could to salvage the marriage. When Marion refused to go back again after the first visit, the college authorities said they were satisfied that I had done all I could.

That fall, one of my classmates, Sandy, did not return after what had amounted to a physical and nervous breakdown the previous year. We had all watched as Sandy was stricken with rheumatoid arthritis, and his life became increasingly painful. Underneath his controlled calm had lurked a terrible bitterness and depression, which he had hidden from most of our classmates. One night, I had gone to Sandy's room, concerned about his absence throughout the day. I knocked persistently at his door, until Sandy got out of bed to let me in to his dark room. He had been sleeping all day. When I asked why, he blurted out a confession: while my wife and I had been out he had climbed the fire escape, entered the small third-floor apartment, and stolen Marion's prescription pain-killers, which he had swallowed. That had been hours ago. Although he assured me that he would be okay, that he thought he had slept it off, I nevertheless insisted that he go to the hospital for treatment. Together with the dean of residence, I took him to the emergency ward; after a thorough examination, he was discharged. His suicide attempt had failed.

Sandy was a good man, thoughtful and self-effacing to a fault. What could have gone so wrong that he would try to take his life? Gradually the mystery unravelled. Sandy had fallen in love with one of the men in the residence, who had thwarted his every advance.

Sandy told me of his struggle for years to repress his homosexual feelings, and of the guilt, fear, and self-hatred that overwhelmed him. God had not heard his cries for help, for release from the feelings that crippled him inside, and so he had tried to end his life.

With my friend's absence that fall, and my failed marriage burning in my conscience, I began seriously to question many of my own beliefs. Was lifelong marriage the only healthy option for Christians who were normal sexual beings? One of my friends had almost died in an effort to deny his sexual orientation. I found I could no longer believe in a God who condemns the homosexual but refuses to remove homosexual urges. What a cruel God, to make someone a homosexual and then condemn him to a life in hell as he struggles to change. The only way to health for Sandy was to accept himself as a gay man, since he obviously had no choice in his orientation, and find some responsible way to live his life. No longer could I condemn homosexuals, especially not Sandy. A radical change had taken place in my understanding. I concluded that the rubber band of inherited sexual orientation had no stretch left in it for my friend. And yet, impossible though it may seem, I still wanted to believe that I had a choice about my own sexual orientation. Despite a brief sexual encounter with one of the men in my class, who promptly ran off in panic to a psychiatrist to be reprogrammed, and my own acceptance of Sandy, I could not yet accept myself.

About this time I got a call from an unexpected source — Marion. She wanted the two of us to talk about the marriage, to see if we could start over and make it work. At first I was angry, but, as I thought about it, I realized that part of my current suffering was rooted in the fact that I had not taken my share of responsibility for the marriage's collapse. As is true of most estranged partners, each of us wanted to blame the other for the marriage breakdown. I knew now that I hadn't fully decided for myself that it was over — I needed to make a final decision of my own, and take responsibility fully. The thought of the two of us doing our own marital counselling seemed ridiculous to me when I thought of the almost three years of daily anguish as we had tried to do just that. I knew we needed a third person to give us an objective reading on what was going on in our lives.

Since Marion had refused to go back to the psychiatrist recommended by the college, I set about finding someone acceptable to both of us. One of my classmates recommended a doctor whom he had found particularly helpful. While not licensed as a psychiatrist, this doctor had vast counselling experience and, most important to my wife, was a committed Christian, unlike the previous psychiatrist, and an Anglican to boot. When he wisely suggested that he thought it best to counsel couples together or separately, depending on their living arrangements, my estranged wife and I began a four-week course of individual counselling. At last I felt I was taking charge of my life, and was on my way to making my own decision about the marriage.

The verdict after a few weeks of honest soul-baring was no surprise; deep inside I already knew the marriage was over. The doctor said he had never seen a case of two people who were so thoroughly incompatible. He found it surprising that the tales my wife and I told, and our individual assessments of what was going on in the marriage, were so similar. Most couples, he said, came in with very lop-sided perspectives of their relationship, but our stories gave him a clear picture of what we already knew: we were two people who should never have married. His opinion was that we had made a mistake; it was the clearest case he had ever seen. We had entered into marriage honestly, but must now accept the fact that we had been honestly mistaken. Having tried our best to make an impossible situation work, there was no need for guilt or recrimination. At last Marion and I were fully agreed, and we put any thoughts of reconciliation to rest.

Knowing that the decision to end the marriage was the right one did not end the pain. I had lost so much: the innocence, the simple faith and trust, and the high ideals of marriage and commitment. Finally, I got angry. I shook my fist at God one night and cursed him. In what I considered to have been the most devout moment of my life three years earlier, I had trusted God, and he had let me down. But in the midst of my fury came an amazing sense of liberation: I could be angry at God without being struck down. With the realization that God was not going to give me explicit directions about the decisions of my life came a new sense of personal integrity. God trusted me to make my own decisions; he might provide options — perhaps many options — but the ultimate choices and decisions were my own. Faith in God's loving presence did not mean believing that he had a detailed plan for all the decisions of my life; nor did it mean that God would desert me if I made the "wrong" choice. Choices were not black and white, good and bad, but a mix. The Bible, which I had previously used as a rulebook to give me black-and-white answers and directions, now became a gracious and forgiving instrument with which to gain insight into the character of human behaviour, including my own. Guidelines rather than rules. I had been honestly mistaken in believing that God wanted me to marry Marion; now I could honestly admit that mistake without self-recrimination or fear of recrimination from God.

◆

At the end of term I got my first real taste of Church politics. I might have peace of mind — albeit tinged with grief — about my decision to end the marriage, but others did not share that peace. The weeks had gone by as I wrote papers and prepared for end-of-term exams with my fellow students' love and encouragement, which was a real healing force. Then I was called into the principal's office and told that I must go back to the psychiatrist at the Clarke Institute. The counsellor I had been seeing was not satisfactory. When I objected, saying that I had already done everything the college had asked, and more, I was told that I must not only *do* everything possible to save the marriage, but must *be seen to do* everything possible. My graduation and recommendation for ordination would depend on it. I felt as if I had been punched.

With a sick feeling, I knocked on the door of the college's professor of pastoral psychology, who I suspected was at the heart of the college's sudden ultimatum. When I told him what had just happened, my suspicions were confirmed. He was not happy with the doctor I had seen; he did not have the appropriate credentials, in my professor's estimation. What if Marion refuses to go back to see the psychiatrist, I asked. Well then, I would be seen to have done my part.

Marion's refusal a few hours later to see the college's first choice of psychiatrist did nothing to relieve the chill that had settled in my soul. I felt betrayed by the very people who I had felt empathized with me. What had happened to change their attitude? Was it mere professional jealousy about credentials, or was it something more sinister? Not only must I *do* but I must *be seen to do* everything possible to save my marriage. I knew that the college council had many very conservative clergy in its membership, and I had heard the rumblings about their concern over the number of marriage breakdowns and divorced students in the college. I remembered a classmate who said he was kicked out after first year because he was a divorcé, and a senior student who had returned after summer placement without his wife, who had run off with her husband's supervising priest! Was my sudden persecution an attempt to allay the concerns of some conservatives on the college council who wanted to maintain "high moral standards" for the college? I began to think that I had become a football in a callous game of professional and political intrigue.

Worried about my future, I paid Archbishop Garnsworthy a visit. I had heard via the student grapevine that the archbishop and the principal were not the best of friends, so I hoped for a positive hearing. When I told Garnsworthy what had happened, especially the threat about my recommendation for ordination, he was furious. With a comment that it sounded like blackmail, he assured me that the principal's recommendation had little bearing on who he did or did not ordain. I was not to worry about it, just get my work done and get out of the college.

I spent my last five months at Wycliffe feeling quietly bitter. I did my schoolwork, and completed my courses, with the support of my classmates. What little energy I had left was taken up with my student placement at Church of the Ascension in Don Mills, where I was supervised by the Reverend Beverley Brightling, a sensitive and caring man known to one and all affectionately as "Bev," and enjoyed a great deal of affirmation from him and his parishioners in my sense of call to ministry. As I preached, taught, sang the services, led a weekly Bible study, and struck up friendships with young and old, the parish community had a healing effect on me. When I graduated in May I was asked to stay on for another year as volunteer assistant at the Ascension.

The ordination of my classmates that spring was a bitter-sweet time, as I struggled with my sense of failure tempered by the archbishop's counsel to wait a year. My life was on hold, in more ways than one. I would have to find work for a year — not a difficult prospect — but more importantly my personal life was on hold. Being separated was like being in limbo. My inner longings for intimacy with men were confined to my fantasy world. The Church was watching me closely, and I knew it. When I went back to my familiar job driving a Wheel Trans bus, an old woman gave me a word of advice. During frequent trips to the veterans' hospital to visit her husband, she had taken an interest in me and shared the sad tale of her parish priest who, a decade before, had been fired over allegations of sexual misconduct with a young man. "Whatever you do," she said, "keep your nose clean."

Clean I kept it. For a year I submerged myself in work, first as a busdriver, then as a salesman of production reporting equipment, travelling the countryside around Toronto to every imaginable sort of factory, from food to steel, and eked out an existence. What really gave me life, however, was my volunteer work at the Ascension. In addition to my other duties, I decided to start a youth group. Maureen, the church secretary, a marvellous, caring straight-shooter who pretty much ran the parish, said it couldn't be done. Nevertheless she offered to phone up every family in the parish who had children in their teens to invite them to an initial meeting. Out of the first meeting with about twenty young people developed a lively youth group that met every Sunday night for a year. It was one of those rare, magic combinations of personalities, aged thirteen to twenty-two (which should never have worked). Love, sex, Bible, God, ethics, school, parents — we covered everything under the sun, in sometimes riotous good times. In short, I had a marvellous time at the Ascension while my year of limbo passed.

It was in early March 1980, when Bev had his annual Lenten clergy party, that I was invited and introduced to a who's who of local diocesan clergy. I particularly remember meeting Archdeacon Arthur Brown, rector of St. Michael and All Angels' Church in downtown Toronto. A jovial man who cut a larger-than-life figure, he regaled me with some of his stories about his old friend Bev, with an engaging mix of humour and respect. Bev had been a meat salesman for Swift's before he went into the ministry, Art said, and when he was a student he always drove a big car. "Swift's Premium Ham" — that described Bev, said the archdeacon: swift, because wherever he went, he was in a hurry; premium, because he always travelled first class; and ham, well that was self-explanatory.

A few days later, Bev told me that he had whispered my name in the ears of a couple of the clergy, including his friend Brown, who wanted to meet me to talk about working with them. I was delighted but somewhat aghast since, for the past few years, the diocese had been making the appointments of newly ordained assistant curates, in an effort to circumvent the old system of horse-trading whereby the parishes with the most money courted and won the best of the new graduates. Shrugging off my reservations about the political process, and knowing that Bev had my best interests at heart, I called Archdeacon Brown for an appointment.

A few days later I sat in the archdeacon's office. Bev had spoken very highly of me, he said. Could we take a look at the idea of working together? As Art described the parish, the congregation, and the work of the clergy team, I was impressed at what a unique opportunity this multicultural parish was for me to begin a challenging ministry with a growing edge to it. Human rights, building bridges between different ethnic communities, reforming people's prejudices, ministering to mostly single parents in the day care centre — an impressive and exciting list of initiatives in a bustling city church. The archdeacon decided he liked me, and that a divorce, though tragic, was not an obstacle for a good man entering the ministry. I was given the evening to mull it over.

The next day I was back in the archdeacon's office, excited and prepared for the challenge, the air full of the sounds of children. A little girl burst through the open doorway, asked her grandfather about something, and was sent bustling off with a kiss. Art told me it got a little noisy with kids all over the place, and I would have to learn to live with that. The assistant curate's office was on a small landing right over the main entrance, in the centre of activities. Could I start next week? I was a little stunned with the haste, but Art was anxious to replace his assistant, who had suddenly left the previous week to return to his native Uganda. I could move into his house behind the church as soon as it was freshly painted.

When I agreed to the offer, Archdeacon Brown picked up the phone and called Archbishop Garnsworthy. After negotiating with the bishop — something I thought was forbidden under the curacy system — it was agreed I could start. My ordination would have to wait until the spring deacons' ordination, and the parish would have to pay my full salary until then, when the diocese would pick up half of it.

April 1 marked my first day as assistant curate of St. Michael and All Angels'. It was the beginning of Holy Week, and also April Fool's Day. An auspicious beginning, I hoped.

CHAPTER 2

THE ART BROWN SCHOOL of Curates was a tremendous experience. I had never met anyone so open to unexpected visitors and events, seeing them not as interruptions but as opportunities for ministry. At any time a person in crisis could walk in the church door and find that "the godfather of St. Clair Avenue" would extend a warm welcome and be genuinely helpful. Street people, illegal immigrants, single parents, clergy in personal difficulty, and politicians, as well as the regular round of parishioners of all races and backgrounds, would find a caring archdeacon willing to move mountains for them. I had heard clergy gossip (and, believe me, the clergy in all churches gossip) about what a political person my new rector was, but if this was what it meant to be political, then my heart was won over.

Oftentimes life at St. Michael and All Angels' Church — often called "St. Mike's" or the more tongue in cheek "All Angles" — seemed chaotic. I had hoped after the turmoil of the previous four years that I might settle into a more ordered existence, but that was not to be. Sunday morning was a time to be open to the unexpected. While the Book of Common Prayer was used every Sunday, alternating week by week between Morning Prayer and Holy Communion, the preacher was the only person informed of their role beforehand. The details of who was doing what were determined just before service, and could change at a moment's notice, even in the middle of the worship service. A visiting dignitary from a sister church, spotted sitting in the congregation one morning, might be asked to take an unexpected role in the service, displacing one of my functions. Or something might be adjusted because the rector had had a brilliant flash of inspiration and wanted to inject some new element.

Day-to-day parish life, planning sessions, board meetings — all were subject to the vicissitudes of the archdeacon's openness to new people, new ideas, new decisions. Overnight there often seemed to be a complete turnaround of what had seemed the day before to be his final decision on some important aspect of parish life. While some people found his unpredictability unsettling, I began to realize that he and I were kindred spirits in the way we approached life.

My marital status was simply not an issue at St. Mike's. It wasn't that Art and I were keeping it hidden, it was just that it was irrelevant and we didn't bother advertising it. Ministry at St. Michael's was a very open-ended affair, where what I thought were the usual rules of a WASP congregation just couldn't be applied. As a skilled mentor, the rector took time with me almost every day to explain the unique circumstances of what was the leading integrated congregation in Toronto. As much as two-thirds of the congregation on a typical Sunday morning were West Indians, from every part of the Caribbean, and their struggle for full dignity and integration in the Church had been a long and often painful one. Most of the bigots in the old congregation had left over the years.

The reality of human prejudice was brought home to me many times there. An old spinster in the congregation had the reputation of being a fire-breather. Every Sunday the folks in the pews would watch as Irene made her pilgrimage up the centre aisle of St. Mike's very long and narrow nave to the altar rail. To which side would she go to receive communion? As she wavered up the aisle, some people claimed they could see her making the mental calculations of rank, colour, and status of the clergy and laity administering the blessed sacrament to determine which side would be least offensive to her. Sometimes, watching parishioners told me, they would place mental bets as to which part of the rail she would choose. The archdeacon knew the prejudice in people's hearts, and not just Irene's, and so each week he carefully calculated what mix of communion administrants would make up each side of the altar rail. Clergy or lay, black or white, male or female, bishop, priest, deacon, or student — representation was carefully balanced to give a mix that could bewilder the most vigilant bigot.

One Sunday, after careful deliberation, I was assigned the north side of the altar rail with two theological students, one a black male and the other a white female. I'm not sure who was on the other side, but my mix must have been better, as Irene knelt and extended her hands to receive the bread. It was at that moment that the black student who had been following me with the chalice decided it was time to hand it over to his female colleague. I caught my breath, wondering how Irene would react to this change. Wasn't white better than black? But was female better than male? It was out of my hands as I continued down the altar rail, but it was reported to me later that Irene had been seen fuming down the aisle afterwards. Several days later I had the misfortune of running into Irene at the bank. "Well," she ranted, pointing at me accusingly, "I'll never take communion from that woman again!"

Besides the parish's ongoing struggle with discrimination, latent and overt, other forms of cultural prejudice had to be faced. I had grown up in a WASP community in Agincourt, where the norms of family were fixed. In my new multicultural setting I discovered that the norms were different. Or, more to the point, while everyone still officially held up the norm of the stereotypical nuclear family, it was honoured more in the breach. One day, Art told me, he had introduced a West Indian woman to another parishioner as "Mrs. Smith" only to have the woman proclaim in a loud voice, "I am not 'Missus.' I am 'Miss.' I have no need of a man except to sire my children!" The woman's five children had three different fathers, all of whom were supporting their children.

Large numbers of parishioners really couldn't stand up to the scrutiny of the Church's traditional moral standards. Many single women had come from the Caribbean, made new lives for themselves in Canada, and sent for "nephews" or "nieces" to put through school here. In a complicated twist of circumstances, in order to break out of grinding poverty and come to Canada, they had had to lie about their children, sponsoring them later as nephews or nieces, and then agonize when their children reached the age of majority over whether or not landed-immigrant status could be obtained for them. They were caught in a catch-22: if they told the truth now about their children in order to sponsor them as family, they ran the risk of being deported for having lied to the immigration authorities in the first place. And so the dreadful secret had to be kept, in hopes that things would work out for the best for all.

I began to feel stirrings of identification with my own situation. I had my own dreadful secrets: I was divorced and, even worse, a man with homosexual desires. Terrible things might happen if those secrets came out. At the same time I was experiencing the need for integrity and the heaviness that comes with having to avoid the truth. Striking though the parallel was, I wasn't ready yet to apply it vigorously to my own situation. But I was opening up to the "irregularities" of others' lives.

In the clash of cultures at St. Mike's, the essential question became very clear: how can the Church be a welcoming, loving, inclusive community? Surely not by imposing white North American cultural standards, but by dealing at a deep non-judgemental level with the realities of people's lives. Breaking through the hypocrisy of stated cultural standards, and living with people as they really were, to ensure a place for them in the community of the family of God, was a major thrust of the archdeacon's ministry. Increasingly I found my own prejudices and rule-bound rigidity breaking down. Some of the most wonderful, loving, spiritual people were those "outside the pale," and they were accorded a significant place in the church family at St. Mike's.

It was from the archdeacon that I learned to think of Church rules no longer as absolutes, but as useful standards of behaviour which must be sensitive to a given context. With a pastor's heart, he made it clear that people came first. Sometimes a gracious disregard for the rules was called for in order for people's real needs to be met. It could be as simple as respecting the spiritual needs of parishioners raised in the Anglo-Catholic tradition in various Caribbean Anglican churches, who felt strongly the need to receive the Blessed Sacrament each Sunday morning. Raised in a spiritual context in which receiving communion at weekly public worship was essential, they felt the biweek-ly Morning Prayer services of scripture readings, prayers, and ser-mon lacked a critical component. The pastor's response on Morning Prayer Sundays was to have communion from the Reserved Sacrament distributed in a separate chapel following the main service, for those who wished to receive. In this way the consecrated elements reserved from the early-morning communion service, or from the previous Sunday's main worship service, could be extended to those in need. Perhaps this was just a stretch and not a breach of the rules.

Once a month baptism was celebrated. In most parishes the impor-tance of baptism as a time of real commitment of faith and incorpo-ration into the church family meant that rigid standards were increasingly in place. Gone were the days when a family could simply show up at two o'clock on a Sunday afternoon with babe in arms and find the parish priest patiently waiting to see if any candidates would appear for baptism. Now there were baptism preparation class-es for parents and godparents, and it was expected that at least one parent was attending church regularly, and would promise to bring the child to church and Sunday school. At St. Mike's, however, the old practice prevailed. New immigrants needed to know there was a place for them in the church, a place where they knew God's people welcomed them, the rationale went. A simple application form dropped into the church office was all that was required to book a place in the next baptism service.

Parishioners were divided over the way baptism was handled. It was common to have as many as eighteen babies squirming their way through the service. If this happened one Sunday every month at eleven o'clock, the main holy hour, regular parishioners would be angry: they felt that most of the "intruders" wouldn't be back until the next baby was ready for baptism. Instead, the service was held judiciously at ten o'clock. That way the requirement that baptism be held at a regular Sunday service could be met, without inconveniencing the regular flock.

May 20, 1980, was a happy day for me. After a year's delay I was ordained deacon with eleven other men and women at St. Paul's

Church in Toronto. My grandparents had flown in from St. John's, Newfoundland, and were bursting with pride. Surrounded by family and friends, it was a joyful celebration. Life was on track, God was in heaven, I was moving into the future. And, keeping a discreet distance, was Peter, a man I had recently met, and with whom I was about to fall in love.

Back at St. Mike's as a deacon, I continued to learn that the conflict between rules and context had to be settled in favour of real people in need. One Saturday afternoon I discovered just how far that philosophy could go.

A couple scheduled to be married at three o'clock arrived at five-thirty: luckily we had hurried through another wedding in the meantime. But the scheduling wasn't the main problem: what we discovered, after the frustration of waiting, was that the couple had no wedding licence! It was not uncommon for couples to bring the licence to the wedding rehearsal the night before, but since someone else had taken this rehearsal the previous evening, it had somehow fallen between the cracks. When I asked the groom for the licence, he said the bride was handling that. Moments later, the bride looked at me in shock and said, "My girlfriend told me that you'd look after it."

By this time there was a church full of people, eagerly waiting for the wedding to begin. With a sick feeling, I wondered what to do. It was too late to obtain a wedding licence, since the registrar's office was closed. Besides, a licence had to be three days old to be valid. I called the archdeacon, thanked God when I found he was home, and informed him of the situation. "I'll be right over," he said. A few minutes later he appeared with a banns form in hand. I knew it was the policy at St. Mike's that every couple must go to city hall and get their own marriage licence. Banns were no longer read in our parish because so few couples met the legal requirement of being known in the congregation where the banns would be read. The banns-reading tradition was an anachronism, dating back to a time when people didn't move around much and the members of the congregation where a couple had grown up would be able to testify that there were no impediments to matrimony. The constant flux of people in a big city parish made the reading of banns unworkable. I knew that no banns had been read for these recent immigrants; if they had been, the marriage would be legally recognized.

I gulped when the rector began filling in the banns form but, why not? I wondered. After all, this couple had booked the wedding several months ago, and if they had understood would surely have obtained the necessary licence from city hall. Their intention had been sound — to enter into a legal marriage — so why penalize them for an oversight? And besides, there was a church full of guests waiting for the ceremony, to be followed by a big celebration. As the archdeacon signed the banns form, I heaved a sigh of relief. Thirty minutes later the beaming newlyweds were on their way.

Through many other irregularities in the lives of parishioners I learned how society filters human reality through a superficial screen of righteousness. The raw experience of cultures and attitudes different from mine held up a powerful mirror to my own — including my own church family. An open secret at St. Mike's revolved around a woman parishioner whose husband, a priest at another parish in the city, was having an affair with another woman. The archbishop wouldn't act unless the wife complained, despite the fact that the situation was common knowledge, a scandal in the church community. As long as it wasn't official, everyone could pretend it wasn't happening, and look the other way. The parish family was amazingly tolerant.

At the same time, my real family was under siege: after decades of marriage, my parents separated, and my mother entered another relationship that turned out to be disastrous. But, in the midst of my growing experience of the brokenness of so many people's lives, some magic was happening in my own. I had met Peter at a church function, and we were drawn to each other. His bright spirit, his laughter, and his devotion to God and the Church were contagious. In the summer after my ordination as deacon, we began seeing each other. Both of us were neophytes in the secret world of gay love, but one thing I knew: the accent was on love, and not on gayness. There was something ineffable drawing us together and forming a bond of love. He never spoke of himself as "gay" because, like me, he was too afraid to expose that part of himself hidden in the safe darkness of repression. But as we touched and held each other we discovered how good intimacy between us could be. Over the months we learned how to make love, and I found for the first time a mutuality that I had never felt with my wife. Real trust, respect, caring, and even admiration coloured our time together as, for almost two years, we saw each other once or twice a week, talked on the phone, and shared vacations.

I began to discover the extent of the gay subculture in the Anglican Church. Of course, I had heard gossip in the seminary about this one and that one, but in my state of denial I had scorned the whole issue. Now I began to realize that I was not alone, that there were many gay clergy in places high and low, as well as enormous numbers of gay laity. It wasn't that I socialized with my gay colleagues, but I was becoming aware of their presence. The Church was involved in a massive conspiracy of silence, I discovered, not unlike the one in my parish, to pretend that everyone was "normal" and living within the stated moral standards. When I was ordained I had been aware that the House of Bishops of the Anglican Church of Canada had recently issued a statement on homosexuality, but I hadn't considered it pertinent to my situation since I wasn't "one of them." The bishops' guidelines on the ordination of gay clergy seemed to be honoured more in the breach than in the observance. I even knew a gay bishop.

How did the guidelines actually work? There seemed to be a tacit understanding between gay ordinands and clergy, and their bishops, that as long as you didn't mention that you were gay and avoided being open or causing a scandal, the bishop would ask no questions, and everyone could get along just fine. As long as the bishop didn't know *officially* what everyone knew *unofficially*, he would look the other way. In the context of my experience at St. Michael and All Angels, there seemed to be a consistent tradition, which many Anglicans used as a simple rule of thumb: the Church permits little and tolerates much. Causing scandal is the ultimate sin for Anglicans.

Early in the new year, 1981, scandal rocked the city of Toronto. In one night, in a massive police operation, every gay bathhouse in town was raided. More than three hundred men were dragged out into the bitter winter air, some naked or half-naked, and bundled into paddy wagons. One establishment had been so badly damaged by the use of police force that it never reopened. Many prominent members of Toronto society were charged with being found-ins or with other misdemeanours. The provincial authorities took the unusual step of asking the press not to report the names of those charged; too many politicians, judges, lawyers, clergy, and others had been arrested, or so the speculation went. The gay community was enraged and, accusing the police of deliberate intimidation of their community, marched in the streets in the thousands. At least one prominent Anglican layman showed up at Archdeacon Brown's door for help, after being arrested and charged as a found-in.

Integrity, a recently formed group of gay and lesbian Anglicans and their friends, sent a delegation to see my rector, headed by one of the men from the parish. Archdeacon Brown was well known in the diocese as the Church's foremost advocate of human rights. Over the years he had built bridges between the different faith communities, had spoken up for the rights of people of colour, and had been the prime mover behind the Cardinal Carter Commission on Race Relations and the Police. No better champion of human rights could be found than the outspoken Brown, whose door was always open.

Brown invited me to sit in on the meeting with the Integrity delegation, as he had with other meetings. It wasn't just an opportunity to educate his curate; we had become close friends and confidants. I didn't know if he had surmised yet that I was gay, although he may have suspected. I had "come out" as a gay man to only a few gay friends, since I had not yet fully come out to myself. In the earliest stages of self-acceptance, I entered the meeting with the "out" members of Integrity.

Brown, who had recently been elected assistant bishop, had been informed by the police, in a private briefing, that a lengthy undercover operation had discovered alleged incidents of prostitution, drug-peddling, and involvement with minors. What could he do? The members of Integrity were furious at the new bishop's inaction.

My mind was in turmoil. While I had never been to a bathhouse, a couple of my friends frequented them, and the day after the raids I was worried sick that one of them might have been caught. Why had the police acted with such brute force? Breaking into a private room, even in a bathhouse, was surely an invasion of privacy, and it was not a criminal act for two men to have sex. If there was prostitution, why not simply arrest the individuals involved, I reasoned. And it was hard to believe that these bathhouses were serious drug dens. I became convinced that the police raids were simply an attack on the gay community, an act of oppression and intimidation. Over the next few weeks and months it became clear: as the gay community organized and provided legal counsel for the arrested, only a half-dozen out of the more than three hundred men charged were found guilty, and most of those pleaded guilty only to avoid the publicity. The police had uncovered no prostitution, drug rings, or corruption of minors.

Where should the Church stand on this issue? It seemed to me quite clear that the raids were an attack on an entire minority community, an act of terrible violence whose intention was to drive fear into people's hearts. I knew that fear. For years I had been afraid of myself, and had struck out, albeit verbally, against those who represented what I couldn't accept in myself. I had myself been victimized over the years by a society that had taught me to hate myself and those like me. Society's homophobia, the hatred I had turned in on myself, had, in the bathhouse raids, broken dramatically into the public consciousness. Part of me wanted the Church to speak out against that terrible violence. The problem was, I was still a victim of my own fear. I couldn't break my own silence; how could I expect the Church to break its?

◆

It may seem a small thing, but in spring of that year I got a dog, an Old English sheepdog named Maybe. Her previous owners had found her too messy indoors, and were regretfully trying to find a new home for her. In her own way, Maybe was to teach me as much as some of my parishioners.

Soon I discovered that being "messy" meant relieving her bowels and bladder. At first I dealt with the daily accidents, but, after a few weeks, I snapped: after Maybe had shat on the front hall floor yet again, I found myself beating her and throwing her out into the garden. I was suddenly aware that I had the capacity for blind and violent rage. What if Maybe had been a crying baby, keeping me sleepless for days on end? The insight was devastating, as I suddenly realized how tired, frustrated parents could harm their own children, as I had just harmed my pet. Never again would I treat Maybe with such violence.

It also occurred to me that the bright, affectionate dog never made messes when she had human company, either at home or when I took her to the office. That night I let her into my bedroom and shut the door.

As the days and weeks went by, with Maybe quietly sleeping beside my bed, there were no more accidents. Every morning, even if I slept late, she would lie peacefully until she heard me stir and get up to let her out. Her early history had been a mystery to me, but this much was clear: Maybe needed human companionship. The world was rosy and happy as long as I or another human friend was there to be the object of her apparently limitless slurpy affection. We became inseparable, Maybe going with me almost everywhere.

I wonder now if Maybe wasn't filling my need for companionship as much as I was filling hers. Peter and I were seeing each other only one or two nights a week, and a house, as pleasant as it might be, could be a very lonesome place. Maybe took the edge off the solitude, and held up the mirror to my own human need. Without knowing it, I was building a different kind of family, under difficult circumstances. Celibate I was not; neither was I a person of solitude. My need for intimacy was wonderfully fulfilled by Peter, and my furry dog filled my days with companionship. I gradually started to reflect on the reality of the widowed and single people I knew, gay and straight, some of whom cheerfully admitted to being celibate, and some to being solitary, but very few to being both. The painful reality is that the Church imposes both these states on the unmarried, or tries to.

In the human longing for community and intimacy, some single women are able meet at least the first of these needs by living together and sharing a house and possessions. In parish ministry I began to connect with a few of these women, who could live without fear of fingers being pointed, or accusations being made of lesbian love. But, for men, I discovered a different standard: men living together were automatically assumed to be gay. It was good that Peter and I lived apart.

As loving and wholesome as our relationship was, Peter would never allow me to discuss the fact of our gayness. He seemed not to be as far along the path of self-acceptance as I was, and while it was irksome that he would not use the word "gay," I understood implicitly that he was in a process of coming to terms with the same reality that I had tried so hard to repress. The homophobia of society had soaked into our bones, and try as we might to move beyond it, it had become a painful part of us. The need we felt to hide our love was like a thick, smothering blanket.

◆

For over a year my "family" thrived, and provided the stable island in the ebb and flow of my professional life. My final year in seminary and my year of waiting before starting at St. Mike's had been a limbo from which I had expected to be delivered when I started in parish ministry. It was not to be. Almost immediately upon arriving at St. Mike's, I realized I was really in an interim ministry. The Diocese of Toronto, the second-largest Anglican diocese in North America, was in the final throes of deciding to divide its more than two hundred parishes into five pastoral units, each with its own bishop, to relieve the impossible burden of clergy care that had fallen for years on Archbishop Garnsworthy and his suffragan (assistant), Bishop Allan Read. There was a tremendous hope that, with more chief pastors, priests and congregations could get the sort of time for care and nurture that was increasingly needed. My rector was the leading candidate for one of the three new episcopal openings.

Nominated by the host of assistant curates he had trained over the years, and elected on the third ballot as the first of three new suffragan bishops, Bishop Arthur Brown was consecrated at a historic service in November 1980, along with Bishops Desmond Hunt and Basil Tonks. St. James's Cathedral was too small a venue for the service, so St. Paul's on Bloor Street, with three times the seating capacity, became the cathedral for the night. It was a glorious and joyful service as my friend and rector became bishop, and special for me as one of four deacons invited to take part in the service. In a historic gesture, we placed giant silver candlesticks onto a Holy Table that had never been graced by candles, converting it into an altar for one night. If there were any gasps in that evangelical bastion from anti-Catholic low-church ghosts, aghast at the papist symbols, they were drowned out by the music. Clearing the table afterwards with a dozen or more priests, we found that the Dean of Toronto had, in his exuberance, consecrated far too much bread and wine for the estimated crowd. Since St. Paul's had no facilities to reserve the Sacrament — doing so would be too Catholic — we each had to consume vast quantities of the consecrated bread and wine. The heavy red wine went down easily, but left us staggering out the church doors after the crowds had dispersed. The low-church ghosts had the final laugh that night.

My first eleven months at St. Mike's had been a period of transition — first getting into and used to a very busy parish ministry, and then helping my rector through the agonizing process of nomination, election, and then departure to take up his duties as bishop. When he left, I was marking time, and I knew it. Because I was two months away from ordination as a priest, Archbishop Garnsworthy appointed an interim priest-in-charge. Day-to-day running of the parish nevertheless fell to me as the full-time parish cleric, since the interim priest was there only on Sundays and one or two nights a week. In the normal course of events I had to submit my resignation to the diocesan bishop when the rector left, with the understanding that I would stay until the new rector arrived, and possibly longer. But I expected my time there would be short since, in the Anglican system, assistant curates are licensed to their rectors, so that when a new rector arrives the decks can be easily cleared. Very deliberately, I decided not to move into the main office of the church, in recognition of my tenuous status. After all, I would only have to move back to the curate's office in a few months.

Two months later, on a beautiful May day, I was ordained priest by Archbishop Garnsworthy at St. Clement's Church, along with the assistant curate there. I had hoped that, in customary fashion, the rector with whom I had worked for the past year could be my official clergy presenter, but because of a disappointing imposition of new rules he was notably absent. It was not permitted to have two bishops at the same event, so Bishop Brown could not be there. Even so, it was a time of celebration; I was surrounded by family, friends, parishioners, and even a few of my passengers from my Wheel Trans days. And, of course, discreetly in the background, was the man I loved.

In June 1980, after I had had three months of interim ministry, the new rector arrived. In keeping with the style of the old rector, the new one was also larger than life. A big, bubbly, enthusiastic man, John Erb was nonetheless different from Brown, and had his own vision of ministry and ways of doing things. I quickly realized that I was in the way at St. Mike's. For months I had maintained the style of the old regime, good for the interim but not for the future. It was time for a change. The new man needed to set his stamp on the place, so after the summer, when I thought I had allowed for a respectable passage of time, I went to see Archbishop Garnsworthy. He was expecting me. My former rector later told me, with a goodhearted laugh, that they'd had bets on how long Ferry would last.

The waiting for the other shoe to drop seemed interminable, but it was only two months before the phone call came from Bishop Geoffrey Parke-Taylor, who had replaced Bishop Allan Read. With the change in diocesan structure, Bishop Read, previously Garnsworthy's lone assistant, had quickly moved on to become Bishop of Ontario Diocese, centred in Kingston, and had been replaced as suffragan bishop by the scholar Parke-Taylor. Would I talk with the rector of St. John's in the east end of Toronto about joining him in a team ministry there and at the neighbouring parish of St. Saviour's? Both parishes were in Toronto East Deanery, a loose affiliation of a dozen parishes. There were twenty such deaneries in the diocese, more or less evenly divided among the five bishops of Toronto Diocese, a vast expanse in southern Ontario of twelve thousand square miles, with the city as its hub. I had been to St. Saviour's once on a deanery walkathon. Toronto East's dozen churches were all within a two-and-a-half-mile radius of a central point. With shifting demography, the east end was now severely overchurched, and it had been decided that little St. Saviour's could no longer support a full-time priest. Since St. John's needed a half-time assistant priest, it seemed like a good marriage, at least to the authorities.

Jeremy Van-Lane, the rector of St. John's and also the newly appointed regional dean (the chief priest of the deanery, if you will), was engagingly honest about the dilapidated condition of St. Saviour's. The building needed a great deal of repair, and the people were in low spirits after a year-long interim during which the previous regional dean had done an assessment and recommended a team ministry with St. John's. It was the only way he could see for the little parish to survive. St. Saviour's might go either way: it would die if it didn't learn how to open up to new people and reach out to the neighbourhood, or it could keep its doors open if it did. The demography of most of the east end had shifted with the influx of different ethnic groups, but it was still very WASP in the Upper Beaches area where St. Saviour's was situated, with lots of retired blue-collar workers and an influx of young white working-class people buying homes in what was then one of the few affordable neighbourhoods left in the city. It would mean quite a shift for me, moving from the bustling multicultural ministry at St. Michael's to the small white working-class parish struggling for survival. It would be a tremendous challenge.

A few days later George, long-time treasurer and churchwarden, gave me a guided tour through every nook and cranny of St. Saviour's. The church proper looked like a little cottage church, complete with gables — a little bit of English country-village architecture that had been swallowed up by the encroaching city. It had an air of history about it. George proudly pointed out the newly shingled roof and exterior painting that had been done the summer before. But it was cosmetic repair, and physical disintegration remained, underneath. The old tumble-down shack that had been tacked onto the back of the church during the Great War was sagging badly. One wall had collapsed and had been rebricked by George, a retired bookkeeper with a feisty temperament but good-humoured glint in his eye, and Ted, a veteran of two world wars that had left him with bad lungs and a glass eye. Ted, an old railway man, had years ago acquired an old locomotive bell; it had recently been resecured and was in use as a makeshift church bell, a thoughtful reminder of the days when the village of Toronto East was a railway town built around the old Grand Trunk Roundhouse, long since replaced by a skating arena. The proud people of St. Saviour's knew how to make do.

A relatively modern addition, the parish hall had been built just before the Great Depression, and its two large rooms on the main floor and in the basement were in good shape, though sorely underused. The church basement was another matter: this rabbit's warren of small and large spaces hollowed out of the earth over the years required a watchful eye if one was to avoid smacking one's head on the overhead beams or tripping over the misshapen steps. Hidden in the rubble in the organ-bellows room was an ancient church sign listing service times from the 1920s. The clutter of almost a century was everywhere.

The church's worship space was warm and intimate. All of the gabled windows had been fitted with stained glass, with the oldest and most striking windows over the altar. About sixty people occupied half the pews on a typical Sunday, George told me. Bitterly he described the process by which he said many parishioners believed the authorities had been trying to close down St. Saviour's. There had recently been a study of Toronto East Deanery with a recommendation that six of the twelve churches there be closed down. One had already been closed, and St. Saviour's was next on the list. Many parishioners, he said, believed that the appointment five years earlier of a Chinese priest in this white community was a deliberate attempt by the archbishop to kill the parish. George described how several priests had already turned down the appointment to St. Saviour's. Control of the rectory, usually maintained by the local parish, had been taken over by the diocese, and one of their staff was living there for next to nothing. According to George, what the parish needed was a full-time priest living in the rectory, which he believed the parish could easily afford.

In spite of the poor sales job from the churchwarden and the dean, there was something about St. Saviour's that captured my imagination. The potential in the neighbourhood, with increasing numbers of young families; the sense of roots and history about the place; the commitment of a dedicated core of parishioners — all pointed to a real possibility of life and growth. Resurrection from death or death-like experiences had become part of the fabric of my being. I believed that, with fresh leadership, a message of hope, and lots of loving care, the parish could trade its siege mentality for a more open and welcoming mindset and practice.

As a recently ordained priest, I knew I had to have a good reason to refuse the bishop's offer of a first appointment. The next offer might be out in Apsley, jokingly referred to by bishops and clergy as "the Siberia of the diocese," and I knew I didn't want the isolation of the far reaches of cottage country. St. Saviour's was a challenge that it appeared no one else wanted. It would be hard work in a depressed situation, but it had potential, and I longed to have my abilities put to the test. When the bishop asked for a three-year commitment, I suggested five, saying that three was hardly enough time to get settled in and make a go of it. Delighted, he agreed, and my appointment was announced the following Sunday.

My first day as priest at St. Saviour's was marked by a surprise birthday cake. December 15, 1981, was my twenty-ninth birthday, and word had gotten around somehow. At the end of my first monthly church board meeting, my new parishioners burst into song as the cake was carried in from the kitchen. The folks were excited about my arrival, having heard good things about me from a family who had been summer parishioners in Fenelon Falls three years earlier. And since everyone seemed to have dogs, the visible portion of my family, Maybe, was also made welcome. Only the week before, after a meeting with the church organist to plan my official welcome service, I had found that my seventy-pound fur ball had joined the choir as it assembled for practice, and was sitting in a choir stall, holding hands with a chorister, slurping her energetically. George's wife, Doris, told me never to come to their house without bringing Maybe along.

I plunged into parish life with enthusiasm. It was Christmas time, a time of hope and joy, and of new beginnings. The people of St. Saviour's welcomed me with great warmth and affection, and together we moved to address some of the problems causing the parish deep concern. The people were not just ready for change, they were longing for it. The altar guild, a small group of women who faithfully each Saturday morning prepared the sanctuary for worship, approached me with a couple of questions, the first and most startling being: when was I going to move the altar out from the wall? I was puzzled at first, until it was explained that, a dozen years earlier, the rector of the day had moved the altar out from the east wall under the main window so that he could get behind it and face the people during the celebration of Holy Communion or Eucharist. It had caused a terrible ruckus at the time, but people had gotten so used to seeing their priest's face during the service, and feeling they were all gathered around the Lord's Table for the sacramental meal, that when the previous regional dean had pushed the altar back a year ago to make room for a couple of Christmas trees, the people felt they had really lost something. The thought of worshipping with my back to the people had been weighing heavily on me, so I gladly gave the women permission to move the altar out two feet, much to their delight. A few weeks later, the matriarch of the chancel guild, Alice, whose husband, Ted, had done the brickwork on the collapsed wall, and her assistant Elma approached me cautiously. They had been to the religious-supplies store, looking for candles, and found themselves tasting different kinds of sacramental wine. Would I mind switching to white wine? After my experience with the thick red stuff most churches purchased from the liquor store, and my hangover after consuming the leftovers after the bishops' consecration at St. Paul's, I had developed an aversion to red sacramental wine. The women said the white wine wouldn't stain the linens, so it was decided. I was amazed at my new parishioners' willingness to try new things, especially since altar guilds are notorious for preserving every jot and tittle of tradition. "As it was in the beginning, is now, and ever shall be" might be a motto for most altar guilds, but not for these adventurous souls.

As soon as I arrived, a small local daycare centre that needed to relocate called, and within a few weeks had moved into the lower parish hall, providing a much-needed service to the community as well as a boost in church income. Some of the women had been complaining for ages about the dim lighting in the main stairwell of the church, which made climbing or descending the stairs treacherous for older people with poor vision, so cast-off fluorescent fixtures from another church that was being renovated were installed. We began to tidy up the clutter and neglect of decades; these many simple improvements didn't cost anything, but raised people's spirits. And, through it all, I preached and encouraged people with a fresh, hopeful vision of what the future could be.

Then we decided to attack the monster in the church basement. Hidden in a cement-lined sunken room was an ancient coal-burning boiler that had been converted to oil. A primitive device, with only one thermostat in the entire church complex, it was guzzling fuel at an alarming rate and heating the whole neighbourhood, or so it seemed. Other than the thermostat, the only control on the massive device was a low-water safety valve, which George informed me sometimes shut down the boiler on the coldest winter nights. The boiler was like the sword of Damocles hanging precariously over the parish's head, threatening to break down any moment and in the meantime consuming a vast portion of parish finances. Within a few months I had arranged grants from the diocese and the deanery, which, together with some modest fundraising in the parish, would allow us to replace the heating system with a brand-new one, without a burden of debt. With some assistance that year from our sister parish, St. John's, it became clear to Van-Lane, the parish, and me that St. Saviour's would be in a position to cut the apron strings and be self-financing by the end of my first year there. However, it took two runs at the College of Bishops, who seemed more intent on consulting with one another than listening to the regional dean and me, before we got permission to sever the team ministry and have my appointment at St. Saviour's made full-time. The deep despair was lifting from the congregation, fresh young faces were starting to appear, and the future was beginning to look brighter.

In the meantime, another sword hanging over my head had been removed. While I had been waiting for the bishop's call to a parish, the three-year separation required for a no-fault divorce had elapsed, and I was preparing to go to court. After three years of marriage and an equal time of separation, it took only sixty seconds for the judge to dissolve the marriage. Accompanied by the chancellor and my close friend Paul, who with his wife had watched the marriage disintegrate, I answered the judge's few questions with a yes or no, and it was done. Three years of separation had put the ultimate questions about marriage and sexuality on hold, but now they came to the fore. What would people think of me as a divorced man? Would they begin to wonder who my next love would be? Was I really gay, or had I simply had a bad experience with one woman? Was I really in love with Peter, or was he just a good friend? Would the bishops or clergy or parishioners begin to wonder if I was gay, and would such a suspicion be an obstacle to normal career advancement? What would they think when I began showing up at parish functions "stag"?

Repressed, internalized homophobia began to well up from where I had so carefully hidden it.

In what was to be my final see-saw of self-repression, I began dating a woman, and saw Peter less and less frequently. Lynn was a beautiful young woman, and I had become close friends with her and her mother over the previous three years. At my side at a couple of parish functions, Lynn probably scotched any speculation about my sexual orientation and established me firmly in people's minds, I thought, as "normal." There was no doubt that we were genuinely fond of each other, and I hoped that things would work out. Peter patiently endured my explanations of the conflict I was going through, trying to go straight. His love was strong and he had his own difficulties with accepting himself as "gay."

Ultimately, Lynn sensed that something was wrong. I never shared with her my deep inner struggle to deny my gay self, but she must have realized that something was missing. Perhaps it was the fact that I never suggested that we make love, although we were intimate. She broke off the relationship a few months after it started, and I felt a sense of relief. I had come to realize that there was no changing my orientation. The rubber band had broken, so far had I tried to stretch it. My gay sexuality was simply a reality. For months I had been plagued with longings for male intimacy that just wouldn't go away, and finally they culminated in a torrid encounter — a one-night stand. In a panic I went to see Peter, to explain what had happened, but by then he had been too deeply hurt by my infidelity. I begged him to give me a chance, but I had driven him away. In the terrible battle to defeat my true self, I lost the man I loved.

CHAPTER 3

THE END OF MY RELATIONSHIP with Peter marked the beginning of a long period of mourning. I buried myself in parish work, partly to escape the pain of loss, and partly because parish ministry was so enjoyable. I had found my niche, and God knew there was more than enough to do since St. Saviour's was in a needy state. Gradually I began to hear via the grapevine that I was turning the place around. In my preaching I tried to be positive and hopeful, so much so that one gloomy old man blurted out one day after Sunday service, "Well, we sure can't fault you for being negative!" For the first time in decades, a rector kept an office at the church. Word got around that something was happening at St. Saviour's: what had looked to many neighbours like a deserted haunted house had a steady stream of people coming and going.

My shaggy dog became a trademark in the neighbourhood as well as the church, since each day I would walk the short stretch from home to the office with her. It's amazing how people won't talk to a stranger on the street, but they'll always stop to talk to an appealing dog. Maybe was very friendly, and it wasn't long before I knew almost everybody on the street. Some of them started to come to church, and the Sunday school started to grow. Before long one diocesan bigwig who lived a few doors from the church began to spread stories about "the young priest who evangelizes with his dog"! One elderly woman decided to come to church again because, she said, after seeing Maybe sitting on the front steps, "I thought things must have changed at the church. If it's a good place for a dog, it must be a good place for people."

♦

While parish life was deeply satisfying and affirming, the grief in my soul would not abate. I worked late almost every night so that I

wouldn't have to spend more time than I had to alone in the rectory. I longed to see Peter, but we could barely hold a superficial telephone conversation, so hurt was he and seemingly intent on avoiding
me. Guilt and remorse were daily companions as I looked back on
what I had done. I couldn't blame him: it was too risky for him to
come near me, as he might get hurt again.

An even deeper grief was eating away at me. Life had changed irrevocably with the final grudging acceptance of my gay self. I had tried
to change, to go "straight," yet the undeniable reality boomeranged
back — the harder I threw my gayness away, the harder it came back
at me. I didn't want to be gay. I didn't want to be "one of *them*" —
a fairy, a faggot, a pervert, or worse. I had prayed, and fought
myself, and married, and dated. In the end I realized I was only lying
to myself: I was a gay man.

It was only with the loss of Peter that I began to make deep connections with the peculiarities of coming out, at least subconsciously.

I'll never forget an eighteen-year-old I had met one summer at the
hospital where I was working as a student orderly. I'll call him Bob.
Bob was lying on a Stryker frame, his body completely limp, following a diving accident that had almost severed the spinal cord in his
neck a few weeks earlier. He knew his neck was broken, his spinal cord
injured, and that he was lucky to be alive. Teeth chattering from a
fever that had set in, with fans blowing on his exposed body to
bring down his temperature, Bob was nonetheless in good spirits.
Nothing could lick him, not even such a serious accident, and he
was determined that he would heal and resume normal life. Bob was
in the early stages of denial: the injury was not serious, just a little
damage to the spinal cord — it'll mend. The reality was that life had
changed forever: Bob would never run or dive again. His life image,
with its ideal picture of the future, was shattered. In the months ahead,
as the reality of his loss hit home, Bob would experience anger at himself, at the world, and at God: Why didn't I check the water before I
dove? How stupid can you get! Why didn't somebody warn me? Damn
God for letting this happen! I don't deserve this. Anger would give

way to bargaining: If only I can get a good doctor, the right medicine, the best surgeon, the most exhaustive physiotherapy, then I'll change my life, I'll do volunteer work, I'll go to church and teach Sunday school. And then he would experience depression, suicidal thoughts, bleak despair, as he realized that he couldn't change the reality of his loss. Finally would come acceptance, as Bob let go of the life image he had treasured for so long, and the process of beginning to construct a new life could begin. The spiral of grief would take him through all these stages, not neatly or even sequentially; for many months, his life would be a bewildering vortex until he reached acceptance. Even then, months or years later, he would have flashbacks of bitterness, anger, bargaining. The reality of his life had changed irrevocably, much as though death itself had come visiting.

It may seem extreme to compare my struggle with Bob's, but, although they differed in degree, they involved the same grieving process. Coming out of the closet as a gay man, even to myself, had been an agonizing, twenty-year process. That ninety percent of the population that is sexually oriented towards the opposite gender does not undergo the trauma of loss that gay men and lesbians experience. Like Bob, I was facing the loss of an entire world, of all the hopes and dreams that had been instilled in me by family and society, of being "normal," fitting in, raising a family, and leading a "normal" life.

Even worse was the fear that I faced as a gay man. It was one thing to no longer deny to myself my deep inner longings, but to reveal them to family, friends, and a hostile world was a terrifying prospect. Would those close to me be disappointed in me, or even worse, despise me? Relatives and friends might wash their hands of me. I might become one of society's outcasts. After all, it was only in my teen years that homosexuals in consenting adult sexual relationships were no longer considered criminals under Canadian law. Society might still call me a pervert, and discriminate against me when I tried to find a job or a place to live. The Church might brand me immoral and tolerate me only in lesser positions, if at all — and the Church mattered as much to me as my sexuality.

And so I felt little joy in accepting the fact that I was a gay man. The parish was going very well, and I gave all my waking hours to it. In spite of my own sorrows, I continued to preach a message of hope to my flock. The once weary and depressed congregation had been transformed and now had energy and hope for the future. With the boiler-monster in the basement slain, small but steady improvements being made in the church's physical structure, a balanced budget, and my appointment as full-time priest-in-charge of St. Saviour's had come a lifting of the gloom. As the people of St. Saviour's constructed a new future, I began the long and difficult task of reconstructing my personal life image into something that could work for me.

Models for the process of transformation were easier to find for the parish than for my personal life, although the spiritual signposts were the same. Many books had been written on the process of renewal for parish life, and my training had prepared me to teach and lead. The parish had had a near-death experience, but the ingredients for transformation had all been there before I arrived: a willingness to change and experiment; an openness to new people and ideas; energy to break the lethargy and begin to tackle problems one at a time; a warm, generous, and welcoming spirit. We knew what a healthy parish could look like, and could envisage a new life image for St. Saviour's. There was a norm out there, in the Church, to which we could aspire, with only modest adjustments.

But there were simply no healthy models of a self-accepting gay man in the Anglican ministry. I had not yet discovered the library of materials written by gay theologians, counsellors, and others — in fact, much of it was just being written in the 1980s — but the same spiritual signposts that spurred me on in leading the parish to renewal gave me personal hope for a future. I didn't know what a healthy self-accepting gay Christian would be like, but I believed intensely that such a life image could be found or built.

In my days as curate at St. Michael and All Angels, I had read a book by a psychiatrist, Jim Wilkes, called *The Gift of Courage*. It was a book I would come back to again and again as if it were a desert oasis. My personal experience of loss in my marriage breakdown, coupled with my earlier spiritual encounter with God, taught me to trust deeply that out of death comes new life. From Calvary to the empty tomb, from crucifixion to resurrection, I believe that God is at work to transform human suffering and death into new ways of being alive to self, God, and the world. In this hope I would find the way to become more fully human, more fully alive. It was what energized my ministry at St. Saviour's, and gave me the strength to admit my personal loss and go on to an uncertain future.

Faith is not certainty. Despite all my efforts to plot my life course and ensure a future, I had failed. I believe that having faith means being able to live in the present moment with all its ambiguities, facing the unknowns of the future with a sense of hopefulness rather than despair. There is a tension in the human journey between having control and being genuinely open to the unknown, of giving up the past for future possibilities. In my attempts to hold onto a life image that didn't fit, I was trying to attain ultimate control of my life and thus find security, certainty, and perfection. What I really needed was the faith — specifically, the courage that springs from faith — to let go of control and a faulty life image. As Wilkes says, "Courage, whatever else it might be, is the capacity to resist the temptation to demand security, certitude, or perfection — the capacity to face an uncertain and ambiguous reality in which action requires risk."

Three images from the life of Christ powerfully bring into focus the process of human growth: Gethsemane, Calvary, and the Empty Tomb. In the garden of Gethsemane on the night of his betrayal, Jesus agonized over the future. The moment had come to decide to keep control of his destiny or give himself up to pain and death in the faith that on the other side of that suffering would be life in all its fullness. Jesus could have ultimate control, as the devil pointed out in his temptations: turning stones into bread, leaping off a precipice to be saved by angels, or ruling all nations meant that Jesus could have control in the personal, spiritual, and political spheres. And yet the suffering of Calvary according to Christian theology, was the way forward for Jesus and humanity. So great was the anxiety of Gethsemane, the strain of living undecided between the letting go and the keeping of control, that it is said his sweat was like drops of blood. Ultimately, Jesus had the courage to confront his suffering, and a sense of calm came over him, which was unsettling to his tormentors. When the awful suffering of Calvary was completed, Jesus' faith and courage were vindicated by God, as symbolized by the Empty Tomb, and Jesus was raised from death to new life. The transformation from suffering and death to life was complete. The courage that Jesus drew from God the Father had seen him through.

I didn't feel very courageous as I let die my image of a "straight" future and entered a period of pain and mourning that was to last for months. But I clung to the hope that God would somehow transform my suffering.

I had never ventured out in search of a gay community, and the only gay men I knew either were not self-accepting or were leading such promiscuous lives that I was horrified by them. The Christian virtues of commitment, fidelity, and love meant the world to me; so, after a year of mourning for Peter, my mind began to turn to the possibility of falling in love with another man.

Finally I worked up enough nerve to venture forth: I had heard that Key West was a gay mecca, so in April 1983 I booked a ten-day post-Easter vacation in a gay guest-house there. The island was gay paradise, in the days before the AIDS epidemic changed things, and the colonial town was abuzz with gay discos; old houses being converted to guest-houses, gay shops, and restaurants; and, everywhere, gay men. It had been twelve years since I had been in a gay bar or disco, and it was a tremendous release as I danced each night away, surrounded by other gay men. Within a day or two I discovered a group of men from Toronto at the neighbouring guest-house, and we became buddies for the next week. Much to my surprise, one of them was a young man I had met at my former youth group in Agincourt, who had since gone into the theatre. There was a tremendous sense of gay community and pride I had never encountered before, as we gathered around one of the older men, John, who had worked in television with my father back home. And the long-repressed adolescent phase of sexual experimentation was compressed into ten days.

When I got home from Key West, something had changed. I had a new sense of confidence as a gay man. I was not alone. I had met some wonderful gay men who were full of life and self-esteem, and had their lives together. Gradually I was beginning to build a new image of what life as a gay man could be, and I began to embrace it. With forays into the gay world of clubs and discos, and dinners with friends, I began to build up a small gay community of my own. And I quickly learned that gay Christians are in a double bind: not only was the Church prejudiced against me for being gay, but gay men had difficulty with my love for the Church. Most gays and lesbians, I discovered, would have nothing to do with the Church, because they had found it such an unhealthy, bigotted place to be. Coming to terms with God and gayness was something few undertook successfully.

I started to wonder about a good-looking young man who had started coming to church the previous autumn, who seemed sincerely interested in becoming involved in the church. Teaching Sunday school, helping with Saturday work parties, acting as groundskeeper the following summer, he showed his seriousness in what he believed was a call to ordained ministry. Les was strikingly handsome, with a sometimes devilish grin, flashing eyes, and a keen sense of humour. Resisting his charms proved more and more difficult, until finally, one October night after the annual college alumni banquet and address by the primate, Archbishop Ted Scott, we connected. It was the beginning of a passionate relationship that was to last two and a half years.

◆

I remember being amused but puzzled as a child by the tale "The Emperor's New Clothes." A paradigm of the many conspiracies of silence in human society, the story has over the years become for me an increasingly powerful image of life as a gay man in a society that would prefer to deny the fundamental reality of who I am. With my

newfound self-acceptance, I ironically moved into a world of greater
secrecy and shadows. People might know on some deeper level who
I was, but as long as I didn't make an issue of it, neither would they.
A strange silence settled over my new gay life, much in the same way
that families keep secrets about all sorts of things: a father's alcoholism,
an uncle's attempted suicide, the grandparents who had to get married, the child who was adopted or adopted out. Such family "skele-
tons" are kept locked up by unspoken consent, until someone,
innocently or not, opens the door. I can remember my mother's shock
when my grandmother's new fiftieth-wedding-anniversary ring trig-
gered some simple arithmetic that revealed that her oldest brother
was conceived before wedlock. My grandparents did what they had
to, and kept the secret from their children for fifty years; when the
silence was finally lifted they were still very much in love, but at least
one daughter was left feeling angry.

Yet, over the course of time, the conspiracy of silence weighs heavily on the one at the centre of it, the one who has the most to lose.
In the end, such a silence crushes the life out of the gay person, if a
way is not found to break it and, at the same time, minimize the loss-
es that result from doing so. The fear is always more or less present
that someone, malevolently or innocently, will break the silence,
with catastrophic results. At first there was some fear when Les moved
into the rectory, but the cover of "providing housing for a divinity
student" seemed to satisfy the parish. It was, in fact, the truth, but
only part of it. The spare bedroom was all set up with his books, clothes,
and personal things, but each night we fell asleep in each other's
arms in the master bedroom. If people had any theories about my
living arrangements they kept them to themselves, much as the emper-
or's townsfolk did.

As I began to feel real joy and delight in my loving relationship
with Les, the silence started to bear down on me. Like most gays
and lesbians, I wanted to share the reality of who I was with close
and trusted friends. I didn't think my father would be any problem,
since he had worked in television for decades, with gay directors,

producers, actors, and others. Dad had a real tolerance for other people, always thinking first about what type of human beings they were and whether or not they were sincere in their work. In fact, I don't remember when I came out to Dad. Mum, however, I had some concern about. I remembered how she had cried when I told her of my "problem" in my late teens. When her new relationship ended and she was broken-spirited and penniless, I had helped her pick up the pieces, finding her a place to live and helping her get settled into a new life. Heartened by my lack of criticism of her behaviour in running off and losing everything, and knowing her own deep sense of embarrassment and shame, Mum opened herself to me. I never pushed her or said "I told you so." We developed a close, caring relationship, and she even started to come to my church Sunday mornings. Finally I told her about Les and me. Tearfully at first, fearing for my safety and future, and wishing that I could someday marry and have children, she was nevertheless willing to wish me happiness with whomever it was to be found. She soon welcomed Les into the family, inviting us frequently for dinner, and enjoying Les's antics and good humour. Eventually I came out to the whole family, one by one; after their initial shock they became accepting, and even supportive.

All those years I had been afraid that I would break my mother's heart. A large part of the dilemma for gays and lesbians is that we love our parents and don't want to cause them sorrow. Many never do come out to their parents. To carry their pain as well as your own can, for many, be too much to bear. Instead, the conspiracy of silence is the best we can do. Fear of rejection and concern for causing them grief together form a powerful incentive to keep the silence.

Nobody knows for sure who knows what in the conspiracy of silence, creating a more or less constant state of tension and dread. In a world where you can't be honest, how do you know whom to trust, whom to be open with, who is accepting? "Speaking in code" provides an answer, a safe way for gays and gay-positive heterosexuals to set secure boundaries in the coming-out process. With Les living with me in the rectory, I was grateful that there were no members of

the congregation living on my street, but I wondered what the neighbours thought. I got a clue from one couple the day the renovation
of the rectory kitchen began. The middle-aged wife had seen the
kitchen wreckage being flung out into the backyard, and called to
invite Les and me over for dinner that night. She and her husband
were wonderful neighbours — warm, caring people. Over a glass of
wine before dinner, the husband, in the midst of our conversation
about the state of society, expressed the opinion that he had no
problem with gays, and that if two people loved each other, he
didn't think it should bother other people. In that moment of graciousness he had communicated three things: that he knew our secret,
that he didn't want to invade our privacy, and that he accepted us for
who we really were. At least, that is how I interpreted his message.
That's the problem with speaking in code — you're never quite sure
what the message means, or if it has been received, if you're the sender.
Les and I did not reciprocate, being novices at coming out to others,
and so we never shared with that good couple the confirmation that
we were in fact lovers. But the test of time was that the two couples
— the middle-aged husband and wife and the two young gay males
— became more than just good neighbours. They had reached out
to us, understanding that silence was necessary, yet found a way to
be encouraging.

Many gays and lesbians never get much farther in the coming-
out process than that discreet keeping of silence on all sides. Some
parents may send coded messages to their gay or lesbian child that
"we simply don't want to know." They are able to tolerate the secrecy, pretending the emperor has new clothes because they are unable,
or feel they are unable, to face the truth. But the question for the
self-accepting adult gay or lesbian is "What price integrity?"
Keeping up the pretence of heterosexuality by maintaining separate
bedrooms in case the parents come for a visit is anything but affirming for a couple that has been together for five or ten years. Gay
children long for acceptance, if not approval, of their relationship and
their loved one, in the same way their heterosexual siblings do.

Underlying that acceptance or rejection is the central issue of acceptance of oneself as a human being. We simply want to be known as we are and loved unconditionally. I felt myself fortunate to have parents who accepted me and my partner, and loved me without bounds.

Eventually, in the development of a new and healthy life image as a gay person I came to the question, "Whose problem *is* this?" A gay relationship can be the moral equivalent of a heterosexual marriage, in terms of love, mutual concern, dignity, respect, trust, and fidelity. The problem lies in the ignorance, bigotry, ancient inherited prejudices, and fear that form the bedrock of homophobia. Like racism, homophobia grows out of people's fear of that which is different from them, or strange or unknown. I knew all too well the weight of homophobia from within, for I had internalized it early in life, and had hated myself. After years of struggling against my own ignorance, my innate fear of what I thought was different, and inherited biblical and societal prejudices, I had finally vanquished the homophobia within, more or less. Something so deeply ingrained can perhaps never be fully expunged. Increasingly it became clear to me that homophobia was society's problem and the Church's problem, and not the problem of the gay person on the receiving end.

One cautious step at a time, I started to come out to trusted friends and colleagues. Brad Lennon and I were ordained together in 1980, and quickly became close friends. We had studied on opposite sides of the street — quite literally, since Trinity College and Wycliffe College face one another on the university campus — and I had discovered in him a person with a keen and challenging Christian spirituality, expressed in concern for social justice and an ability to recognize and penetrate oppressive social barriers. I sensed in my married colleague a kindred spirit with whom I could trust my innermost being. He was the first straight person I came out to, other than my family. With real love and respect, Brad encouraged me to be as true to myself as I could be in an institution that required the opposite of me. Over the course of months and years I developed a stance that allowed me to have personal integrity in the Church: I would be discreet about my sexuality and not push it down the Church's throat, but if challenged directly would never lie about who I was. The refusal to lie would eventually have catastrophic results, but for many years it served me in good stead.

♦

The need to be known and loved as I really was was more than psychological; it was deeply spiritual. In my readings of Scripture I found in Jesus a man who loved the outcasts of society and those sneeringly rejected by the religious elite as "unclean." In one of the healing stories, I especially identified with the woman who, suffering from a hemorrhage for years and in poverty after spending all her money on doctors, reached out to Jesus in a crowd and secretly touched the hem of his garment. She found herself instantly healed. Spinning around, Jesus asked who had touched him, knowing that power had gone out from him. Trembling, the woman came forward, only to be told: "Daughter, your faith has made you well; go in peace, and be healed of your disease."

Today we would recognize that the woman had a medical condition and provide proper medical treatment, but in biblical times her bleeding was an occasion for prejudice. Women were considered unclean when they bled; not only could a husband not have sexual relations with his wife during her menstrual period or for six weeks after her giving birth, but during those times she was untouchable. Anyone who had contact with her would also be unclean. A second layer of prejudice existed in the theological assessment that her continuous hemorrhaging was a punishment from God for her wickedness. (God could reveal in such fashion a terrible hidden sin.) And, finally, she was just a woman, and unfit to be in the company of good religious men.

The woman broke through the silence of her outcast status at considerable risk. She feared that even Jesus would reject her, and so, not wishing to draw attention to herself, had simply touched the hem of his garment, hoping and praying to be healed. When Jesus spun around to find the intruder, she expected to be chastised. Instead of rejection, Jesus congratulated her for her faith, and made the bold declaration that it was her faith that made her well, that empowered her to reach out for healing, to break the barriers of silence and prejudice. That faith, and courage, ultimately brought her release from her outcast status.

I, too, had touched the hem of Jesus' garment with considerable fear. Trained by society and the religious authorities to believe that I was unclean, I found in the bleeding outcast woman a spiritual ancestor to give me the courage to reach out to God for healing. Years earlier I had reached out for healing of my homosexual orientation, never to receive it. Now, instead, I received healing of my homophobia. And, like the woman, who though physically healed had to return to a condemning and prejudiced society, I had to return to work and live in a Church and society that failed to see the healing hand of God at work. My dilemma as a gay Christian was that I felt deeply that God loved me as I was and called me to form a loving intimate gay relationship, while the Church labelled me a sexual outcast.

Not all gay persons are able to break free of their own internalized homophobia, and those who don't and are in positions of power can be very dangerous. One day a retired bishop invited me for lunch at his home. I had heard via the grapevine that he was "one of the boys" and had a penchant for younger men, so I entered his house with some nervousness. After a lunch of scotch whiskey and macaroni and cheese, and some pleasant conversation, I was on my way home, thinking to myself that his must be a very lonely life and that perhaps all he wanted to do was befriend me. The second lunch a few weeks later was not quite so platonic. After more scotch than I would normally have in a week, and more macaroni and cheese — a creature of habit, he always had macaroni and cheese on Mondays — he grabbed me in his front hallway and started to kiss me passionately. I hadn't really thought ahead about what to do if he made such an advance, and he *was* a bishop, so I didn't want to make a fuss. Just then, there was a knock at the front door; the bishop opened the door immediately to a startled Les. I had arranged with my partner to drop me off at the bishop's while he went to an interview, and then pick me up on his way home. His timing was perfect. I introduced Les to the bishop and made my escape.

In the car, Les suspiciously asked what had been going on. The door had been opened very promptly, and there were both the bishop and I in the front hall, with me looking flustered. He was furious when I told him what had happened. A week or two later the bishop called to invite me for lunch again. It was early morning, and I was barely awake, when he suggested a day and time. Pretending to fumble for my diary, I told the bishop that that time was no good. After two alternatives were rejected, with me pretending to consult my busy schedule, the bishop hung up in disgust. I heaved a sigh of relief, hoping I would never hear from him again.

More stories surfaced about the retired bishop, and how he used his status to try to collect all the young male deacons and priests within reach, while at the same time publicly espousing a homophobic position. One of my young colleagues had an experience similar to mine, but had had much more presence of mind. After being malted and macaronied by the bishop, he was asked by the old man outright if he was gay. When the young priest replied, "Yes. Are you?" the old man spluttered, said no, and that was the end of it. My colleague wasn't invited back again.

Several months after my encounter with the bishop, I got a mysterious call from one of my gay colleagues. "I've just had cocktails with Bishop X," Keith said, "and he said something that I think you ought to know." I braced myself. "He's just back from the House of Bishops meeting, and said that Archbishop Garnsworthy is all upset because there's a young priest in the diocese who has a first-year Trinity student living with him." A sexual relationship was clearly implied.

After the call from Keith I wondered what to do. I could only guess where the story originated. Was the old bishop angry because I spurned his advances, and trying to ruin me? Or had word gotten around some other way to my diocesan bishop, Lewis Garnsworthy, that Les was living with me? Or was the old man just trying to make my life miserable with rumours? Any way I looked at it, it did not bode well. Still, I reasoned, I had not been directly questioned, and things were going so well in the parish that my area bishop would be unlikely to act on rumour when there were no actual complaints against me. Perhaps the spurned bishop was just making noises. I decided not to dignify the gossip, and never heard any more about it.

I avoided the gay bishop from then on, except on those occasions where a brief hello was necessary. I understood the dynamics of his own oppression, having been in a similar space once myself. He hated his homosexual orientation, but it was too powerful a reality to deny altogether, and so came out in sick ways from a twisted soul. Some of the most virulent homophobes in public and private life are those men who are so deeply closeted that they cannot admit even to themselves who they are, and carry on secret sex lives, taking advantage of young men. And this bishop was of an era when all sexuality, not only homosexuality, was not to be spoken of openly. He was paying a terrible price for society's homophobia and, in turn, exacting a toll on others.

◆

In my first few years at St. Saviour's, as I became more fully self-accepting, I developed my first deep adult friendships outside of my circle of gay friends, family, and gay-positive colleagues. Ellen and Pat were two parishioners almost as new to the parish as I was, and I drew them into church activities on the suggestion of others. It was preparing for the church auction that initially brought us into enough close contact for real friendship to develop. We had a riotous time, sweeping through the old building to find hidden treasures, and combing the neighbourhood streets together on Tuesday nights when people put out surprisingly good things for the city's weekly pickup of household refuse. They were bright, articulate, full of imagination and fun, and we became best buddies, with the approval and encouragement of their husbands. One of the real signs of good friends is that they keep you honest. Pat and Ellen did just that, sometimes at parish board meetings, never letting me get away with anything.

All three of us enjoyed a marvellous friendship, which other parishioners found hard to appreciate. Many suspected that I was sleeping with my two friends, and spread rumours to that effect. And some of the women were openly jealous. Little did they know.

My two "girlfriends" were the first parishioners I came out to. As close as we were, it was still not easy to tell them who I was, since the roots of fear run deep. Ellen made it easier. She told me about a gay friend, his struggles to accept himself, and how much she loved him and hoped he would find the right man to love. Speaking in code, she opened the closet door for me so that I could safely come out to her without fear. I discovered, of course, that she and her husband had known I was gay for years. She and Pat had been getting impatient, waiting for me to come out to them, she told me.

Thinking Pat would appreciate the humour, I took her to a gay bar that had an outdoor patio, intending to come out to her there. Instead, she burst into tears. I hadn't taken into account her emotional state in the midst of the breakup of her own marriage. Learning how to come out to people is a difficult process, with no handy models to work with, and I had mishandled it. Over the years Pat has never let me forget that night, although it wasn't long before we were able to laugh about it.

As the months of Les living with me passed, tension grew in the rectory. In the course of his theological studies, Les was becoming more and more disenchanted with the Church as a whole, and especially with the lifestyle of his parish priest and partner. His withdrawal from Trinity College marked the beginning of the end of our relationship, as Les became increasingly unhappy with the life of a clergyman's spouse. One of my parish-priest mentors had, years before, warned me that the work of a priest was hardest on his family, and that he always felt that he sinned most against them. The meetings three or four nights a week, the conflict I had to deal with from parishioners — about things as simple as flowers and as complicated as starting up a daycare centre — and the constant demands on what would be off time for the average working person brought Les to the point where it seemed he hated the Church, what it did to me, and the amount of time I gave to it. And, as he came out of the closet to himself and others, he increasingly saw the Church as an oppressor. The two-and-a-half-year relationship that began passionately ended similarly. He couldn't accept my lifestyle as priest, and I couldn't give it up. Torn between the two loves of my life, I resented having to choose between them. Les and I painfully agreed to break up.

Shortly after Les and I broke up, in the spring of 1986, Rod, a young priest on leave, appeared one Sunday at St. Saviour's and asked if he could talk with me. Two years earlier, on the brink of a nervous breakdown, he had dropped out of parish ministry after being an assistant curate. Long before that time he had come to the realization that he was gay, and his coming out had precipitated his personal crisis. Now, after two years of leave from the Church, it was time for him to make a decision about resigning his holy orders as a priest, and Bishop Brown wanted him to find a parish and priest with whom he could be comfortable, to go through the process. Rod told me that Bishop Brown, my old rector, wanted to keep him in priestly ministry, and had suggested me as one of several priests in the diocese whom he thought were probably gay but were functioning well and staying in the Church, and for whom things were still good because no one had made an issue of their sexuality. In that connection, Rod said, Bishop Brown had made very positive comments to him about my ministry. After some discussion I assured Rod that I would be glad to take him on, once I had a conversation with the bishop, who had only recently been transferred to my area of the diocese. Coincidentally, the bishop was coming for his annual visit and a service of confirmation the following Sunday, so I suggested Rod attend.

After the confirmation service, Bishop Brown told me how pleased he was to see Rod there, looking so much better than he had some months earlier, and that perhaps Rod could find a place to function for a while at St. Saviour's. He asked me to call him, so the next day we had a frank conversation about Rod's predicament, in which Brown indicated how much he hoped that Rod could find his place in our Church. He had recently been playing organ at the local congregation of Metropolitan Community Church, the so-called "gay" church, ironically located only a few blocks from St. Saviour's. The bishop, opting for political safety, never officially appointed Rod as my honorary assistant but kept the arrangements very informal, with a letter a few weeks later confirming our conversation.

I felt trusted and affirmed in the way my bishop and old friend was handling the situation. Believing that he knew I was actively gay, and that he trusted me, I understood that Brown was hoping I could save for the Church a valuable gay priest who had much to offer. While we never spoke directly about my sexuality, I felt we had danced around it often enough that we had an understanding. The 1979 guidelines from the national House of Bishops hung in the air like a heavy scent, but were never alluded to. As long as I didn't come out to the bishop, I was safe. Only if I came out to the bishop *might* he have to be responsible for what I was sure he already knew. And so I didn't volunteer any personal data. I kept in mind his old saying that it's easier to get absolution than permission. The Church's conspiracy of silence was working well for me and my bishop.

Over the months of counselling with Rod, it became apparent that silence could not work for him. He had already come out to the bishop, and understood that to remain in the ordained ministry in the Anglican Church he would have to lie to the bishop and promise to be celibate. Having broken the silence, he was unwilling to turn back. Despite five happy months and the appreciative comments from parishioners about his preaching and musical talents, this gifted man could not find his place in the Church because he was gay, out of the closet, and unwilling to give up the possibility of loving intimacy for the rest of his life, or to lie about it. In the process of coming out he had lost his sense of calling to the Anglican Church. Without apparent bitterness, Rod made the decision to resign holy orders.

Not long before meeting Rod I had read a book that prompted me to reflect theologically on the predicament of gays and lesbians in the Church. *Embracing the Exile* by John Fortunato had a profound effect on my Christian understanding, helping me to live with the tension of being in a Church that would reject me if I was honest about who I was. Considered a misfit by prevailing religious standards, I was in good company. Other misfits — patriarchs, prophets, and Jesus himself— though exiled from homeland, synagogue, or even life itself, were nevertheless at the very heart of God. I came to understand that, like these people, I had a homeland not yet reached, but which some day would be mine. In essence, Fortunato suggests, every human being is in a state of exile, having not yet reached that homeland where God will be known as fully as God already knows us. It is in the embracing of the exiled status that courage and strength are found for the journey home. God's gay and lesbian children are, in fact, he insists, more spiritually aware than the average person because of the undeniable reality of our current exile, the pain of being labelled misfits by Church and society. It is in embracing that reality and not denying it that the journey towards wholeness is accomplished.

Counselling Rod through to the point where he could embrace his exile ultimately by resigning his orders left me in a predicament: I was the same as him, only I hadn't broken the silence. For me, to embrace the exile meant deciding to stay in a Church that might officially reject me if I was completely honest and beginning to educate myself and a few others about the predicament of those who loved with "a love that dared not speak its name." It seemed obvious to me that God had called me and equipped me to be a priest, so much affirmation did I receive from bishops, clergy, and laity. At the same time I knew that God had made me a gay man. It would be a precarious tightrope walk, trying to juggle the church's conspiracy of silence with the need for greater openness and integrity. I wasn't able to set my foot on the highwire by coming out of the closet to everybody, but I *was* convinced that many people secretly knew that I was gay. Perhaps by being a quiet but insistent witness in terms of the ordinary goodness of my life, I could help a few people along the way to learn to love people like me more honestly and openly. I prayed that God would keep my foot from slipping.

CHAPTER 4

LOOKING GREASY, UNWASHED, and in clothes both ill-fitting and in dire need of cleaning, a heavy-set man wandered into church one summer day in the middle of service and sat down. There was a none-too-subtle shifting of bodies in the pews as he selected a seat and dropped into it. It was like the ripple effect in a small still pond when a heavy object lands in the water. I continued with the service as though nothing had happened, but out of the corner of my eye took in my people's reactions. The discomfort of the folks in the pews was most evident later as the intruder came forward with the rest for communion and knelt to find he had lots of elbow-room at the altar rail. And then, just as suddenly as he had appeared, he was gone. As he returned from the altar he passed by the pew where he had been sitting and went straight out the door.

The mysterious visitor provided the opportunity in my sermon the following week to speak about the ways in which we encounter Christ. Hadn't Jesus intimated that we would encounter him in other people, especially in the way we treat them? The hungry, the naked, the thirsty, the sick, the imprisoned — our response to them is a response to Christ himself. As the king says in the parable of the day of judgement: "I was hungry and you gave me food, I was thirsty and you gave me something to drink, I was a stranger and you welcomed me, I was naked and you gave me clothing, I was sick and you took care of me, I was in prison and you visited me. . . . Truly I tell you, just as you did it to one of the least of these who are members of my family, you did it to me."

Perhaps, I suggested, the greasy mysterious visitor of the previous Sunday had been Christ himself. Did we pass the test of the Christ encounter in the way we treated him?

Moments later, during the singing of a hymn, our visitor suddenly reappeared. The congregation was electrified. As he plopped down in a pew, one of the women leaned over to give him her hymn book, nervously pointing out the verse of the hymn we were singing. Everyone was watching. He didn't sing, although he seemed to follow the music and the service, and then, after communion, he disappeared as suddenly as before. People were perspiring, and it wasn't from the heat.

In the following few weeks our mysterious visitor appeared again, finally to be nabbed one Sunday at the end of worship and plied with cookies and lemonade in the narthex. He didn't speak much at all, and his absence after a few weeks left us none the wiser about his origins. There were many group homes in the neighbourhood; perhaps he came from one.

The recognition of my exiled status left me with a keen sense of the inclusive character of the gospel message, especially in the teachings and actions of Jesus. My sermons became more thought-provoking, as I seized every opportunity to motivate my congregation to reflect on the issue of who is "inside" and who is "outside" God's family, and how we make those sorts of assessments all too easily. One Sunday, when the reading was about a woman labelled an adulterer (and why is it that only women are labelled and punished?), I opened my sermon by asking, "Would you hang around with prostitutes?" and was startled by the suddenly beet-red faces of a couple of the men, before I could blurt out, "Well, Jesus did." If it is true that a person is known by the company he or she keeps, then Jesus really was a misfit. What a rag-tag collection of fishermen, tax collectors, women, and other "sinners" he drew about him. I felt I was in good company: the company Christ kept certainly was a gathering of those considered outside the pale by the "insiders" of the first-century religious community. Confident that Jesus loved me and accepted me fully as a gay man, I felt sure of a fundamental reality: in the family of God there are no outsiders, even if the self-righteous label them as such.

Sometimes it is as simple as the shoes you wear. I had taken to wearing dress shorts and sandals in the summer months under my

Sunday vestments, since it could get unbearably hot in a poorly ven-
tilated church. With the arrival of Michael Bedford-Jones, the new
rector in the neighbouring parish of St. Aidan's, we made a happy
arrangement where, by shifting service times a little at both churches, one of us could cover all the services while the other was away on
vacation, and we didn't have to hire a summer supply priest. The
first hot summer day I had donned my sandals and, as I distributed
the communion bread at the St. Aidan's altar rail, noticed some folks
were paying peculiar attention to my feet. Later, Judi, the assistant
curate, said, "Jim, do you know what you've done? Just a couple of
weeks ago I had a strip taken off me by some of the old ladies
because I was wearing brown shoes instead of black. And here you
are wearing sandals!" Not so innocently I asked what they would do
if Jesus appeared, sandals and all, and we laughed as we realized that
because I was a visiting priest I could get away with it.

For church people who don't want you to look different or do
anything new or different or strange, the underlying issue is a deep
resistance to change. How much change you can get away with is a
major issue in churches especially. At a time in society when everything changes so rapidly that change itself seems to be the only constant, church people tend to look to the church as the place of
escape, the final bastion of security in a changing world. "As it was in
the beginning, is now and ever shall be" has become in many
churches no longer an ascription of glory to the God of eternal love,
but a hardened expectation of every aspect of church life. Anglicans
forget that our Church began its separate life four centuries ago in the
crucible of the Reformation, when no aspect of the church's life was
left unchanged. It wasn't just that King Henry VIII needed a divorce,
it was the crying need for reform of a decrepit institution that foment-
ed rebellion and produced the Book of Common Prayer. Worship in
English, married clergy, separation from Rome, new theologies and
worship styles — all were tremendous changes and deeply resisted
by many people. In spite of the fact that the founders of the Church
of England wrote in the founding articles: "It is not necessary that

Traditions and Ceremonies be in all places one, and utterly like; for at all times they have been divers, and may be changed according to the diversities of countries, times, and men's manners," many Anglicans treat the Book of Common Prayer as if it were written in stone, immutable for all time.

The Passing of the Peace is a case in point. At one point in the service, the priest says to the people, "The peace of the Lord be always with you," to which the people reply, "And also with you." In the prayer-book tradition there was no accompanying action, but in the contemporary rites people and clergy exchange simple signs of peace — a handshake, a hug, or a kiss — with the appropriate words. The people at St. Saviour's had found this behaviour fairly easy to learn, but not those at St. Aidan's. After several summers there I was surprised one Sunday in July when the folks at St. Aidan's early-morning service turned to one another at the words of peace and began shaking hands. Thinking the parish had learned a new thing, I innocently exchanged the peace at the next service an hour later, to looks of alarm. One churchwarden in choir robes shook my hand limply with a look that said "What do you think you're doing?" With a sinking feeling in the pit of my stomach I realized that the new learning had not yet been transferred to the late-morning congregation, but I couldn't stop then. Working my way through the choir's hands, I reached one older man who thrust his hands behind his back and, eyes glaring, shook his jowls at me. The congregation stood in frozen silence, arms glued to their sides.

Flaring nostrils and looks of shock — I couldn't have had a worse reaction if I had just set off a stink bomb, I thought. The following week they got a rousing sermon on the meaning of "the peace," and I continued to pass the peace, even though some received it like a hot potato. When Father Michael returned from vacation he carried on the tradition, relieved that he didn't have to take the flak for having introduced the exchange of peace himself.

Michael and I had become good friends, and occasionally, over a good scotch, we would bemoan the state of Christendom, and wonder how we might induce the Church to break its lethargy. The Church had been in decline for the past two decades, especially in Toronto East Deanery, and we shared our common struggle of how we could help our parishes to be more open and accepting of new people and new ideas.

In the midst of decline one might reasonably expect that congregations would be very open to exploring change in order to find new ways of drawing people into the local parish, but when the initial period of upset over the prospect of imminent closure has passed, some parishioners want to settle down to the old ways. Shaking hands, smiling, and saying "Peace be with you" may seem like a small item, but churches have had roaring fights about less. At St. Saviour's we used to fight about the altar flowers and where best to position them.

The changing face of parish life was grounded in the fact that parishes had to find new ways of being in order to minister to the needs of a changing society. Many folks nostalgically longed for the good old days when parishes were alive with all sorts of activity. Churches had been the neighbourhood community centres for a previous generation, and with the loss of that function were in a state of decay. Tragically, too many parishioners associated that decay with "change" itself, as though there was an immutable cause and effect at work, instead of seeing that appropriate change could bring about growth and renewal. The old hymn "Abide with Me" characterizes that melancholy mindset, especially in the lyric "Change and decay in all around I see; / O Thou that changest not, / Abide with me." For many, change was a demon to be resisted at all costs, instead of a life-giving force for renewal. Changes large or small could raise the hackles of good people in ways completely out of proportion to the issue at hand.

A parish family is like any family, made up of individuals with often-conflicting needs and personalities. Some families develop a marvellous ability to negotiate conflicts as they arise, while others are almost totally dysfunctional. Most families get by with some level of dysfunction.

Clergy learn to live with some level of dysfunction in parish life, developing coping mechanisms with greater or lesser success. Art Brown once said to me, when I was his curate, that he didn't know anybody who had it *all* together. Parish families are no exception. The place of children at Holy Communion, the Christian family table, is a prime example of a family trouble spot. Until the 1970s the Church upheld the Victorian tradition that children were meant to be seen and not heard, and thus relegated them to the church basement to children's classes until the age of thirteen, when they could be confirmed and join their parents at worship — all this despite the imposing presence in most parishes of stained-glass windows of Jesus surrounded by children of many nations, bearing the inscription, "Suffer the little children to come unto me, and forbid them not, for to such belongs the kingdom of heaven."

In the 1960s and 1970s came a growing awareness of issues relating to human rights, specifically the dignity of every human being, and since then the Church has been teaching that, at the communion, no one can be excluded on the basis of age, gender, colour, or whatever. The requirement of confirmation before receiving communion was dropped, and individual parishes were encouraged to begin educating adults as part of the process of implementing children's inclusion at communion. There was some dissension at first, but years later it would be hard to find a parish that does not welcome children at the Lord's Table.

The Church has always dealt with other contentious issues in similar fashion. In the early nineteenth century, it was through the efforts of English Evangelicals that the movement to abolish slavery in the British Empire was successful. Until that time the slavery of black races was an accepted norm, supported by good Christian people citing obscure biblical texts as a rationale. For fifty years the remarriage of divorced persons was debated, until, in 1967, the Anglican Church of Canada changed its policy to allow the faithful a second, and sometimes a third, chance. Clergy have had second and third marriages approved by their bishops. Ten years later, after much acrimonious debate, the Church finally approved the ordination of women as priests on an equal basis with men. For a few years a "conscience clause" allowed dissenting bishops to deny women ordination in their own dioceses, and clergy and laity to refuse to receive the ministry of a woman priest, but even that form of discrimination has been ended, at least officially. In all these instances — slavery, divorce and remarriage, the place of children, and the ordination of women — men have historically quoted Scripture to undergird their theological justification for the practice of excluding vast portions of the human race from full inclusion in Church and society.

The point is this: there has been a fundamental shift in how the Church defines who belongs and who has what rights. The defining principle is now one of inclusivity, with the burden of proof falling to those who would *exclude* some, not those who would *include* all people. The day has come upon the Church that St. Paul hinted at when he said, "There is no longer Jew or Greek, there is no longer slave or free, there is no longer male and female; for all of you are one in Christ Jesus." Does this mean there is no longer gay or straight? Or is sexual orientation the last barrier of distinction?

After five years at St. Saviour's, I went to see Bishop Brown to suggest that it was time to think about a move. I was beginning to feel restless, and was ready for an evaluation of my ministry and the parish's, so that I could begin to think about what directions to move in. I felt patronized by the bishop's response that all he needed was feedback from the other clergy to know what sort of a job I was doing. In short, I was doing a superb job and, the bishop said, "You'll be a hard man to replace." Perhaps it wasn't yet time, I reasoned, and so I resolved to put off for another year any thoughts of moving on. Perhaps it was best, I thought, since the issue of gays and lesbians is heating up in the United Church, and spilling over into our Church. In the meantime I was counselling Rod, and that was important.

It was after Rod resigned holy orders that I felt the need to delve deeper into my own sexuality and my place in the Church. *The Church and the Homosexual* by John McNeill had already become a classic, and drew together from the many perspectives of church history, tradition, theology, scripture, philosophy, and psychology, a compelling picture of discrimination, misinterpretation, and oppression of gays and lesbians from the beginning of the Christian era. Already familiar with some of the perspectives of psychology and convinced that my sexual orientation was a given, I found McNeill's focus on Christian tradition and the Scriptures particularly intriguing.

In the time of the early Church, and in the time in which the Old and New Testament Scriptures were written, McNeill points out, there was no concept of such a thing as a homosexual person. That concept was invented by Freud at the turn of this century. As McNeill puts it:

> *Strictly speaking neither the Bible nor Christian tradition knew anything of homosexuality as such; both were concerned solely with the commission of homosexual acts. Homosexuality is not, as commonly supposed, a kind of conduct, but a psychological condition. It is important to understand that the genuine homosexual condition — or inversion, as it is often termed — is something for which the subject can in no way be held responsible. In itself it is morally neutral. Like the condition of heterosexuality, however, it tends to find expression in specific sexual acts; and such acts are subject to moral judgement . . . . The real moral problem of homosexuality has to do with judging the moral value of sexual activity between genuine homosexuals who seek to express their love for one another in a sexual gesture.*

It is clear that the Bible condemns heterosexual persons who engage in homosexual acts, but it is not at all clear what the Bible has to say about sexual intimacy between true homosexuals.

The traditional interpretation of the story of Sodom from the book of Genesis is a case in point. For generations it has been interpreted to justify a blanket condemnation of homosexual activity, and the word "sodomy" has been given a permanent place in the English language as a descriptive term for homosexual intercourse. (Interestingly, in some places, such as the state of Georgia, sodomy laws criminalize not only homosexual acts, but also anal and oral intercourse between a husband and wife.) On closer inspection, many scholars have found that the Sodom story has little or nothing to say about homosexual activity, but much to say about the sin of inhospitality.

In this ancient story, God warns Abraham about the imminent destruction of the cities of the plain, Sodom and Gomorrah, because of their great wickedness, and Abraham pleads with God not to destroy the righteous, however few, with the wicked. So God sends two angels to check out the city's inhabitants, and Lot, a resident alien, invites them to his home for the night. The men of Sodom surround Lot's house, demanding to have the strangers brought out to them "that we may know them," and Lot offers to bring out his two virgin daughters instead. The men refuse the offer, accusing Lot the foreigner of trying to play judge. The two angels reach out and rescue Lot, then blind the men of Sodom. In the morning, the angels rescue Lot with his wife and children, and Sodom and Gomorrah are destroyed in a rain of sulphur and fire.

What was the sin of Sodom? The Genesis story doesn't actually specify. Over the ages, Christians have inferred the sin of Sodom to be homosexual activity, but a growing number of scholars have come to a consensus that Sodom's sin was inhospitality, a grave crime in a land where there were no hotels and travellers caught outside city gates at dusk could become the prey of wild animals or thieves. In fact, hospitality is still one of the most sacred of duties today for the people of the Middle East. Some scholars suggest that Lot exceeded his jurisdiction as a resident alien by taking in strangers without having their credentials checked by the natives. The men of Sodom wanted to examine them or "know them." There may or may not have been an intention to rape the two strangers. If the intention was to rape, that act should not be construed as homosexual, but as one of violence and degradation. Rape is not a sexual act, but an act of violence, regardless of whether the victim is a man or a woman. When Lawrence of Arabia was captured in this century, he was raped. For a man to be used sexually as a woman was (and is still) considered to be the ultimate act of degradation and humiliation. It was common in Middle Eastern cultures for victors to rape their prominent male captives to render them despised outcasts even among their own people.

The conversations among biblical scholars can get quite technical, but this much is clear: Jesus himself identified the sin of Sodom as inhospitality. In the gospel of Luke, Jesus, discussing the problem of the inhospitable reception of his disciples, is recorded as saying: "But whenever you enter a town and they do not welcome you, go out into the open streets and say: 'The very dust of your town that sticks to our feet we wipe off in protest. But understand this: The Kingdom of God is at hand!' I tell you, on that day Sodom will fare better than that town!"

Other passages of the Bible traditionally interpreted as being against homosexuals or homosexuality do not fare much better under serious examination. The ancient prejudices and cultural biases of the people who wrote the various books of the Hebrew and Christian Scriptures, as well as the similar prejudices of the men who have, over the centuries, translated and interpreted them, form a thick barrier that is difficult to penetrate. And yet similar barriers, relating to the issues of race, gender, and divorce, have been eliminated. Christians no longer appeal to obscure texts about Ham, the son of Noah, who for his crime was sentenced with all his progeny to eternal servitude to his brothers' tribes, in order to justify slavery of the black races. We don't appeal to Paul's statements about women keeping silence in church and wives obeying their husbands to bar women from ordained ministry. Nor do we quote Jesus' admonition that whoever marries a divorced woman makes her an adulterer. But we still quote Leviticus against homosexuals, calling an abomination any sexual expression of love between two men. Interestingly, the Old Testament is completely silent on lesbian sexuality, probably because it involved no waste of "seed" but also because of the low status of women, who were little more than property.

What then should Christians appeal to in making decisions about the moral character of gay and lesbian relationships? The answer seemed obvious to me. Since there is really no substantial difference between the mechanics of intimacy for couples of the opposite or same gender, then it must be a question of the manner in which the two persons relate. In heterosexual relations, loving mutuality is of key importance: equal consent, equal concern for the partner's well-being, lack of force or violence, fidelity, and a shared intention to make a life-long commitment. All of these sound Christian and biblical virtues could characterize a gay relationship as much as a heterosexual one. I determined that I would seek out a person with whom I could experience that quality of relationship, even though the obstacles in Church and society would be considerable.

Ancient prejudice, fear of those who are "different," unquestioning adherence to received traditions, sheer ignorance, reluctance to accept new ideas and perceptions — all form the almost impenetrable bedrock of resistance to change. Yet another complication in the process of change, of coming to new ways of perceiving, and being, and doing, is the issue of who mediates change. Who makes the decisions, who is involved, and how are those decisions made?

In the Anglican Church in Canada there has long been tension between episcopal authority, the authority of a hierarchy of bishops over priests and lay people, and the principle of democratic government. The fundamental unit of the Church is the parish, where lay people have the most input and power. Parishes are clustered in small units, such as deaneries, with little power, and they in turn make up a diocese. In Canada there are thirty dioceses, divided into four ecclesiastical provinces, which in turn make up the national Anglican Church. The parish, the diocese, and the national Church are where things really happen, the other levels being weak links. But the most power resides with the diocese, and its bishop and once-a-year synod.

The Anglican Church of Canada is not like a corporation with one head office and thirty branch plants, but is more like thirty head offices with a loose central affiliation. Sometimes authority and power flow from the top of the pyramid, the diocesan bishop, down to the bottom, the folks in the pews. At other times the flow is reversed, at least theoretically — for example, in the meetings of diocesan synods, which convene annually to make important decisions, especially about budgets. In a diocese as large as Toronto, with a synod composed of more than five hundred lay representatives from more than two hundred parishes, plus all the clergy, the unwieldy body is often charged with being nothing more than a rubber stamp for "the boys downtown who make the real decisions."

I had always considered myself a team player, supportive of a large and all-too-complex system, so when I found myself caught up in a unilateral power-play, I was more than disappointed, I was angry. In June 1986 I was summoned by the archbishop's office to a special meeting of the diocesan ministries fund. This eight-member committee had its roots in the disestablishment and sale of churches struggling with harsh economic realities in the east and west ends of the city.

A decade earlier, the funds from the sale of a church in Toronto West Deanery had been put in a deanery ministry fund held in trust by the diocese. Similarly, money from the sale of Church of the Nativity in Toronto East had been invested. The closure of Nativity had been heart-rending for its parishioners, and could be accomplished only with the promise that half the proceeds would help establish a new Nativity in the suburbs, and the other half would remain in the deanery so that, in some sense, the original parish's ministry could continue in some form. Over the years, Toronto East Deanery had put its money to creative uses: hiring a chaplain for a local hospital and a youth worker for the deanery churches, and even in helping St. Saviour's replace its ancient boiler. Most recently, it was used to hire a deanery evangelist to help the churches to reach out and grow.

In 1983 the diocese, concerned that its own special fund and those of the two deaneries could be better administered jointly, proposed a trial merger of the three funds for three years, at the end of which time we would evaluate the situation. Toronto East Deanery Council debated the issue hotly, and agreed to the proposal with the understanding that Toronto West hadn't been using its funds in a planned or efficient manner, and the trial system would serve as an incentive to them, as well as freeing up funds for other needy situations in the diocese. An eight-member committee was struck, with four representatives appointed by the diocese and two each by the deaneries. I was one of the Toronto East representatives.

For almost three years the committee met to consider applications for funding — Toronto East had to apply like everyone else — and we doled out money to worthy applicants. Then a sudden call went out to meet with the archbishop. No agenda for the meeting had been sent out, so those of us who had been summoned could only surmise that something drastic was about to happen. When we got there, we found all five bishops, the chancellor, and the secretary-treasurer of the diocese waiting for us. It was a Wednesday, the traditional meeting day for the college of bishops, which the chancellor did not usually attend. The tension in the room was palpable. Then came the bombshell. Diocesan financial arrangements had been under study, we were informed, and a committee had recommended the dissolution of the special ministries fund. The money, over one million dollars, was to be absorbed into the diocese's investment fund.

For a few moments there was a stunned silence. Awkwardly, the representatives from Toronto West broke the silence, and in what was a surprising turnaround for them, acquiesced to the proposal. There was an almost audible sigh, a relaxing of the tension. Then all eyes were turned on Don and me, the Toronto East representatives. They didn't expect trouble from us, but what the bishops hadn't counted on was that Don wasn't just any deanery representative: he had been churchwarden when Nativity was sold, and remembered all the promises that had been made. There was some argument about whether promises had been made at all, whether they were written or oral, official or unofficial, and whether or not they had to be honoured ten years after the fact. Then I screwed up what courage I could and suggested that, as a representative from the deanery, I would have a difficult time selling the idea to the people at home. For years the deanery council had operated with the understanding that Nativity's money was a sacred trust, and it had been almost the only reason to come together to dream and to plan for the future. In a deanery where most of the dozen parishes were struggling for survival, it had been a tremendous encouragement to us. How could the diocese take it away? And, just as importantly, we had entered into the three-year trial by formal agreement, only to be told unilaterally that our money was gone. Why hadn't we been invited to be part of the evaluation process, since we were equal partners at the beginning?

There was a pregnant pause. I knew I was taking a terrible risk in speaking out to the bishops and chancellor, even in a just cause. It seemed clear they had already made their decision, and to them it was just a matter of damage control. Finally, one of the four diocesan representatives timidly but courageously tried to rephrase the concerns expressed by Don and me. It was a tremendous relief to realize that we had been heard by somebody. The rector of St. Clement's Eglinton, who was still a new kid on the block, having arrived from another diocese and jumped the clergy queue for the largest parish in Canada only three years earlier, was taking a risk. I was grateful to soft-spoken Terence Finlay, the man who in a few short months would himself join the ranks of the purple.

In the end, a compromise was imposed. The ministries fund was dissolved and the two deaneries' monies returned, not to each deanery, but to two of the bishops, to be shared by us with the neighbouring deaneries in the two bishops' areas. And I learned an important lesson: episcopal authority wins out in the end.

♦

"The rectum is not designed for sexual intercourse!" declared one of my United Church colleagues. Monthly meetings of the multidenominational Beaches Ministerial Association rarely got exciting, but that day became an exception when the two ministers from neighbouring United Church congregations got onto "the issue." The clergy from other denominations meeting that day at the Baptist church watched from the sidelines as the hitherto in-house battle became public. When the liberal cleric had commented that gays have a right to enter loving relationships like anyone else, the conservative had responded: "Faithful marriage or loving chastity, that's what the Bible calls for!" Obviously the two men had been through this acrimonious debate before, as the liberal went on to challenge the other over rigid interpretations of scripture entirely out of keeping with his colleague's usual approach to the Bible. When pressed to the limit he finally blurted out his view on the use of the rectum.

I was sitting by, furious but hamstrung by the closet I was still in. Quietly I asked, "Don't husbands and wives sometimes have anal intercourse? Is it wrong for them?" Not to be stymied my colleague went on to describe the diseases he believed were rampant because of such "deviant" and "unnatural" practices. I was boiling inside, but I let it drop. Why is it, I asked myself, that when you push someone who has strong anti-gay feelings to defend his or her position the argument turns to bodily mechanics? Ultimately it seems so often to boil down to physical revulsion. Again and again people like this who don't know me or understand me reduce my loving relationship to a mere animal act in order to condemn me for it. I wondered how he would like to have his marriage described solely in terms of the position he assumes in bed when making love with his wife; not in terms of deep love, commitment, caring, fidelity, or any moral quality, but just the sheer mechanics of penetration. Surely, I thought, he must have recognized that there is no significant difference in what same- or opposite-gender couples do in bed.

Angry and humiliated, I could not speak up. I feared becoming known as the Beaches Ministerial's token faggot. Instead I comforted myself with the warning of Jesus that you should not throw your pearls before swine.

This ignorant man had undoubtedly assumed that I was just one of the boys, "normal," married with children. Would he have behaved differently if he had known that I was gay, or would he be a danger to me? Would I have quickly become the subject of gossip and wound up on the unemployment line? The dilemma for gays is agonizing at times. People don't recognize the ordinary goodness of our lives, and instead cling to stereotypes of gay people as perverts and child-molesters. If only sexual orientation was like skin colour, at least we would be a visible minority instead of an invisible one. Some gays and lesbians dream of the day when every one of us would turn purple — no family, no workplace, no church would be left untouched. The unknown would be known. The "faggot" or "dyke" would no longer be a loathsome creature of the dark but everyone's son, daughter, sibling, friend, or neighbour.

By 1987 a dark cloud of fear and hostility had spread throughout the Canadian church scene. The question of sexual orientation and ordained ministry had become a very public debate throughout the 1980s in the United Church of Canada, the country's largest Christian church other than the Roman Catholic. Beginning with the Hamilton Conference's refusal to ordain a self-declared lesbian, the issue was passed on over the years to increasingly higher Church jurisdictions until it reached the national level of General Conference. In the process, conservative forces formed an organization called the Community of Concern whose primary goal was to prevent the ordination of self-proclaimed gays and lesbians. The national church had begun a study of sexual orientation designed to involve ordinary church people from city and rural congregations — a grass-roots process which many hoped would result in a genuine welcoming of gays and lesbians as full members of the Church.

The sensitivity of the issue quickly became apparent in the polarization within presbyteries, conferences, general conference, and parishes, of which my two Beaches Ministerial colleagues were a prime example. Media focus on "the issue," as it came to be called, drove the tensions in the debate to a fever pitch. Dire predictions were made that the United Church would come untied when the issue came to a vote at the 1988 general conference, and that hundreds of congregations would leave the Church. The Community of Concern fanned the flames at every opportunity.

None of this furious controversy was taking place in a vacuum. Indeed, the same controversy was generating considerable heat south of the border in many denominations in the United States. John McNeill, the Jesuit priest who had written the landmark book *The Church and the Homosexual*, had been silenced by the Vatican. The U.S. Episcopal Church (sister to the Anglican Church of Canada) was divided, although a few brave bishops had ordained "open" lesbians.

Canadian Anglicans were keeping a low profile. Smugly, we told our United Church friends that their public family feud was no way to handle a sensitive issue. It should be dealt with discreetly, behind closed doors. That's the problem with the congregational system of church government, we said wisely: you have no hierarchy to guide you through the minefields of contemporary issues.

In fact, I had felt some pride at the way my Church had handled a sensitive issue, at least early on. Instead of opening the discussion up to the general public in a way that would have resulted in violent and divisive debate, the Anglican bishops of Canada commissioned a task force in the summer of 1976, composed of eleven people from a variety of backgrounds, to present an advisory report to "assist the bishops in their deliberations." That commission, headed up by Dr. James Reed, a psychotherapist, Anglican priest, theologian, and professor at Trinity College in Toronto, would devote almost two years to writing and rewriting their report. It was to be an arduous and ultimately not very rewarding task, with continual criticism from at least some of the bishops who tried to keep the debate in-house by holding their discussions *in camera*.

Charges of pre-empting the bishops' commission were directed in October 1976 against *The Canadian Churchman*, the national newspaper of the Anglican Church of Canada. In an effort to open up the discussion to the Church public, eight full pages were devoted to a section entitled "Understanding Homosexuality," the result of a year of research by the author Ann Benédek. In a wide-ranging series of articles, people from all perspectives were interviewed: bishops; a closeted gay priest in a five-year relationship; Bob Wolfe, the pastor of Metropolitan Community Church of Toronto, which has a special ministry to gays; Ellen Barrett, the first open lesbian to be ordained in the United States by Bishop Paul Moore of New York; George Hislop and Michael Riordan, who were prominent gay activists in Toronto; former moderator of the United Church of Canada Bruce McLeod, a member of the Ontario Human Rights Commission's review committee then conducting hearings about the inclusion of sexual orientation in the Ontario Human Rights Code; Tom Warner from the Gay Alliance Toward Equality; Konnie and Chris, a lesbian couple; and psychologists who indicated that homosexuality is not necessarily an illness. It was the most in-depth coverage of the issue that Canadian Anglicans would see for the next fifteen years.

A year later, *The Canadian Churchman* responded to mounting criticism from within the Church with an editorial titled "Lid Should Be Taken Off Church Sexuality Report." The newspaper was condemned by several sources inside the Church structure for anticipating the work of the task force, and this was cited as a reason for the attempt to delay publication of the articles. There was immediate reaction across the country. One diocesan organization urged withdrawal of funds from the *Churchman*. But some correspondents found the issue helpful in dealing with their own homosexuality, and that the articles had stimulated discussion in their parish.

Debate in the House of Bishops in February 1978 was lively. Three points of view emerged, which the primate, Archbishop Edward Scott, tried to meld into a common statement. Some bishops wanted to support gays and lesbians in loving relationships in some significant fashion. Other bishops were virulently opposed to homosexuality and any intimate expression of it; it was, for them, a perversion contrary to Scripture, Christian tradition, and the laws of nature. Still other bishops, perhaps the majority, wanted to ease the burden put on gay Christians without coming right out and supporting them, for fear of dividing the Church — tolerance rather than endorsement. The primate was working furiously to bring the disparate factions together.

At the same time the bishops were under a great deal of public pressure to declare their position after much coverage in the Canadian media. At the end of a week, after considerable debate and amendment, a statement was agreed upon and released to the media.

> *We believe as Christians that homosexual persons, as children of God, have a full and equal claim, with all other persons, upon the love, acceptance, concern and pastoral care of the Church. The gospel of Jesus Christ compels Christians to guard against all forms of human injustice and to affirm that all persons are brothers and sisters for whom Christ died. We affirm that homosexual persons are entitled to equal protection under the law with all other Canadian citizens. It is clear from Holy Scripture that only the sexual union of male and female can find expression within the covenant of Holy Matrimony. In the heart of biblical teaching about creation we discover insights into the nature and purpose of sexuality. Rooted in God's creative purpose is the fulfillment and completion of male and female in each other, together with the procreative function of sexuality. Thus the Church confines its nuptial blessing to heterosexual marriages, and we cannot authorize our Clergy to bless homosexual unions. We are aware that some homosexuals develop for themselves relationships of mutual support, help and comfort, about which the Church must show an appropriate concern. Such relationships, though, must not be confused with Holy Matrimony, and the Church must do nothing which appears to support any such suggestion.*

A brave statement in 1978, it provoked a furious debate in Church circles as well as the press. "Bishops Support Gay Legal Rights," cried the front page of *The Canadian Churchman*. The bishops had affirmed the full and equal claim of gays to acceptance in the Church, even going so far as to advocate protection under civil law. Opponents of equal human rights protection for gays were set on their ears by the call for equal protection under Canadian law. Even worse in some eyes was the bishops' recognition of the goodness of at least "some" homosexual relationships, going so far as to advocate the Church's showing "appropriate concern." While explicitly refusing to put gay relationships on a par with heterosexual marriage, they appeared to be trying to find a way to validate and support lesbians and gays in loving relationships. Nowhere in the bishops' statement was to be found any statement explicitly condemning homosexuals or "homosexual activity."

Inside that issue of the *Churchman*, an editorial raised questions about the meaning of ". . . equal protection under the law. Do the bishops restrict themselves to the law as it now stands, or to the law as it may in future be amended?" Would a bishop be able to dismiss priests who admitted to their congregations that they were gay? "In such situations, the priest or ordinand would have legal redress and the onus would be on the bishops to demonstrate that heterosexuality was a *bona fide* requirement of priesthood." The human rights issue raised by the bishops' statement had serious implications for the future.

In an effort to address the concern about secrecy, the National Executive Committee of the Anglican Church of Canada a few months later, "after considerable debate, gave approval to the drafting of a study paper which would deal with the issue of human sexuality, with particular reference to homosexuality." It was to be based in part upon the confidential report of the bishops' commission. There was great reluctance to produce any document at all.

Rancorous public debate went on for months until the House of Bishops' meeting in February 1979, when the church's leaders held an in camera debate about the report of their commission, and how they should respond to it and the public furore. Finally a resolution was passed that endorsed conditional ordination for homosexuals. The press had a field-day. Headlines screaming that the bishops had approved the ordination of homosexuals sent them scurrying to do damage control.

Within the week, Lewis Garnsworthy, the Archbishop of Toronto, had a pastoral letter read in Anglican churches across his diocese, berating the media for "the misleading and distorted reporting in the press" by which "you would come to the conclusion that the Church is taking some new action." Denying that anything had changed, Garnsworthy attempted to assure the faithful that all the bishops had done was to state candidly what the traditional practice of the Church had always been. They were not condoning homosexual activity since that was sex outside of marriage.

On the national scene, Archbishop Scott issued his "Pastoral Letter to the People of the Anglican Church of Canada," informing them of the recent resolution of the Canadian House of Bishops "concerning the ordination of persons with homosexual orientation." Considerable backtracking had to be done after the bitter complaints of some of the faithful about the bishops' 1978 statement, which they saw as throwing the doors open to homosexuals. In an apparent about-face from the previous year's statement, the resolution of the House of Bishops stated, "We accept all persons, regardless of sexual orientation, as equal before God; our acceptance of persons of homosexual orientation is not an acceptance of homosexual activity." Love the sinner, hate the sin. In this inherently contradictory statement, the bishops put behind them the "appropriate concern" they had only a year earlier espoused for gays in loving relationships. To make sure the public got the point, they made it explicit: "We do not accept the blessing of homosexual unions." The door slammed shut for those seeking full acceptance for gays in the foreseeable future. In a moral and theological contradiction, the bishops put themselves in the unenviable position of saying both that homosexuals have a full and equal claim on the Church's acceptance and that for such persons to express themselves sexually in a gay relationship is a sin. The gay community might well wonder what it meant to be fully accepted as gay human beings who were nonetheless never to act on that state of being. This appeared to be no acceptance at all, but a cruel and arbitrary distinction between being gay and doing gay. And the buzz among some of the gay community was that the Church was against gay relationships and therefore was in effect encouraging back-room encounters and promiscuity.

Knowing that the rancorous voices would be only somewhat mollified, the bishops went one step farther: "We will not call in question the ordination of a person who has shared with the Bishop his/her homosexual orientation if there has been a commitment to the Bishop to abstain from sexual acts with persons of the same sex as a part of the requirement for ordination." Once again, love the sinner, hate the sin. This appeared to be the clear stand that the conservative elements within the Church were seeking: practising homosexuals (an obnoxious phrase; we never speak of practising heterosexuals) would not be ordained. And the bishops announced that the issue of homosexuality would be broadened "within the larger study of human sexuality in its totality." The bishops vacillated about issuing the report of their commission on homosexuality, and in the end affirmed their decision to commission special study materials on the general topic of sexuality.

"A double standard," charged *The Canadian Churchman* in its editorial the following month. While the statement represented a step forward into a previously ignored area, in many ways it fell short. "There is a contradiction in the bishops' acceptance of homosexuals. We accept all people, they say, regardless of sexual orientation, as equal before God. But they then say their acceptance of homosexuals is provisional; they do not accept the sexual activity of homosexuals and, in fact, they require the homosexual ordinand to abstain from this expression of homosexuality. And so this guideline sets up a double standard between the homosexual, and the heterosexual whose ordination is not dependent upon a promise of abstinence." And the guidelines also set up a double standard between Church and society: "Now the bishops appear to be saying that while they expect society to abide by one set of rules, the church will abide by another set." The editorial charged that gay clergy were offered no hope of an honest pastoral relationship with their bishops. The bishops had not come to grips with the issue of sexuality. "In theory, the bishops' statement offers a promise of equal acceptance to Anglican homosexuals. In practice, it does nothing substantial to erase the mistrust, alienation and fear that is a constant companion to every homosexual person in the church."

Once again the primate had to respond to bad press — this time from the Church's own newspaper. In an interview printed the following month, Archbishop Scott reiterated the bishops' position, that they were merely stating clearly what had always been the Church's stand. In a fine balancing act he tried to leave the door open to future changes in "the mind of the church." "Our statement is not meant to be, in any way, legislation or a final doctrinal statement. It is a pastoral statement and we intend it to assist us in the exercise of our pastoral ministry within the church." The *Churchman*'s charge that a double standard was in place would be true only "if it were completely clear that homosexuality is totally genetically determined. Only then could homosexuality and heterosexuality be viewed as completely equal conditions."

While the Church public may have thought the bishops' stand was perfectly clear, bishops and clergy, like the *Churchman*'s editors, knew that the Church's familiar and historical duplicity was simply being restated. The cleverly worded phrase about ordination left both bishops and gay clergy free to function in an almost-explicit conspiracy of silence. Written in large letters, visible only to clergy eyes, was the word IF. In his letter the primate assured Anglicans that nothing had really changed; the bishops were merely making explicit the "standards that had always been expected of all clergy." And, indeed, nothing had changed. "*If* a person seeking ordination shares with the bishop his/her orientation" left both bishop and ordinand considerable latitude. There was no obligation for ordinands to reveal their sexual identity, nor was there any obligation for bishops to inquire about it. Silence of both parties secured the conspiracy. In the unlikely event that a bishop had heard from other sources that a candidate was gay, he could write it off as "gossip" and, with a wink, turn a blind eye as long as it had not become a public scandal. Even if a bishop should ask or a candidate should volunteer the personal information, the candidate could simply promise "to abstain from sexual acts with persons of the same sex" with fingers carefully crossed behind the back. After all, no one would actually know what a priest was doing in the privacy of the bedroom. In an attempt at compromise, the mutually exclusive views of bishops who were anti-gay, pro-gay, and somewhere in-between came together in a guideline that was so vague and inherently contradictory as to make it almost unusable. Someday it would implode from its own flaws.

◆

I had not taken much notice of the bishops' statements when I was ordained in 1980, as I was, at that time, still in a deep state of denial. But as I became more aware of the statements and of the large number of gay clergy in positions high and low, I came to a deeper understanding of the Church's conspiracy of silence. Life went on as before for gay clergy. Being discreet, long an Anglican virtue, now became a necessity. While most bishops did not initiate homophobic witchhunts, a few bishops interrogated single ordinands about their sexual orientation, forcing gay candidates to lie or face the prospect of being refused ordination. "Ask me no questions, I'll tell you no lies" and "Don't tell me anything I'd have to act on" had long been the modus operandi. The difference now was that it was enshrined in a resolution of the House of Bishops that was "meant to be a pastoral guideline for the Bishops, as they consider persons to be admitted to the Church's ordained ministry." Those previously ordained heaved a sigh of relief, thinking the guideline was not retroactive and, at any rate, dealt only with the decision making of the bishops in the ordination process. It was a guideline for bishops, not for clergy, and the bishops clearly used it at their individual discretion. In fact, at neither of my ordinations, as deacon in 1980 and as priest in 1981, was the issue raised by Toronto diocesan authorities, nor was it raised at any point in the process before ordination, to the best of my recollection.

As for me, like many of my gay clergy colleagues I saw the House of Bishops' statements and guidelines as inherently contradictory and unjust. Yet I still believed that they provided a way forward, however inadequate, as the Church came to terms with the reality of gay sexuality. At least the Church was talking about it, and the door had been left ajar for future discussion. The bishops had committed themselves to continuing study of the issue, and had shared that mandate with the national executive committee.

But the Church didn't want to talk about it — or, at least, not the bishops and the national executive (NEC). A new task force headed by Dr. James Reed, which had been given the mandate to produce a study resource for the whole Church, was passed back and forth like an unwanted child for eight years. The only thing the bishops and the NEC could agree on was that there *should* be a study resource; what sort of materials it should contain was a matter of deep division. Concerns about people's divergent views and the role the media would play were of paramount concern. Again and again the resource papers were sent back for revision, until, in the end, little was left of materials from the study commissioned in 1976 by the bishops. None of that commission's recommendations was allowed to be published. Could the people in the pews be trusted with the same information that the bishops had received in 1978?

Church and secular media fell silent on the issue, at least for Anglicans. After all, the United Church was providing a much more interesting *public* debate. But behind the scenes the deliberations of bishops and the NEC were just as heated. As late as February 1985, when the sexuality task force reported to the House of Bishops, there was fevered debate over the study guide's two chapters on homosexuality. Dr. James Reed and Phyllis Creighton were raked over the coals by some of the bishops, who charged they were advocating homosexuality, contrary to scripture and tradition. The authority of Scripture was being compromised, they charged. One bishop even claimed that "one of the major social problems we are facing is the romanticizing of homosexuality. . . . children are being bombarded with romanticization of homosexuality and protection of the young from a pervasive evil is the responsibility of the church." According to the minutes of the bishops' meeting in February 1985, the primate, Archbishop Scott, "reminded the Bishops that the Church was requested to study sexuality and homosexuality and that we must try to prevent discrimination and seek the truth. He said that, if the study guide is published with no reference to homosexuality, that, in itself, will carry a message." The pressure continued on the two authors to dilute the offending chapters.

While it is impossible to delve into the inner thoughts of a bishop, there was real difficulty on a personal level for more than one bishop who had gay children. Chief among these was Lewis Garnsworthy, the Archbishop of Toronto, whose son Peter had recently come out to him as a gay man. Like many parents of gay and lesbian children, Garnsworthy had a hard time coping with his son's sexual orientation for a number of years, complicating both his personal thinking on the larger issue, and the House of Bishops' deliberations which he influenced greatly. Avoidance of the issue of gay sexuality personally and in the House exacerbated the delay in the publication of the study guide on sexuality.

When finally *A Study Resource on Human Sexuality* was published in 1986, there was little fanfare. The study documents circulating in the United Church of Canada on "the issue" were provoking angry public debate, with the Community of Concern leading the fray. Anglicans — bishops, clergy, and the people in the pews — were content to stand back and watch the United Church ripped apart, shaking our heads and lamenting that our sister church didn't have the good sense to follow our example and keep such a contentious issue under wraps.

Despite the smugness of the imagined safe Anglican perch, down in the trenches gay priests knew the real dangers at hand. Some gay clergy avoided the line of fire by getting into some "special ministry" that afforded them some protection against the sharp-shooters commonly found in parish life. Chaplaincy, teaching, or even an administrative position at national or diocesan headquarters was a safe haven for clergy who could no longer stand the stress brought on by the vulnerability they felt in parish life, where their comings and goings could be watched by nosy or irate parishioners. If I had not enjoyed parish ministry so much, I too might have retreated to a safer form of ministry. One summer, in fact, that became an option.

I was finishing my summer vacation with my first-ever visit to Montreal, in late August 1987, when I ran into an old acquaintance. Andrew Hutchison had been director of the parish training program in Toronto Diocese, and had seen me through my difficult summer almost ten years earlier in Fenelon Falls as my marriage was breaking down. Now he was Dean of Montreal and rector of Christ Church Cathedral there. Sunday morning, after the main service — I usually attended Sunday service while on holidays to see what the rest of the Church was up to — as we shook hands he invited me to attend Evensong later in the afternoon and join him for a drink afterward. I gladly accepted.

Later that evening, Andrew described the exciting ministry at the cathedral. There was an opening coming up on staff; would I be interested in moving to Montreal to take up "a ministry to singles" at the cathedral? There were lots of young people, singles, gays, and divorcés, as there were at most cathedrals, and as I was a "single person" he thought I could be very effective there. Having lived my entire life in the Toronto area, it was a tantalizing idea: a new city, a different culture and language, a new experience. Since I had been unsuccessful in my few attempts at dating and hadn't formed a new relationship, it seemed like an opportune moment to make a move. And, most important of all, I wondered if there were quotation marks around "single person." I couldn't know for sure, but I assumed that the dean knew I was gay. A ministry that included a real outreach to the gay community stirred my imagination. And I was restless and ready to move from St. Saviour's after six years there.

In the ensuing weeks Andrew and I talked on the phone and agreed to begin the necessary process. I typed up my résumé and sent if off to Montreal for his parish committee to peruse. My area bishop, Art Brown, hadn't taken my request to think about a move very seriously, and I feared I could be stuck where I was forever. Andrew agreed to talk to his bishop, Reginald Hollis, and ask him to make the courtesy call to Archbishop Garnsworthy to let him know that Andrew would be talking to me.

A few days later a shocked Dean of Montreal called to tell me that it was off. When his bishop had asked my bishop if it was okay for Andrew and me to talk, Garnsworthy had simply said, "No." That refusal had come as a complete surprise, since the request had been mere protocol. In the ordinary course of events a bishop is not supposed to block the movement of clergy to another diocese, even though he may think of it as poaching. A few days later I called Art Brown to vent some spleen over the archbishop's unwarranted roadblocking. Quite simply I was too good a man to lose, I was told. Well, I thought, the archbishop could at least have talked to me about it, instead of being so autocratic and paternalistic. But, on one level, I was flattered. Perhaps now the bishops would take my desire to move seriously, and begin putting me on some interview lists for vacant parishes.

I didn't have long to wait. A few weeks later, one of the other bishops called to ask if he could put me on a list for a parish in his area. After reading the profile the parish selection committee had put together, and going to an interview, I knew it wasn't the right fit. But at least I knew that things were moving. I sensed that my ministry was strongly valued and that, even if the bishops knew unofficially that I was gay, it was not going to be an obstacle to future opportunities in the parish placement process. With renewed vigour I gave myself to the busy parish life I had nurtured for six years.

CHAPTER 5

FOR MONTHS I WAITED FOR a call from a bishop. In theory, the process of clergy moves is democratic. Each month clergy vacancies are listed in *The Diocesan Link*, a monthly newsletter from headquarters sent out to all the priests in the diocese, with an invitation to speak to their bishop if they're interested in any of the advertised openings. In practice I knew you had to be naïve to think you could simply apply for a parish — the bishops kept tight control, and with a patriarchal attitude from another era held the parochial placement cards close to their chests, dealing them out pretty autocratically. I had tried once to express an interest in a vacant parish near the "gay ghetto" in downtown Toronto, only to be told that the parish really needed a "married man, this time." Spoken in code, I understood the message: they didn't want one gay priest to follow another. I realized that all I could do was await the bishops' pleasure, however long that might take.

When Bishop Pryce called in spring 1987, I was taken by surprise. Half a year had passed since my last placement interview, and I was being asked to "go on the list" of St. Philip's, Unionville, a booming parish in an affluent young suburb just north of Toronto. I knew it was considered a plum assignment. Still, having been through the process once before, I asked if I could first see a parish profile to see if it had the potential to be a good fit. The bishop wanted an answer there and then — three other good names were on the list and I wasn't committing to go there, just to be interviewed, he said. Assured by the bishop that he believed I had the gifts for St. Philip's and would bring a much-needed spirituality to a parish that had been too consumed with the nuts and bolts of putting up a new building, I could hardly refuse. Indeed, it was exciting to be considered for rector of one of the prominent churches in the diocese.

On paper, St. Philip's was challenging: almost four hundred families, a large Sunday school, dozens of active parish groups and committees, senior and junior choirs as well as a children's chorus, a church secretary and an administrator on staff, all sorts of parish programs, and a brand-new million-dollar complex with a hefty mortgage. Wisely, the rector was not expected to do everything single-handedly; the next task the parish had set itself was to find an associate priest to share the busy workload.

During the months of May and June, the parish selection committee tried to discreetly check me out at little St. Saviour's. It's hard to be inconspicuous in an intimate setting with only twelve rows of pews usually half-filled by the sixty stalwarts! The people of St. Saviour's welcomed the visitors warmly as they appeared, usually two at a time, and pressed coffee into their hands as they tried to escape unnoticed at the end of the service. Finally the phone call came, asking me to meet the committee in Unionville.

It was a sweltering July evening, but I sat shivering in Carolyn's tastefully decorated but overly air-conditioned living-room in my usual summer clothes — dress shorts and sandals. With relief I noticed that one of the men was similarly attired. After all, I had been told to come casually dressed. The six members of the parish selection committee were a fascinating lot: two churchwardens, a deputy churchwarden, two lay delegates to diocesan synod, and a woman elected by the parish just for this committee. Someone had warned me that a parish interview was like a blind date — the whole point was for the two nervous parties to get to know each other. Since the committee had had the opportunity to see me in action on Sunday mornings, and had read my résumé, they had a good idea of who I was, so I asked them if they would first tell me something about themselves.

Cathy sat comfortably draped over a hassock. A young mother with two preschool-age daughters, she talked easily about her faith in God, her love for the church, and her musical work with the children in Sunday school. One of the parish's delegates to diocesan synod, she enjoyed her busy life at home and church. Tony, a man my own age with a noticeable English accent, teased our host, Carolyn, in a good-natured way, eyes twinkling. Father of two young children and vice-president of a financial institution, he was the appointed rector's warden and was charged with overseeing the parish's finances. Carolyn had a take-charge air about her. An imposing middle-aged woman with striking red hair, this mother of one adolescent daughter had almost single-handedly overseen the construction and decoration of the new church. I could see that contractors would follow instructions from this strong-willed woman, the elected people's warden with responsibility for overseeing personnel and buildings. Her soon-to-be successor, Claudia, had stuck out like a sore thumb one Sunday at St. Saviour's. A good-natured housewife and mother of three teenagers, she was never at worship without a hat, a distinguishing mark given up by most women years earlier. Not a hint of guile about her, the down-to-earth deputy people's churchwarden could be disarmingly honest about how she saw things. The other lay delegate to synod, Darrell, came across as a strong, decent, caring man, committed to the well-being of the parish. Married, as were all the committee members, with two young daughters, he had a keen interest in the parish's commitment to justice issues, especially in their active outreach committee. Jean, the final member of the selection committee, specially elected for that purpose, was a soft-spoken woman of deep spirituality. A middle-aged mother of three young adults, she was devoted to the Bible-study group and concerned for the spiritual well-being of the parish. I couldn't have imagined a group that better represented the parish.

The interview went well. Many of the skills and programs I had developed in my first parish seemed to dovetail with the needs of Unionville: the committee seemed impressed with my preaching, the way I conducted worship and included the children, my successful fundraising experience, the warm friendly atmosphere at St. Saviour's, and my involvement with the larger Church and community. It seemed to be a good match.

Later that evening I received the royal tour. The church was perched on a hill just north of town, overlooking miles of rolling countryside. To the north and east, farmland was still under cultivation; to the south was one of the most affluent growing suburbs in the Toronto area. Attempting to recapture the best of small-town Ontario life, yuppies had built up a suburb centred on the old main street of Unionville, which they had gussied up with fresh paint, cobblestones, enormous barrels every ten feet brightly spilling over with flowers, and antique-style lampposts sporting hanging planters. Most of the old houses had been converted into restaurants and expensive boutiques — altogether it was a big splash of overstated charm and affluence.

The new church on the hill reflected the optimism and affluence of the new gentry, a modern edifice built in the old style on the site of the original St. Philip's, which had been planted there a century and a half earlier. In fact, the new church was the third St. Philip's: the second building had been put up during the First World War, right in town. For various reasons, it had been decided to move the new church back up the hill. It was a shining example of a successful marriage of old and new. With the brick exterior of the parish hall and church, and the pitched shingle roof of the worship area with interior exposed beams, the new facility was ingeniously designed with all the modern amenities, including air-conditioning, to form an architectural amalgam that captured the feel of antiquity while providing a large modern space that lent itself to contemporary worship and parish life. The half-million-dollar mortgage was a reflection of the fact that no cost had been spared in building the parish's new home. I knew what one of my major tasks would be — fundraising.

I liked the people of the Unionville committee. They had bright hopes for the future — none of the gloomy siege mentality that had greeted me almost seven years earlier at St. Saviour's. St. Philip's looked to me like a real hothouse environment to test the skills and vision that I had developed in the smaller parish. Could this place, where vibrant Christians formed a loving community, become the sort of church every parish priest dreams of? The parish's statement of purpose said it beautifully: "Inspired by the love of God, and led by the power of the Holy Spirit, St. Philip's seeks to be a welcoming, caring and accepting community ministering to one another and to the wider world, through worship and prayer and by sharing our gifts and love in the service of our Lord and Saviour, Jesus Christ."

I was amazed to find a parish that could articulate and adopt such a broad and inclusive mission statement. I wondered, though, if it was inclusive enough to call me, a single male who was known to be gay in at least some circles of the diocese. Would this group of married suburbanites, all with two or more children and two cars in the driveway, be able to set aside the Unionville yuppie ethos and value me simply as a human being with gifts for ministry and a successful track record?

Two weeks later I got my answer. The parish selection committee was unanimous in its decision to call me to be their rector, the bishop told me. It was the middle of July and I had just begun my summer vacation, so we agreed on an October 1 start date, and I returned briefly from vacation the next Sunday to tell my congregation at St. Saviour's that I would be leaving. They were saddened but not surprised by the news; after seven years they had suspected I was theirs on borrowed time. But letting go of them proved to be more difficult than I had anticipated. A priest's first parish is always a special place; I had made many friends and a few enemies, and the parish family had patiently and lovingly endured my early mistakes and helped me to grow into a competent pastor. We now had to let go of strong bonds of affection as I moved on to other challenges.

Buoying me up was a deep sense of vindication: I had been selected unanimously over three married men for the new parish, and was going to be with people who valued me for being a person with the gifts and abilities they needed in a pastor. The subject of my private life had never been raised, so I concluded that it wasn't an issue; I could live with discretion in my personal affairs, trusting that my new parish family would not be intrusive.

"The issue" blew up just as I was in the throes of winding things down at St. Saviour's and making arrangements for the move. It was Wednesday, August 24. The headlines screamed: UNITED CHURCH COUNCIL VOTES TO ORDAIN HOMOSEXUALS. For the previous week the media had thronged the Church's biannual General Council in Victoria, British Columbia, pumping up the issue of gays in the Church almost beyond recognition. In the end, a carefully worded motion had been passed after exhausting and sometimes nasty debate in the wee morning hours: "That all persons, regardless of their sexual orientation, who profess Jesus Christ and obedience to Him, are welcome to be or become full members of the Church" and "All members of the Church are eligible to be considered for the Ordered Ministry."

The subtle difference between "all are eligible to be considered" and "council votes to ordain" was obliterated by a press hungry for sensational news, and the Community of Concern prophesying the breakup of the United Church.

I heaved a sigh of relief that I was an Anglican, yet I still felt suspicion around me. And it was on the day that the headlines appeared that I met Ahmad. For two years, off and on, I had dated men, hoping to find someone, but to no avail — I had given up on the idea of falling in love. Most men were scared off when they found out who I worked for — Holy Mother Church — and understandably so, given the amount of suffering and alienation the Church had caused them.

Then came Ahmad. Introduced by a mutual friend who said that Ahmad wanted to talk about faith and homosexuality, we fell in love at first sight. Ahmad was a handsome young immigrant with dark Mediterranean good looks, and I was swept away by his charm, his smile, and the sincerity with which he shared his personal struggle to love God and accept his sexuality. There was a powerful magic between us from the initial meeting, which grew over the following weeks as we saw each other more and more often. Bubbling over with good nature and love of life, Ahmad's vitality was contagious.

What a time to fall in love, I thought, just as I was moving to a new parish. But, unlike other men I had dated, Ahmad had a tremendous respect for my vocation, which made me love him all the more. At last, a man who was unthreatened by my love affair with the Church and who was willing to share me with her! As the move approached, Ahmad spent many hours helping me pack, freeing me up to deal with the many details of saying goodbye to one parish and hello to the next. Caught up in the vortex of change, my body began to object to the stress of the move, while my heart was vacillating between the joy of new love and fear of the unknown. My life was changing course in more ways than I could have imagined just a few weeks earlier. A discreet man by nature, Ahmad would, I hoped, not be a problem for my new parishioners. At any rate, he wouldn't be living with me, and there were no parishioners living within view of the rectory to watch my comings and goings.

With the church beautifully decorated for the Harvest Festival, the parish pulled out all the stops in celebration of the new rector's arrival. The choir sang my favourite anthem — John Rutter's "The Lord Is My Shepherd." Brad Lennon, one of my dearest straight clergy friends, preached, and the church was filled with parishioners old and new, clergy colleagues, family and friends, as Bishop Taylor Pryce inducted me as rector with all the pomp and circumstance befitting the occasion. Also in the crowd was Ahmad, sitting inconspicuously with my good friend Pat. The welcome was overwhelming.

During the next few weeks parishioners poured into the church office to greet the new rector and share their concerns with him. It seemed that most parish organizations had been waiting with bated breath to see what the new priest was like before making decisions about their programs — study groups, outreach, the Sunday school, and the choirs, had kept much of their lives on hold, hoping the new pastor would support their particular visions and plans and encourage them in their efforts. So constant was the stream of people to the church office that I joked to the church secretary that I needed a number dispenser on the door. My early evaluation of the parish was confirmed: it was running over with bright, talented, articulate, and energetic Christian people, representing a broad spectrum of spiritualities.

All had strong points of view about what should be the primary focus of parish life, from prayer to Bible study, to social justice, to worship, to fellowship. I learned quickly that I couldn't possibly play a leading role in every activity, as I had at little St. Saviour's, but should act as support and resource to the many competent lay people who formed and led most groups. I had to make a major shift in my ministry style, from leading and energizing most things to acting as facilitator for most groups and leading in only a few crucial areas.

The support staff were wonderful. At the centre of action was the church secretary, Cheryl, who was universally loved and respected in the parish. A mother of two teenagers, married to a corporate executive, she was the church secretary clergy dream of — good-natured, knowledgeable about everything that was going on in the parish, sensitive, caring, and hard-working, she was a delightful resource and a loving support to me. The soft-spoken devoted parish administrator, Les, was semi-retired but fully engaged in overseeing the nuts and bolts of the day-to-day operations of the parish facilities. A gentle man, he had been a parishioner for several decades and had given leadership many times. Ridley, my honorary assistant, had entered seminary after retiring from a successful career in the insurance industry, and after ordination and surgery for two detached retinas, settled into the volunteer position at Unionville. A deeply spiritual man of wisdom and marvellous dry wit, he steered me through much of my orientation to the parish and the town.

Despite the tremendous outpouring of welcome and the appearance of a healthy parish, all was not well at St. Philip's. Between the announcement of my appointment in July and my arrival in October, the churchwardens had called a special vestry meeting to deal with the parish's financial crisis. Givings were so far under budget that the wardens decided to remove the promised assistant priest from the budget. Attendance and givings had been declining since the beginning of the year, because of the economic recession, the lack of new housing starts in the town, and other economic factors. As well, the gild was off the lily as the euphoria surrounding the building of the new church wore off. The parking lot could accommodate only half of the potential congregation and there were no side streets for the overflow, so many people got fed up and stopped coming.

The move up the hill had left a legacy of bitterness and anger, and a divided parish. Within days I learned the details of the agonizing process of deciding to sell the old church and build the new one out of town. Many blamed "the boys downtown" — the bishop and the Church development board — for forcing an unnecessary move. And in the process of designing the new facilities, terrible battle lines had been drawn, with the choir seeing itself as the big loser. To make matters worse, I began to hear of the power struggle that had gone on for years between the parish priest and the choir over, of all things, worship — how it was done and who controlled it. Almost immediately upon my arrival, I felt I was walking through a minefield of volatile emotions and unrealistic expectations. The parish selection committee had put its best face forward during our courting process — but then, so had I. The honeymoon was over sooner than expected.

The explosion happened only a month and a half after my arrival. Outraged at the sudden resignation of the choir conductor, precipitated by weekly arguments she and I had about details of the service, the choir boycotted communion one Sunday morning. Instead of coming up to the altar rail to receive the sacrament at the usual moment in the service, they remained seated and glowered. Eventually, two choristers broke rank and came to the altar rail. The following Sunday the choir abandoned its accustomed place and sat in the back row of the church, glaring angrily. I couldn't have imagined a worse action against a priest than to refuse communion from his hands. I was grateful that the organist hadn't been part of the uprising, although he, too, was feeling betrayed by the choir's action.

"Thank God, Jim, we finally got a priest who was willing to stand up to the choir. This should have happened years ago. We're sorry you had to be the one to deal with this." For weeks before the blowup I had heard from many among the parish leadership about the years of turmoil with the choir, and now I had their overwhelming support.

But knowing I had the backing of most of the parish did little to alleviate the pain as weeks went by and the possibility of coming to a constructive resolution grew dimmer. The choir appeared to see me as the new gunslinger hired by the churchwardens to attack their leader, rather than as the new kid on the block, trying to deal with old animosities. Despite weekly telephone conferences with my bishop and assurances of his support as I tried to work through the trying circumstances, the impasse could not be broken. I had been through parish conflicts before, but nothing of this magnitude. A sense of failure haunted me as I recognized my impotence to heal the years-old rift that had fractured so violently. The entire parish was in pain.

It was the following June before things got back to normal, after a Christmas and Easter with no choir. During that time we had to rely on a substitute organist when ours was lured to a nearby United Church whose massive pipe organ was a giant step up from our small electronic one. Through it all most parishioners maintained an embarrassed support for me. The busy parish life went on more or less as usual, although tinged with a deep sadness. Then Ted arrived. The new music director, who combined conducting with organ-playing, brought a wealth of choral experience from his years singing in the renowned Toronto Mendelssohn Choir, as well as a sound knowledge of liturgy — the structure of worship. From his first Sunday the grey-haired early-retired schoolteacher brought a vitality to worship with his stirring organ-playing, which quickly lifted the thick pall of sadness from the congregation. Like many musicians, Ted had a mercurial personality and very definite ideas about how the liturgy should be shaped, so he came prepared to take me on. I think he was surprised to find that our understandings of worship were so similar and that I was giving him a freer rein than he had experienced in previous parishes.

In September, choral music once again beautified worship at St. Philip's. Raw recruits from the congregation — all but two of the old choristers had left the congregation — were trained to read music, breathe and project properly, listen to each other, and keep in tune.

The new choristers were so enthusiastic about the music director's choral skills that some even rearranged business schedules so they wouldn't miss a choir practice. Under Ted's careful tutelage they blossomed into a competent choral group. By Christmas time and the Festival of Lessons and Carols, long-time parishioners were commenting that they'd never heard such fine singing at St. Philip's. Even so, the sense of achievement was tempered for me and for many by the pain of the previous year's upheaval, a wound that never quite healed.

The upheaval with the choir wasn't the only crisis that happened in Unionville that first year. Down the road, at Central United Church, a major storm was brewing. David Reeve, the senior minister there, was a kingpin of the Community of Concern. A pleasant older fellow who preached vigorously against his Church's stand on gays, he didn't seem to recognize me as "one of *them*." Our relations were always cordial, and I detected no tinge of suspicion on his part. In the meantime he was dividing his own congregation to the point where some parishioners, outraged at their denomination's pro-gay stance, resigned from Central United and moved up the hill to St. Philip's, thinking it was a safe haven from "the issue." One family in particular became fans of mine to the point of bragging to their former fellow parishioners at Central about the "fine young priest" at the Anglican church. The irony didn't escape me or my new colleague, Debbie Savage, who was the assistant minister at Central. A young, recently separated mother, she became one of my best friends. It wasn't long before I came out to her, and we laughed over the terrific irony of people who were so anti-gay and yet couldn't see the gay man right in front of their noses. It felt good to be free to be myself with at least one person in Unionville.

There was one woman, however, with whom I knew I could never be free. Suzanne hated homosexuals and didn't mind telling anyone who would listen. From my first month at St. Philip's, Suzanne filled my ears with frequent outbursts of loathing, judgement, and hatred for homosexuals. She had even gone so far as to act as an undercover agent in a lesbian bar. "You don't know what they're like, Jim," she told me the few times I tried to suggest that maybe not all gays were that evil. "You don't have the experience I've had. I can always tell if someone is gay," she assured me several times, with a knowing look. Her frequent tirades were virulent and nerve-wracking, yet she seemed to be oblivious to the sexual orientation of her parish priest. I intended to keep it that way, sure that she would stop short of nothing to drive me out of the parish if she ever found me out.

Others raised the issue of sexuality more subtly. In the summer of 1989 I supervised my first student in the Toronto Parish Training Program, the same program in which I had been a student a decade earlier. Ruth was a mature student, about fifty years old, with five grown children, some of whom had children of their own. Having gone into seminary after raising her family, this caring, empathic woman brought a listening pastoral touch to the parish. In one of the weekly supervisory hours for which she was to decide the agenda, she brought up the topic of homosexuality. She knew a number of gay students at Trinity College, and was struggling with her understanding of their place in the Church, especially after getting to know and respect them. For an hour we reflected on the nature of sexuality, what the Bible says and doesn't say, modern scientific knowledge, the Church's duplicity in looking the other way, and the conspiracy of silence that both protects and oppresses gay people. One mature student she had studied with had opened her mind to the possibility that gays like him and his partner might live in a moral Christian relationship, yet at the same time her stomach rebelled at the thought of what two men did together. At the end of the session I lent her my copy of McNeill's *The Church and the Homosexual* without giving any hint of my own sexuality. That might come in the future.

A few weeks later one of my colleagues died from AIDS-related causes. An outrageously funny gay man, Keith had had an effective ministry to seniors, and at the hospital where he was chaplain. His death was a terrible blow to many, especially the gay clergy. Bishop Finlay, who had taken office a year earlier as diocesan bishop after several years as a suffragan bishop, had visited Keith every week at Casey

House, the AIDS hospice in Toronto. We had all watched with growing admiration as this sensitive chief pastor faithfully cared for our
dying friend. But Keith wouldn't admit he was gay or dying with AIDS,
binding us all with his silence. Only in his obituary was there a veiled
reference to his secret — which was really a very open one, since
most people knew the reality — with a request for donations to Casey
House in lieu of flowers. In his funeral sermon, the bishop carefully
danced around the silence by thanking the staff at Casey House for
their extraordinary care of Keith. Then, reflecting on the appointed
Scriptures for that Sunday, Bishop Finlay made a sensitive comment
that touched everyone in the packed church. To the passage where
Paul states that, in Christ, "there is no longer Jew or Greek, there is
no longer slave or free, there is no longer male and female," Finlay
responded that Paul would today no doubt have added to that list
— moved to tears, I could hear the unstated "there is no longer straight
or gay." "For all of you are one in Christ Jesus," continued the reading from St. Paul. My respect and admiration for Bishop Finlay grew
that day. Here was a bishop, I thought, with tremendous sensitivity
to the plight of gays and lesbians in the Church.

The following Sunday, at St. Philip's, with the same appointed
readings, I had the courage to preach on the bishop's theme, only
somewhat more explicitly. Careful not to personalize my message, I
preached of the deathly silence that separates gay Christians from
the straight majority, and of the Christ who breaks down the barriers
that people erect to divide humanity. From the response after service, I knew it was one of my better sermons and had touched many
hearts that day. No one looked at me suspiciously. I had successfully
danced around my own secret, or so I thought.

Often it's the little things that catch you by surprise. One day
that summer, Cheryl, my faithful secretary, said with a big sigh that
she had something to tell me that I wasn't going to like. One phone
call she could ignore, but with the second she had to speak to me.
People were asking if Father Jim was gay. They had seen my name listed as celebrant for an Integrity service in *The Anglican*, the diocese's

monthly newspaper. Exasperated, I asked what difference it would make if I was gay. Shaking her head and with a shrug of her shoulders, Cheryl said that it wouldn't make any difference to *her* relationship with me. Besides, I went on to point out, all sorts of clergy — men, women, and married people, including every one of the bishops — had celebrated a service for Integrity. It didn't mean a thing. I left it there, hanging. I didn't want to put Cheryl in the awkward position of having to keep my secrets, even though I trusted her more than anyone else in the parish. Maintaining the silence was difficult enough for me; I couldn't impose it on her.

Soon one of my parishioners would find herself caught in a secret both similar and different. Sandra came to me because her best girl-friend at college had recently come out to her as a lesbian. Perhaps it was my sermon about Keith that opened the door for her to share her struggle. She wanted to understand what it was all about. After an hour together in which I found a surprising openness in this otherwise conservative woman, I lent her my treasured copy of the first "gay" book I had read, John Fortunato's *Embracing the Exile*. When she returned it a month later, a deep acceptance of her friend appeared to have settled in. It was later that I found a handwritten note tucked into the book: "*Yes! to second-last paragraph on pg. 107.*" Intrigued, I looked it up. "I noticed a curious thing about a year ago: straight people who have traveled a while on the spiritual path are remarkably untroubled by a gay person's sexuality. It is simply a non-issue for them." I wondered if she was trying to tell me that she was a safe person to confide in.

The next time Sandra came in, she wanted more to read, so I recommended McNeill's book. She had to hide it in her purse, afraid her husband might find it. This woman with two young children lived under a threat: her husband had told her that if she ever publicly supported homosexuality, he would take the children and leave her. When I came out to Sandra some time later, I knew my secret was safe with her.

◆

My first anniversary was a joyful occasion. Everything was coming together in the parish. With the new choir making beautiful music, the gloom had lifted. The parish was bursting with all sorts of activity. Recently instituted new children's programs were up and running.

During my announcements at the end of service, all of a sudden the congregation burst into laughter. Following their eyes I turned to see one of the lay assistants, eyes rolling, standing right behind me, holding a cake with one lit candle. Blushing, I realized that sometimes I did get a little long winded with the announcements. As the choir burst into a rendition of "Happy Anniversary," people in the congregation were beaming, and I think we all believed that the future for St. Philip's was bright.

The only sadness I felt was for Maybe, who had become as much a part of St. Philip's as she had been at St. Saviour's. She wasn't well, and soon, I'd have to have her put to sleep. Thank God for Ahmad, who had loved and supported me through all the turmoil.

Another year passed in good order, as the parish bustled with activity.

CHAPTER 6

"**J**IM'S A HOMOSEXUAL and we've got to get him out of here!" Gabe and I were sitting in the Swiss Chalet, eating barbecued chicken, normally my favourite fast food, but I was picking at it. The bombshell was more of a shock than anything I had expected. It was only under pressure that Gabe uneasily blurted out what he had heard from Suzanne. I continued to push food around on my plate with my fork. Dear God, I thought, how am I going to deal with this? My worst fear was being realized.

The meeting the night before had been a mild tremor in comparison. As one of the parish power-brokers, Suzanne had requested a meeting with two of the churchwardens and myself, excluding one of the three wardens. She was concerned about troubles in the parish. Suzanne said that Gabe, after a year as deputy warden, was not handling them very well. I soon regretted having that meeting without him.

Gabe was new to his responsibilities, Suzanne said, and was creating problems. He wasn't dealing with people's complaints, and instead was only encouraging gossip. And what complaints were these? I probed. People were saying that I was not doing my job, and they wanted action taken. When pressed, Suzanne said there were complaints about my preaching and "goings-on at the rectory."

My heart started to race that night as I realized the direction she was pursuing. Who were these people with the complaints? Of course, she told us, she couldn't break a confidence. When I asked what, exactly, the "goings-on" at the rectory were, she shrugged and shook her head. She didn't know. She knew only that a few people were very upset.

As far as the preaching went, I was charged with not being forceful enough. People expect answers, clear direction. Yes, I thought, it gets pretty uncomfortable when the preacher makes you think about your life. Meaning, purpose, responsibility, difficult decisions, faith in the midst of complex lives — some people wanted hell-fire and brimstone while others wanted pablum. Making people think, questioning their faith, and taking responsibility for leading Christian lives had always been my focus. Some parishioners never forgot my first sermon the day I was inducted in Unionville when I told them that part of my purpose was "to comfort the afflicted, and afflict the comfortable."

Darrell, my rector's churchwarden, laughed at the accusation about my preaching. Claudia, about to finish her term as elected people's warden to be succeeded by Gabe, looked amused. They had heard nothing but compliments about my preaching. The "goings-on," however, were a much more serious matter. No amount of cajoling would force Suzanne to be more explicit. Since Gabe hadn't passed on to the other wardens any of the complaints she had heard, he was derelict in his duty, she charged. I determined, then, that I would sit down with Gabe privately the next day.

That meeting at the Swiss Chalet was tense. Gabe was understandably upset that Suzanne had forced a wardens' meeting to talk about him. He was as good-hearted a man as one could find; generous with his time, his money, and his affection; and full of love of God and people. The backbone of a previous and much smaller country parish, he was finding the churchwarden's job in Unionville far more complicated than he was used to. Dealing with a highly educated professional congregation whose people had no reservations about forcefully expressing their own points of view was proving a little intimidating. Getting Gabe beyond his hurt to the issues burning in my mind was like pulling teeth.

People were talking, Gabe said. Of course, I thought, churches are wonderful places for gossip. So, what were people saying? After much coercion, Gabe said that it wasn't important. He didn't believe rumours anyhow. So what was Suzanne on about? I asked. What about these "goings-on"? I hoped my rising anxiety wasn't apparent as I pressed Gabe for more detail.

Finally, Gabe blurted it out. Suzanne had approached him at

coffee hour after service the previous Sunday, and they'd begun to share "concerns" — a code word for gossip. With some encouragement from Gabe, who had a penchant for gossip, she had finally spit out, "Jim's a homosexual and we've got to get him out of here!"

Gabe was very apologetic. Of course, he didn't believe rumours. He shouldn't have said anything to me at all, since he didn't believe it. But . . . I could see the flicker of doubt in his eyes. I agonized for a few moments about whether to come out or not. Could Gabe be trusted with my confirmation that I was gay? Would he reject me, or hate me, or join forces with Suzanne to get rid of me? In that moment I decided to do what I had always done: I neither confirmed nor denied the accusation. Nonetheless, my life changed course inexorably.

I continued to probe the source of Suzanne's accusation. All she would tell Gabe was that an unnamed woman had found incriminating evidence in my house — discovering a book on gay love-making had almost driven this anonymous woman to leave the church. I couldn't believe my ears. I rarely had anyone into the rectory, since I visited with people almost exclusively in their homes or at the office. On rare occasions I had groups over for prayer or parties, but I couldn't imagine who would go snooping through the house. I suggested to Gabe that such a woman, if she existed at all, might have found any one of a half-dozen books I had in my bookcase on homosexual issues. I could point them out in my office that day. Of course, Gabe agreed, any pastor worth his salt should be prepared to counsel all sorts of people and do the necessary reading.

After Gabe's revelation, I called a meeting with all the church-wardens, including Gabe, to discuss how gossip should be handled. Without mentioning Gabe's particular revelation we agreed that gossip is gossip; it should not be dignified. Nameless complainers could not be allowed to sway our actions, but any serious complaints from people willing to speak for themselves should be heeded. We left it at that. My peace of mind was, however, shaken.

Gradually I began to make associations. I remembered an evening, a year earlier, when I had had the choir over to the rectory for a Christmas party. It had been a joyful evening. Under the tutelage of the new music director the group of inexperienced parishioners had been transformed, in a few short months, into a competent choir. The advent service of lessons and carols had been beautiful, and every-one was in high spirits.

Preparing for the party had been a chore, but had been made much easier by Ahmad. He wanted the house to be spotless, and came over and spent the day cleaning from stem to stern. Always thought-ful, he knew that a bad disc in my lower back made heavy housework a hazard. By the time the crowd arrived, the house was aglow, and Ahmad was ensconced upstairs in the study, working on a paper for his engineering course.

Later that night, when the last reveller had left, Ahmad made a startling revelation. During the party, the study door had cracked open and Suzanne's head had appeared. Oh!, she had excused herself, she didn't know he was there! She was only looking to see what Jim had done with the rooms since he'd settled in. The two knew each other since both had been part of the large moving and unpacking crew a year earlier when I had arrived at Unionville. Suzanne hadn't seen Ahmad since then, but she clearly hadn't forgotten him.

The penny dropped as I remembered the choir party. The only person who had been caught snooping around my home was Suzanne herself. The unnamed woman was most likely her. Many months later, when I recounted this story to a choir member, my suspicions were confirmed. She had been seen stomping down the rectory stairs that evening, and had been heard to say to her husband, "I've seen all I want. Let's get out of here!"

It was now January 1991, and I had been at St. Philip's for almost two and a half years. Often during that time I had listened to Suzanne spew her venom about homosexuals. I had never encoun-tered such prejudice and hate in my life, but I had thought I was safe. She didn't suspect that I was gay, or so I had hoped. Obviously Suzanne's penny had finally dropped, and I saw her statement to Gabe as a declaration of war. She was a powerful force in the parish, and used to getting her own way; I wondered how long it would take her to find a way to "get me out of there."

January is a busy time in any parish. Once you had recovered from the Christmas rush, you got caught up in the onslaught of preparations for the annual vestry meeting. Preparations of reports, finalizing the budget, lining up officers for the church's myriad committees all but consumed my waking hours. In the midst of it all, word came from Gabe of another disgruntled parishioner, this time a man. Disgruntled parishioners are commonplace in every parish, but again, there were troubling suggestions about my sexual orientation. When I called the man's wife, there was no hint about concern over my sexuality, only that he was upset about my preaching and about troubled parish finances. Why didn't I speak to him?

While Suzanne was virulently homophobic, I wasn't sure about Fred. He was a busy executive, with a wife and children, and I hadn't seen much of him lately in church. Our relations had been cool but amicable, so I decided to call him up and arrange a meeting. When he came into my office the next evening he was noticeably uneasy, but willing to talk.

I got right to the point. I had, I said, heard that he was unhappy with me about a few things, and I thought we should talk about it. Fred asked what I had heard. I told him I was aware that he had some concerns about my preaching and about church finances.

Fred exclaimed that there was too much preaching about AIDS and homosexuality. I was stunned for a moment. After a deliberate pause to collect my thoughts, I reminded him that the last time I had preached on AIDS or homosexuality was a year and a half earlier, hardly overdoing it! But Fred was not mollified. No, even that was too often. It should never be mentioned in church, not with children present. I pointed out to him that the last time I had preached on the topic was on AIDS Awareness Sunday, a day called by the primate of the Anglican Church. Disdainfully, Fred insisted that it had no place in the church, even so.

He let the topic drop, and we moved on to parish finances, which Fred believed were in dire straits. Relieved to talk about something that was not solely my responsibility, I pointed out that the parish's finances had been in decline before I arrived in Unionville, burdened with a large mortgage for the new church facilities, and that we needed his leadership in financial management and fundraising. Why not let his name stand for deputy warden? I suggested.

Although Fred declined my suggestion that he become part of the parish leadership, and seemed more co-operative in the following weeks, I was left with an uneasy feeling. What connection, if any, was there between Suzanne and Fred, or were these isolated incidents? With the stress of preparations for the annual meeting I had no time to think deeply about my vulnerability. I prayed to God that nothing would come of Suzanne's threat or Fred's anger. I decided that I was not prepared to discuss openly with the churchwardens the reality of Jim Ferry the gay man. Not yet. I needed some space to reflect on the Church's conspiracy of silence regarding gay priests, and whether or not I could continue to hold up my end of the bargain.

♦

It was a relief to be in Atlanta the last week of January. Three hundred Episcopalians — Anglicans in American lingo — were gathered together at St. Philip's Cathedral for the annual conference of the National Episcopal AIDS Coalition. Two colleagues and I from Toronto Diocese's AIDS committee formed the Canadian contingent. For the first time I found myself in an Anglican context where I felt completely accepted as a gay man. It wasn't that everyone there was gay, by a long shot, but love and acceptance were in abundance as we found a place where gays and straights, people with and without AIDS, white and black, male and female could find a place in the heart of the Church. I wept during the evening liturgy as most people went forward for anointing and prayer for healing. People with AIDS were touched, embraced, and kissed. People in ministry to those with AIDS felt gathered in from the margins of Church life, to the very centre. God's presence was palpable. As I went forward, longing for healing in my wounded spirit, I experienced for the first time in an Anglican church a sense of God's complete love and acceptance for me as a gay man. For once I felt I could be totally present in God's house, and not have to leave my sexuality at the door. I wept and prayed for Bruce, a parishioner's son who had died of AIDS several years earlier in a trauma of self-loathing. When I returned to Unionville, I felt more deeply at home with God and myself as one of God's beloved gay children.

The annual vestry meeting a few days later was unremarkable, as most parish priests would hope. The most controversial item — the proposed reorganization of parish structure to spread responsibility and accountability more widely among the people — was passed without conflict. No one took on the pastor on the issue of his personal life. I heaved a sigh of relief.

In February the parish held its first-ever retreat at a beautiful place in the Hockley Valley. Perched on the valley's edge, the old farmhouse, updated and enlarged, had a warm homey feel, conducive to quiet conversations and reflection. Led by a former Dominican who was now an Anglican, thirty of us sang and prayed and talked our way into a spiritual high. In a quiet corner, during a break, one of the women looked deep into my eyes, sighed, and told me that I was such a mystery. Was I really holding so much of me back? I wondered. I knew that she cared deeply for me both as a priest and as a human being, but could she bear knowing me fully? In that moment of grace I was as honest with her as I felt I could be at the time. Many people would probably not accept me if they knew who I really was, I told her. Prejudice was a reality, even in the Christian family. Lorna hugged me for a long time, and told me that she understood, and loved me, all of me. But for the rest of the retreat I couldn't help wondering what the others would think or do if they knew I was gay. A feeling of alienation was gnawing at my soul, even as my sense of God's loving presence grew.

The parish retreat initiated a period of deep reflection, as I began to feel more deeply the dilemma I was in. Most parishioners never asked probing questions about my personal life, and I was convinced couldn't care less if I was gay or if I had a love-interest. As long as I was effective in the parish, my personal life was for them exactly that — *personal*. Some, I believed, would go so far as to be happy for me if they knew. But would there be anyone willing to face the denizens of prejudice if my sexuality should become an issue? In the shifting sands of Christian attitudes I believed that the Church — or at least most of the Church — had already moved to the point of tolerance for gays, if not support. Even the bishops had stated in 1978 that homosexuals should be protected by civil law against discrimination. Yet the same Church was making me a potential target of acts of prejudice, even extortion or blackmail, by turning a blind eye to its numerous gay clergy, in a cruel double standard. That stretch of land between "no homosexuals, period" and "we accept homosexuals" was proving to be a minefield of "but's." The Church's official position had not yet caught up with its unofficial practice.

The Church's conspiracy of silence was killing me by degrees, as I began to realize that not only was I set up for blackmail, but that the very silence that was supposed to protect me was impairing my ability to relate to people fully. How can you connect deeply with people when one of the most important parts of yourself, something integral to who you are, must be kept shielded from all eyes? It was Ruth who put her finger on it for me. A very empathic intuitive "feeler," she had stayed on after her summer training experience, and then had been ordained deacon for St. Philip's. She was a great parish visitor, and the women flocked to her for personal counselling. Some of them were having a hard time relating to me, she told me; they sensed a wall. I realized they were right, at least some of them. While I had made deep friendships with many women in the parish (in fact, my best friends were women), there was a deep sense of reserve in many. I had rationalized that some of it was a hangover from the choir upheaval, but with Ruth's feedback I began to think it was more than that. The pall of secrecy was preventing some from knowing and trusting me.

I decided that I simply had to take the risk of letting a few parishioners really know me. But who could I trust? The dilemma for every gay and lesbian, in our families, circles of friends, at work, and at church, is the same: how do I know who can be trusted with the knowledge of who I really am? Worst of all, will the disclosure completely disrupt relationships? There really is no "safe place" for gays, I knew, but I hoped I could make a small safe circle of a few people I trusted in the parish. And I had to know if I really would be all alone if Suzanne unleashed the threatened storm.

An important change had taken place in my life over the past year. Amidst the busy and fulfilling parish life I had found time to do further reading on gay issues and go on my first retreat for gay Christians. The further insights into the mystery of sexuality and my experience of a whole gathering of loving, articulate, faithful gay and lesbian Christians had a profound impact: no longer did I see my gay sexuality as just something I had to live with grudgingly. It was a gift from God, as valuable as any other. Not a curse, but a blessing. And that meant I belonged at the heart of God and God's church, not at the margins to which so many of my gay brothers and sisters felt themselves relegated. No longer ashamed of who I was because I knew in the depths of my soul that gay was the way God made me, it rankled that there were still some who wanted to thrust me to the outer darkness. My inner life was being transformed in a way I had never dreamed possible, yet I still had to live with the perils of the political realities of the Church world.

Ahmad was threatened by my newfound confidence and self-acceptance. A young man from a very conservative religious and cultural background, he really seemed to believe that, as much as he loved me, it was still a sin to express that love sexually. It was agony, caught in the clash of my joy and his guilty feelings. For five months we had lived together while he worked in a small city north of Unionville, and the dark cloud of guilt and shame hanging over the bedroom had become intolerable. It was with deep mutual disappointment that he moved out to work and live in Toronto. Even so, we could not stop loving each other, and we continued to see each other regularly. We had come to mean so much to each other over two and a half years.

When my mother died suddenly in July 1990, he was there to weep with me at the cancer hospital as I held her rapidly cooling hand. Mum had loved Ahmad and had always asked me to bring him with me when I came for dinner, yet he had to be hidden in a back row at her funeral. He couldn't hold me when I burst into tears as the St. Philip's choir followed her casket into the church. Sometimes the injustice is overwhelming as gay loved ones must hide at the times of greatest need in order to protect themselves and the people they love.

Grief had followed grief in 1990, but my assistant, Ruth, helped me through it all. I had come out to her, a trusted colleague and friend, after she raised gay issues several times in the autumn after my mother died. Taking a leap of faith, I had assumed that she wanted to hear my truth and could deal with the knowledge. Other parishioners had supported me too: a young woman psychotherapist who had told me of marching in the Gay Pride Parade with some gay friends; Barbara, a delightful loving "pillar of the church," whose only response was to give me a hug and say it didn't matter to her; and a married couple with a counselling practice who had supported me through the crisis with the first choir. All had responded supportively when I told them I was gay, and seemed to love me all the more. I felt secure in their love, and in the knowledge that I could be safely fully known to a few.

Trusting the Church hierarchy was another matter. The conspiracy of silence weighs almost as heavily on the bishops as it does on the gay clergy. In fact, in conversation with my old friend Bishop Brown shortly after Keith died of AIDS, Brown had discouraged me from coming out to him. I was frustrated by the silence surrounding his death, and, in sharing this with the bishop, was about to tell him of my own reality when he stopped me short by warning me that I shouldn't tell him anything that he would have to do anything about. He might know that I was gay, but he didn't want it to be official.

Bishop Finlay seemed to be different. First there was his beautiful sermon at Keith's funeral. Then I had lunch with the gay classmate of Ruth's who had so impressed her. Art was a charming, soft-spoken older man who, like Ruth, had gone into seminary later in life.

He had made no secret of his sexual orientation or of his decade-long relationship with his partner, Bill, during his studies at Trinity College. Art had been struck by Bishop Finlay's concern at the bishop's dinner for the graduating class. All the students had introduced their significant others at the dinner table, and he had introduced Bill simply as his "other." As the couple had left quickly after the dinner, and the sea of classmates and spouses seemed to part to give them a wide berth, the bishop rushed to catch and stop them at the door. Both Art and Bill had been deeply touched by the bishop's dramatic gesture and his apparently genuine warmth and good wishes in what must have been a sensitive political milieu.

Another sign of Bishop Finlay's sensitivity to the church's gay membership occurred the following month. In *The Diocesan Link*, the monthly newsletter for clergy, the bishop urged all his clergy to obtain and study *Our Stories/Your Story*, a study resource from the Gay and Lesbian Task Force of the national Church's Human Rights Unit. For over a decade now the national House of Bishops had roadblocked open discussion about homosexuality. The 1978 report of the Primate's Commission on Sexuality, subtitled *A Study on Homosexuality*, still bore the warning, "CONFIDENTIAL — *For the House of Bishops only*" and its recommendations were still a well-guarded secret. In addition, the Church's Human Rights Unit had been thwarted since its inception at General Synod — the national Church's legislative body — where, in 1980, it was decided to establish a program on human rights. With national staffing and a budget, it was to involve the Church at every level in work on human rights issues, to develop "a theological statement to both support and criticize our work, and to be involved in a major gathering to reflect on and celebrate human rights."

After a decade of bouncing between the House of Bishops and the National Executive Council largely because of a clause in the Proposed Human Rights Principles for the Church, which included protection from discrimination on the grounds of sexual orientation, the Human Rights Unit was getting nowhere. In frustration they had set up a subcommittee, the Working Group on Gays and Lesbians and the Church, which in turn had produced *Our Stories/Your Story* as a resource to familiarize Anglicans with the experience of gays and lesbians in the Church. An end-run around the bishops and Church structures, the document was an attempt to tell the personal stories of nine gay and lesbian Anglicans in a low-key manner that could be easily studied by parishes and individuals.

Bishop Finlay's exhortation to the clergy to obtain and study *Our Stories/Your Story* was backed up in March 1991 in *The Anglican* by a major news item, "Gay and Lesbian Anglicans Tell Their Stories": "The Rt. Rev. Terence Finlay, Bishop of Toronto, urges church members to read the booklet and to make their comments on the questionnaire included with the resource. 'As far as I am aware there is no anticipated change in our church's position. This is an attempt to help people understand and to encourage informed discussion. It is important to hear these stories,' said the bishop, 'and to reflect on the pain people experience in their life, and at the same time to search for God in the midst of all this.'" While there was a double message from the bishop — that we should change our understanding but not our official position — gays and lesbians saw it as a tremendous encouragement. Thank God, one bishop was at last drawing attention to the plight of gay Christians and encouraging understanding. It was a good start, though long overdue.

Encouraged by the bishop's public advocacy of the study resource, I passed a copy of *Our Stories/Your Story* on to St. Philip's Outreach Committee. One of the finest outreach groups in the diocese, they had already held parish forums on a variety of social justice issues, including Native rights. With their involvement in Amnesty International, the Primate's World Relief and Development Fund, and ecological groups, and their sponsoring of a refugee family, I suspected that this group of justice-seeking individuals would be keenly interested in the resource. Little did I know what other parishioners were already doing with it.

Jan was angry. "What does the bishop think he's doing?" she raged over the telephone. She had seen the article with the bishop's comments in *The Anglican* a week earlier. At first I thought she was angry at Bishop Finlay for raising the issue, but as she vented her spleen I realized that her anger was directed at his double message. "Why does he tell us to get *Our Stories/Your Story* and read it if he's already decided the Church isn't changing its position? What's the point?" For what seemed like half an hour she vacillated between anger and cool logic as I tried to point out how significant it was that the issue was being raised at all by the leader of the largest diocese in the country. In the end I had to admit the inherent contradiction in the bishop's exhortation, but only after Jan had given her impressions of the nine stories, which had touched her and moved her to call me. I was delighted that she had taken the initiative to obtain the human rights resource and taken the time to read it thoughtfully. And I wondered if, through her openness to the stories, she wasn't sending me a covert message of understanding and support for my personal dilemma. Could she be speaking in code? I was careful not to disclose my own story, while at the same reassuring her that these were real people whose stories she had read — I had known three of them personally as classmates and colleagues.

The only person to whom I had given a copy of *Our Stories/Your Story* was Louise Briggs, co-chairperson of the outreach committee and the wife of Darrell, the rector's churchwarden, so I wondered if she had lent it to Jan, with whom she had frequent conversations. Hanging up the phone, I slipped into the secretary's office next door to mine and remarked to Cheryl that it was great that Jan had taken the initiative to read *Our Stories/Your Story.*

"No, Jim, it's not great," said Cheryl, with a look of concern. "They're passing it around the parish." She paused, and with a sigh added, "They're trying to figure out which of the stories you wrote."

For a moment I was stunned. After swallowing, I said, "Well, Cheryl, I can give you the definitive answer on that." I paused. "I didn't write any of them . . . but I could have."

The flood gates burst open. Cheryl had suspected for a long time that I was gay; why hadn't I told her? Didn't I trust her?

I tried to explain the dilemma of the conspiracy of silence, and how I trusted her more than anyone else in the parish. I knew her love was genuine. But I didn't want to put her in the stressful situation of having to lie to protect me. What she didn't know she didn't have to be responsible for, and I had simply tried to keep her out of what could be a compromising situation.

What a relief it was to be able, at last, to be open with Cheryl. I wasn't sure if she really understood why I hadn't come out to her earlier, but we did agree on one thing: my private life was my business, and she would continue to refuse to answer any questions about it. Let them ask me if they had the nerve. Of course, nobody ever did: gossip and innuendo didn't take much courage, but confronting me might.

◆

In search of an oasis, I started to attend the Christos congregation of Metropolitan Community Church several Sunday evenings a month. One of two MCC congregations in Toronto, they were part of a larger denomination founded over twenty years earlier in Los Angeles by a gay minister, Troy Perry, after he was ejected from the pulpit of an evangelical church. Congregations with a "special ministry to the gay community" — composed, in fact, mostly of gays and lesbians — had sprung up across the United States and Canada, and around the world. God's loving presence was there at Christos MCC in a way it wasn't in the Anglican Church; however, I found I had some difficulty with the "ghetto" nature of a Church that was composed mostly of gays and lesbians. It was a relief to feel that I could worship without having to leave my sexuality at the door, but it also rankled that such a Church should be necessary at all.

Despite attempts at recruitment by Susan Maybe, the Christos pastor, and my own pain in the Anglican Church, I couldn't make a shift to MCC. I was a part of the Anglican family. Period. And I knew that, at heart, my Church family was one of the most inclusive in Christendom. It could and should include me. I wanted to stay in spite of the harassment to which I was being subjected.

Blackmail. I was sure it was only a remote possibility, until it happened to Ed. My exhausted United Church colleague finally returned my Friday phone call on Sunday evening. "Oh Jim, I've had a terrible time," he said, his tone of voice coloured by pain. He was in the midst of an uproar involving the police and lawyers — someone had threatened to expose him as a gay man if he didn't deposit a large sum of money in a certain bank account. I couldn't believe what I was hearing. A gentle, caring, and successful pastor, he had been too honest with someone he was counselling, and a few days later, under the threat of blackmail, he realized he had been set up. A call to United Church headquarters revealed that they were well prepared for just such an eventuality. After spending a day with Church officials, police, and lawyers, and an anxious weekend, the threat never materialized. The blackmailer apparently was scared off, leaving a shaken minister behind.

Ed wasn't the only one who was shaken. His blackmail experience struck me hard. I felt more vulnerable than ever. The United Church was prepared to support its clergy against the violence of harassment and blackmail, but were my Anglican bishops?

After a few sleepless nights, I poured out my soul in a brief agonized written response to *Our Stories/Your Story:*

> *Some days I feel like Yentl. Have you ever seen the movie by that name, starring Barbra Streisand? Set in Eastern Europe at the turn of the century, it's about a Jewish girl of marrying age who stays home to care for her widowed father. Yentl loves God and her father, and is filled with a deep thirst for God and the things of God. Her father, a teacher of Talmud, breaks with religious tradition by allowing Yentl to read books only men could read, and teaches her Talmud, all in secret.*
>
> *When Yentl's father dies, she cuts off her hair, binds up her breasts, and dons boy's clothes in order to enter the Jewish school from which girls are excluded. Her longing for*

*God and study of God's word leads her into a life of mas-
querade as a boy — a time of great turmoil, fear and secret
humiliation. . . .*

*Sometimes, as a gay Christian, I feel a lot like Yentl. Forced
to wear "straight" clothes, I masquerade as a heterosexual in
order to find acceptance in the religious community, and continue the journey to the God I love. I know that God loves
me. I feel God's call, and the rest of the community affirms
that call powerfully, but I dread the possibility of being stripped
so that people can see all of me, and reject me. For I am different. I am gay.*

*Early in the movie, Yentl's father one evening gives in to
her eager request to study, and as she shutters the window she
says, "I don't know why we have to hide from the neighbours.
. . . God knows what we're doing." "Yes," father replies, "I trust
God, but I'm not so sure about the neighbours." As a gay
Christian, I know that God knows me and loves me just as I
am. It's my Christian neighbours who can't understand and
love me — unless of course I pretend I'm just like them. . . .*

*When will the Church leave behind centuries-old cultur-
al stereotypes and prejudices? Is it really a question of biblical
authority, or is it something darker, like fear of the strange or
different, or fear of change, or lust for power over others, or
fear of the ambiguities that lie deep within every human heart?*

*I long to be free of the painful bonds that are an unjust
necessity to survive in the Church. People are beginning to
guess who I am, and I don't know what's going to happen if
they rip off my bonds. These are difficult times for closeted gay
Christians, after the United Church upheaval. And now
the resource* Our Stories/Your Story *is beginning to circu-
late in the parish, underground. Some are trying to identify
me as one of the nine authors. Some want to expose me.*

*Suddenly the allegory of Yentl is shifting. Now the story
of Lazarus comes painfully to mind. I've heard the voice of*

Jesus calling me from death to life. I hear him saying to the others, "Unbind him, and let him go!" The smell of death is all around me. Who will unbind me with loving hands, so that I can come out into the light, and breathe the fresh life-giving air of real freedom?

Quickly, unbind me, please! I'm smothering, and some would keep me that way. I must decide soon whether I will choose life with Christ or death in the Church. A terrible sadness is overtaking me. Should I leave parish ministry after all these years as a faithful priest? It's a terrible choice. Will someone unbind me?

Writing down my feelings brought some relief; at least God had heard my cry. But I needed more than that. My cry had to be heard by the Church, but in such a way as to protect my identity. A few days later I sent my "response" anonymously to the Human Rights Unit, which had been the force behind publication of *Our Stories/Your Story*. They needed to know the jeopardy in which their innocuous document was placing potentially hundreds of faithful gay clergy in the hostile climate in the Anglican Church of Canada.

To the few to whom I had come out in the years before the Christmas bombshell, I added a couple more. Darrell and Louise didn't bat an eyelash. The outreach committee meeting at their home had dispersed, and Louise's suggestion that the committee have a study on *Our Stories/Your Story* had been well received. Over a beer I came out to them, expecting that this young couple who had become close friends wouldn't flinch. I wasn't disappointed. The gender of the person I loved was simply not a problem for them. So completely at ease were they with my sexuality, it dispelled much of the panic I had been feeling.

With my response to *Our Stories/Your Story* burning in my back pocket, I decided to share it with one trusted parishioner. Lorraine was married to Gabe, who had a few months earlier graduated to the position of full-fledged people's churchwarden. In various ways this woman who had recently begun part-time studies at my alma mater, Wycliffe College, had impressed me with her genuine love and openness. I felt implicitly that she would understand, and I hoped that she could be a personal support to me. One evening, after a meeting, I gave her a copy of my story with a warning to be cautious with it, that it was very personal and sensitive material. She tucked it away to look at later.

What I didn't count on was Lorraine's own panic and fear. She shared what I had written with two women with whom she met weekly in a small support group, and they invited me to meet with them.

The three women were on pins and needles. Janice already knew I was gay from the conversation I'd had with her and her husband, who together had a counselling practice. Irene, however, hadn't had a clue. Like Darrell and Louise, the three women had no personal difficulty with me being gay, but there was one catch: they were worried on my behalf, and they wanted to protect me from harm. When I told them about Suzanne's threat, they were alarmed. They didn't know if they were ready for a fight if the enemy should carry through on her threat. Over the next few weeks their fear abated little, until they wisely decided to get on with other concerns and not let "the issue" consume them.

It wasn't long before Gabe took me aside. With great affection this gentle man told me that his wife had shared my story with him, and that it didn't make any difference to him. "People are people," he said. "What does it matter if someone is gay or straight?"

Now that the two churchwardens — Gabe and Darrell — knew I was gay, as did Barbara, who had become deputy warden, I began to relax. Thus far I had encountered nothing but loving acceptance.

At the next meeting of the outreach committee the group decided to sponsor an evening reflection on *Our Stories/Your Story* for the whole parish. Copies of the resource would be provided from the church office for anyone who intended to come that evening, and the event would be advertised in the parish bulletin with other items of note, but I decided that I would not make any announcements at

Sunday services about it — I wanted to have little visible connection to it. Perhaps someone from the Gay and Lesbian Task Force of the Human Rights Unit could be contracted to come and facilitate the evening. My friend Brad agreed — he was a safe, straight married man, and a priest already familiar to the parish, having preached at St. Philip's at my induction and in the years before my arrival as a guest of the previous pastor.

In the meantime, a marvellous change had come over the man I loved but whom I had been seeing less frequently. I don't know what happened inside Ahmad, but he seemed to have experienced a breakthrough in his dark feelings about being gay. We began to see each other more frequently as summer approached and the love that had seemed dormant burst into full bloom. Re-energized by Ahmad's love and laughter, and nourished by his frequent visits and daily telephone conversations, I found I could face the parish and its tensions with greater calm and sense of purpose. At the same time, having come out to all the churchwardens, my secretary, and a handful of trusted parishioners, I had experienced their full acceptance and love. It was good to be fully known and loved — so much so that a new sense of security began to grow. I could face the future in a church where the people most important to me supported me fully.

There was a joyous service in May that confirmed my hopes. In an historic service on the second Sunday of May — Mother's Day — our curate, Ruth, and three other women were ordained to the priesthood at St. James' Cathedral. One of those women was the first female cleric on staff at that previously all-male bastion of tradition. In an ironic twist, there was not one male ordinand in sight as the four women knelt on the chancel steps before the Bishop of Toronto. The preacher spoke of the historic import of the event, a culmination of the Church's movement towards greater inclusivity. Standing at the bishop's left hand, I chanted the litany for ordination — a special set of sung prayers — an honour for the young gay male rector of one of the candidates.

As June 19 approached — the date set by the outreach committee for the study of *Our Stories/Your Story* — two other events fuelled my optimism that the Church was indeed moving towards the realization of Christ's inclusive vision: the biannual conference for all diocesan clergy at Trent University in Peterborough, followed by my second June retreat for gay and lesbian Christians at Kirkridge in Pennsylvania. At the Trent conference, Henri Nouwen, a famous writer, theologian, and speaker, had led a powerful spiritual retreat for three hundred Toronto clergy. For the first time I heard the predicament of gay Christians raised at a diocesan gathering when the chairman of the diocesan "marriage and family life" committee asked our famous speaker during question period if he had a word of hope for the Church's singles, including homosexuals. After a meandering response, another priest bravely got up and put the question about gays and the Church more boldly. All I could remember hearing of Nouwen's response was his saying that we were asking the wrong questions about gays, and instead of asking whether homosexual *acts* are right or wrong, we need to focus on issues of *being*. The reality of persons of gay *being* is the primary consideration. I thought I heard him driving at what I already knew: if we accept homosexual persons, then we must accept that there is a positive moral context in which they can *act out* who they *are*. None of the five bishops of Toronto sitting in the lecture theatre that evening rose to dispute Father Nouwen.

Buoyed up by the Trent conference and the Kirkridge retreat the following week, I faced the outreach event anxiously but optimistically. Twice I'd had to make the trip downtown to replenish the stock of *Our Stories/Your Story* that disappeared from the church office in the weeks before the study session, so I expected a crowd. The atmosphere was tense as parishioners gathered for the eight o'clock event on Wednesday evening. The start had to be delayed a few minutes while extra chairs were set up to accommodate the last of the thirty or so parishioners who showed up. The outreach group was buzzing proudly about the large turnout. Suzanne and Fred were seated together with sullen expressions, looking as if they would breathe fire any moment. Later I saw that Darrell had seated himself deliberately between them.

Brad began the evening nervously, explaining the genesis of *Our Stories/Your Story*, drew up some questions for reflection, and divided the thirty people into small groups. As the evening progressed it was apparent that there were many opinions about the place of gays in the Church. Every small group had at least one member who was strongly pro- or anti-gay, while the majority were somewhere in-between. Surprisingly, Sandra, the parishioner to whom I had lent the books and to whom I had come out, started to quote the Bible like a fundamentalist — perhaps her husband's threat had won out. I felt betrayed.

The tension was heightened when the large group re-gathered to hear reports from the small groups, common concerns were identified, and Brad tried skilfully to wrap up the evening with a group consensus on where to go with things. Fred tried to end the discussion there, saying angrily that the parish should not be wasting its time, but should be focusing on evangelism and church finances. Suzanne sat there, glowering but speechless, as young progressive voices made their points of view known. Finally, most agreed that there were two concerns to address: how the Bible is interpreted, and getting to know some gay people. It all came together when an older woman volunteered to be part of a small planning group to arrange future events on the two topics. The woman in front of me suggested that we should try to find a homosexual so we could talk to one at another meeting. I almost chuckled as I sat, invisible, right behind her.

The outreach organizers and Brad and I heaved a collective sigh of relief as the meeting broke up and parishioners dispersed in small groups, some in animated conversation. The evening had been a success, in most people's terms. A controversial issue had been raised, and the world had not ended. In fact, the majority of people wanted to pursue the issues that had been raised, and had made arrangements to follow through.

Hoping I could stand back while parishioners gave leadership on the issue so close to my heart, I began to think optimistically about the future. I could envision staying in a church where there were so many people willing to be open to their gay brothers and sisters.

The next few days were busy but joyful. The choir's end-of-season pool party was a high-spirited celebration, and was followed in the next two days by rehearsals for weddings. The wedding of an old school chum was followed by the "wedding of the year" on Saturday afternoon, as the son of Gabe and Lorraine was married with the help of four clergy. John had just finished first year of theological training and wanted all the important priests in his life to have a role in his wedding to Janice. The joy of the occasion seemed unmarred, but it was the calm before the storm.

The blow was delivered unwittingly by Ruth after the last parishioner had cleared out of the church following the Sunday service. Ruth came into my office and kept saying how sorry she was. She had arranged for my support group to meet that night; would it be okay if the women brought their husbands? I looked at her, puzzled.

"What are you talking about?" I asked.

"Hasn't Gabe or anyone told you?" she asked incredulously.

"Told me what?" I asked, beginning to be alarmed.

"Oh no!" she said, starting to cry. "They want you to resign. They're going to go to the bishop, if you don't. I'm sorry, Jim. You're going to have to resign. There's nothing else you can do."

Ruth burst into tears and threw her arms around me, but it was no comfort. I was stunned, completely taken by surprise after the success of Wednesday evening's event. Eventually I composed myself enough to extract more details from the sobbing woman. "They" — led by Fred — had delivered the ultimatum to Gabe on Tuesday, and in five days no one had told me the terrible news. I guessed everyone must have hoped that someone else would be the messenger.

"And why am I supposed to resign? Did they give any reason?"

"They're unhappy with your ministry, and the way the parish is going."

Those are pretty broad strokes, I thought. They must think I'm a fool not to know what they're getting at.

"Well, I can't be there tonight. I'm going to be preaching at Christos MCC. It's the first time and I can't not go." What did she think she was doing, arranging a meeting behind my back, even of a "support" group? Did everyone but me know what was coming down?

"You'll be with your own people tonight. I'm so glad," said Ruth, wiping away some tears.

I asked her to arrange for the group to meet the following evening, and went home, heart filled with despair. Bitterly I thought of her phrase: "My own people"! After Ruth's two years with me and all the insight she had gained, didn't she know that my parishioners were "my own people"? Against some odds I had worked for years at the centre of the Church's life, refusing to be consigned to outcast status. Was I suddenly to be relegated to an untouchable caste, fit only to associate with "my own"? The theme of my sermon that very morning had been that God's love knows no human barriers.

Monday morning Barbara and I met with Gabe at his office. Darrell was at work, so only the deputy churchwarden could go with me to confer with the people's warden. I had to hear it directly from Gabe's mouth. He was beside himself. Fred was calling every hour to see if Father Jim was going to resign. The list of complaints he had presented were trivial: the expense of my moving out of the rectory and into a condominium; the innuendo that I was hiding my comings and goings; the parish's financial difficulties; and my taking too many holidays.

None of the complaints held water, and Gabe and Barbara knew it. I had moved into the condo so that we could house Ruth and her family in the rectory — one person didn't need that big house. And it was ludicrous to suggest that I could hide anything when half a dozen parishioners lived in my new building. Every parish was having financial difficulties in the economic recession; and, as far as holidays were concerned, for the first time in ten years I had taken the two weeks of professional development that was the diocesan standard. The complaints were obviously a smoke screen, and the timing the day before the outreach study of gay stories could be no coincidence.

Reluctantly, Gabe admitted that Suzanne had joined forces with Fred, and that she was threatening that if I didn't resign quickly she would go to the bishop herself. He could barely restrain her, he said. Abashedly, Gabe admitted he hadn't told me sooner because he couldn't find the right moment — he had been so caught up in the preparations for his son's wedding, and then he thought that someone else must have told me. After more than an hour of agonizing over the situation, I said that I would meet with the support group that evening and make my decision.

The meeting with the "support group" was disheartening. They were afraid. In the preceding weeks, all of them had acknowledged their full acceptance of their pastor as a gay man, yet in the face of parish conflict they could see no alternative except resignation. I was so disappointed, yet I understood their fear intimately. It was as though I had taken some of my fear and given it to them. As my fear had dissipated, theirs had gained force. A potential large-scale battle was more than the parish could face, they said, especially with the wounds of the upheaval with the former choir barely healed. They might not be homophobic, but they were too afraid to face those who were. Unwittingly they were giving the enemy far more power than it really had. Only Darrell and Louise, and Maggie, a woman from the outreach group, thought that resignation was out of the question.

The decision was made that I would go to see the bishop. But I couldn't help wondering if things would have been different if I had been black instead of gay, or if I had been a member of an ethnic minority, or a woman, or a priest undergoing marital breakdown. Under any of those circumstances, would my friends be deserting me in my darkest hour?

CHAPTER 7

B ISHOP TAYLOR PRYCE, MY area bishop, was on sabbatical for the summer, so I searched through *The Diocesan Link* to see which of the other four bishops was on duty. I heaved a sigh of relief when I saw that Terence Finlay, the diocesan bishop, was on for a couple of weeks. Of all the bishops he was the one I trusted most with my particular agony. Late-night drinks at clergy conferences, meetings we had shared, my work with him in chaplaincy concerns, his visiting with Keith at the AIDS hospice, his dramatic gesture at the Trinity graduates' dinner, and his advocacy of *Our Stories/Your Story* — all led me to believe that the man I knew to be sensitive, open, and down-to-earth would not be dismissive or authoritarian if I went to see him. In fact, I already knew one priest who came "out" to Finlay before he became a bishop, and had been met with only a deep concern for his well-being.

Still, I knew that my job and my future were on the line. As far as I knew, Finlay's personal approach to the guidelines had not been officially tested, and what he might think and do privately could be very different from his public actions. For a day and a half I agonized about what to tell the bishop, but I could come to only one conclusion: the time had come to be honest. For years I had been discreet, not forcing my issue on the Church, but trying to simply be me with a cautious integrity. Bishop Brown had known my track record and trusted me enough to send a gay priest to me for help. Only the previous week I had made the decision, mindful of the support of the handful of parishioners and friends who knew I was gay, to continue to live and minister discreetly in the Church. Now enemies had decided to break my silence.

For half a year since Suzanne's threat I had felt harassed and lived in fear. Now that the situation had intensified, I felt as if not only my privacy but my being was being violated. Finlay would understand, I hoped. The key to my future was in his hands, and I could only trust that he would be just and loving in what he did with it.

The recommendation of most of the "support group" had been that I go to the bishop to resign. No, I thought, that would be pre-determining the bishop's response. I would simply tell Finlay the truth, completely and candidly, and trust that he would find some way to support me through the turmoil. I thought I knew how the late Lord Bishop of Toronto, Lewis Garnsworthy, would have handled it: *tell the troublemakers to come and see me — if they have the nerve.* Garnsworthy had enjoyed a reputation of caring, first and foremost, for his clergy, and protecting them from harassment.

It was a bright summer afternoon, June 26, when Darrell and I sat down in the bishop's office. I felt I needed moral support, so I took with me the only man in the parish who I was absolutely certain had no qualms about my sexuality. My friend was also rector's church-warden, but that was beside the point in my hour of need.

Ahmad, my beloved partner, was frightened, but supported me in my decision to go to the bishop. I knew he had gone to work that morning in a very anxious state, praying and totally preoccupied with my meeting with the bishop and its outcome. He had never come out to anyone, not even a friend, and felt keenly the terrifying prospect of coming out to one's boss.

After a brief exchange of pleasantries with the bishop, I got right to the point. "Terry, there's a small group of people in the parish who want me to resign. It's a serious matter, and I've always gone to the bishop when there's trouble so he's not caught by surprise. They have a short list of complaints, but too trivial to be the real thing. The real reason they want to get rid of me is because they suspect that I'm gay." I paused, mustering up all my courage. "And it's true. . . . I am gay. In fact, I have someone that I love very much." Surely, I thought, he must know what it is like to love someone as I loved Ahmad.

The bishop paused in his note-taking, and suddenly seemed a little pale. Then he asked, "Jim, are you aware of the bishops' statements on these matters?" The fatal question.

My heart sank as I realized the direction he was taking. I had feared he would ask the question about the "guidelines."

"Yes, I am."

"And where do you stand with them?"

Sighing, I replied, "Well, I'm certainly not celibate. I love someone. Why would I be celibate? The time has come, Terry, when I simply have to stand up and tell you who I am. The conspiracy of silence in the Church is killing me, and I can't live with it any longer."

I poured out my soul — the agony of years. "It's very painful to me that the Church refuses to hold up to me the same standard of faithful love that it holds up to everyone else."

"The Church isn't ready for that, Jim."

"The Church oppresses gays and lesbians."

When the bishop protested that it wasn't so, I explained at length the Church's conspiracy of silence, and the jeopardy in which it puts every gay man and lesbian — especially clergy. For half an hour the bishop listened attentively, asking few questions, as I described my struggle over the years to live with the silence and be an effective pastor while trying to maintain some sense of integrity. I even described how Bishop Brown and I had nurtured Rod through the decision to resign his orders, together trying to keep this gifted young gay priest for the good of the Church, but failing in the end.

The man who held my future really cared, I thought, as with growing confidence I shared what was in my heart. I felt an enormous load being lifted as the bishop listened with an expression of thoughtful concern on his face. When he asked how Darrell saw things in the parish, Darrell told him about the positive outcome of the meeting with Brad the previous week, and said that he was optimistic that the parish could work things through — it was only a few parishioners who had problems with homosexuality.

By the end of the hour, Finlay seemed deep in thought. He congratulated me and thanked me for coming to see him and making sure that he was the first to hear about the trouble. He assured me he was not a homophobe.

"Nobody is going to push me into a hasty decision, Jim. I'm going to need some time to think and pray about this." The bishop paused reflectively.

"The homophobes in the parish will probably complain that the bishop is taking too long to pray. But you tell them," he said, with a thoughtful glance at Darrell and me, "to just cool it down — the bishop is praying."

Darrell and I left the diocesan office feeling hopeful. I had not been fired on the spot, and there were to be no hasty decisions. Over a couple of cold drinks in the afternoon sun, we celebrated the fresh hope I'd found in a bishop who would not be pushed into action by homophobes. My cry for help had been heard.

Darker thoughts returned with the night. Why had the bishop felt it necessary to ask the question about the guidelines? I had long understood that the guidelines on ordination of gay persons were to be used entirely at the discretion of an individual bishop. I knew of no one who had been fired after years of ministry because of them, and I knew that they were coming up for review at the House of Bishops' meeting in a few months' time. But still I was uneasy with the fact that Finlay had raised the question with me.

♦

Days passed while the bishop prayed. Word began to get around the parish that I had gone to see him. And the bishop was right — the homophobes did think he was praying too long. Gabe was getting frequent calls to see what was happening, and the stress was showing. The Sunday services were tense. Suzanne and her husband showed up for the early service, glowering with hostility, but were protectively sandwiched by some of my "support group" like thorns between roses. The fuming couple stayed for the 10:30 service and were joined in a front pew by Fred and his wife. I felt a wall of hatred as I led the service and preached my way through as best I could. It was baptism Sunday, always a favourite service for me after working for weeks preparing young excited parents and godparents for the big day. I couldn't help wondering as I held the children in my arms and poured water over their heads, in the name of the Father, the Son, and the Holy Spirit, if theirs would be the last baptisms I would ever conduct.

Monday morning I heard about the scene in a local doughnut shop after the Sunday service. Fred and Suzanne had asked Gabe to meet them, and he had wisely taken his wife and Barbara, the deputy warden, with him. Things had gotten so out of hand with Fred and Suzanne and their spouses, and the Norberts, a young fundamentalist couple who were friends of Suzanne, that voices were raised in anger. I was sickened — my sexuality a topic of loud angry discussion in a public place! Darrell, who hadn't been invited to the meeting but found out about it afterwards, was furious; the complainers kept bypassing him, he was sure, because they knew he wouldn't stand for their homophobic witchhunt.

Finally, the phone rang on Wednesday afternoon. The bishop had prayed exactly one week — or until the next weekly Toronto College of Bishops meeting, I thought cynically. When the bishop's secretary asked me to come to see Finlay the following Tuesday, I was filled with foreboding. Why hadn't he called himself, as was his usual custom? Had he made a decision without any further conversation to see how I was doing? I tried to hold onto the memory of the caring reception I had gotten the week before, but I feared the worst. A few days later, when I called the bishop's office to let him know I wanted to bring the churchwardens with me, I was told that they had already been contacted and would meet with the bishop separately. Was it divide and conquer? Or would he pray for another week?

There were signs of a growing smear campaign being run by the enemy. Reports got back to the church office that a letter-writing campaign had begun. I heard about a distraught young woman whose husband had been stopped in the street to be told the news that "Father Jim is a practising homosexual." The bearer of bad tidings was the same man whose family had moved up the hill from Central United in a fury over "the issue" three years earlier, and who had been so proudly telling people in his former congregation about the "fine young priest" at St. Philip's. The enemy had obviously been recruiting. Worst of all was the use of the word "practising." I had told no one but the bishop and Darrell that there was someone I loved. I felt brutalized having my love sneeringly spoken of as mere sexual activity.

On Sunday, July 7, tension filled the church. Again Fred and Suzanne were sitting near the front with their spouses, and if looks could kill I might have been struck dead. Suzanne was so full of rage that when she came up for communion and extended her hands to receive the sacrament from my hands she was noticeably shaking. In spite of the uproar these hate-filled people were fomenting, my pastoral duty called me to minister to them as I would to anyone else. How could they come up to the altar rail seething with hatred? Even the former member of the United Church who had been stopping people in the streets to attack me dared to look me coldly in the eye as I inducted his young son into the servers' guild.

The gospel reading for the day was a story of rejection — the rejection of Jesus by his own hometown people. "And they took offence at him. Then Jesus said to them, 'Prophets are not without honour except in their own town, and among their own kin, and in their own house.' And he could do no deed of power there."

I preached passionately on the Church's rejection of people throughout the ages: of Jesus, who dared to say that we should love our enemies; of Galileo, who dared to say that the earth wasn't at the centre of the universe; of the African peoples enslaved for so long by Christians; of divorcés and women denied for two millennia their full places in the Church. It was not by scripture or tradition — the first two pillars of Anglicanism — but by the third pillar of reason that the Church had repented of its rejecting ways. Still, there were many outstanding issues. I went on:

> *We will have to deal with issues like abortion, in Church and society. Issues like "Is there a just war?" and how we justify things like that. What about the place of gays and lesbians*

in the Church? What about capital punishment? The Holy Spirit is moving in our lives. The Spirit is moving in the Church. To this point there is no consensus, but we cannot deny the fact that God is moving. The Spirit of God has yet to reveal to us the totality of the divine will and purpose for our lives.

The Church today is struggling; I think everyone knows that. The Church is dwindling all over the place. But the Church can be renewed if it becomes the community of love and justice. Read the parish statement of purpose on the back of the Sunday bulletin:

> *Inspired by the love of God, and led by the power of the Holy Spirit, St. Philip's seeks to be a welcoming, caring, and accepting community, ministering to one another and to the wider world, through worship and prayer, and by sharing our gifts and love in the service of our Lord and Saviour Jesus Christ.*

What a powerful, wonderful purpose! Inspired by God's love, and led by the power of the Holy Spirit, to become a community, welcoming caring and accepting. . . .

Gingerly, I talked around the central topic and the tragedy I feared was about to take place. Only a handful of parishioners knew what I was driving at, both friends and enemies, while everyone else was oblivious to the events that were threatening to disrupt the parish. I had made no allusion to my own predicament that the uninformed would pick up, because I still had to trust the bishop to make a good decision. To have come out to the congregation would have been a breach of that trust, I reasoned.

On Monday, the day before I was to meet with the bishop to hear the outcome of his prayers, the churchwardens took action, led by Jack Fricker, one of two lay delegates to Diocesan Synod. Jack and his wife, Carolyn, nearing retirement age, had been pillars of the parish for more than two decades, and had given leadership in most parish roles over the years. They lived in my condominium building and had become dear friends, often inviting me for dinner. Distraught, I had shared my predicament with them a few days earlier. Jack, never one to sit back and watch events overtake him, and in fact a leader in Church justice issues, penned a letter to Bishop Finlay with help from Darrell and Gabe:

> *Dear Bishop,*
> *We the undersigned would like to appeal to you regarding your forthcoming decision concerning the Reverend Jim Ferry.*
> *In the Diocese's Mission statement it states as its purpose "to embody . . . God's reconciling love, justice, compassion and liberation. . . ." The issue before us is seen by a large number of parishioners as a justice issue and as such Father Jim has a great deal of support. We trust that your decision will reflect that support and the intent of the Mission statement.*
> *Questions have also been raised about the legality of any decision, particularly if Father Jim is relieved of his duties as a parish priest. Could this leave the Church open to legal action under the Ontario Labour Law and the Canadian Charter of Rights?*
> *We appreciate that this is a difficult decision for you and the College of Bishops. We are confident however of the support Father Jim has at St. Philip's and that our parish could be an example of living the Diocese's Mission statement.*

The letter was signed by the churchwardens and the lay delegate and hand-delivered to the bishop's office on Monday morning.

Monday was the start of Vacation Bible School, a week-long morning program of fun, crafts, songs, and Christian teaching attended by dozens of children. The school was organized and run by some of the women of St. Philip's; I was to play a key role each morning at gathering time, and to take photographs the first day of each child for a collage they would make later in the week.

Camera in hand, I ran into Norbert as I passed through the church office on the way to the parish hall. He was just dropping off his children for the morning. With a strange expression on his face he said, "Jim, I just want you to know that the letter I've written to the bishop isn't to be taken personally. You and I just have a difference of opinion on an important issue."

I was infuriated. This was the same man who had been shouting about me in the doughnut shop a week earlier. "How dare you call this a difference of opinion!" I spat. "You're trying to destroy my life and take away my future!" I stormed off to the parish hall, shaking and trying to compose myself for the waiting children. I was supposed to talk to them about how God loves everyone, regardless of their differences.

Tuesday morning I arrived at the bishop's office, gripping the hand of one of my trusted friends from the parish. Maggie, one of the dissenting voices at the final "support group" meeting, had volunteered to accompany me to the bishop's office for my second interview. Active not only in parish outreach but also at diocesan and national church levels, she was known to the bishop for her work. I had heard years before in the clergy gossip mill that you never faced a bishop alone if there was a crisis, and that bishops would try to get you alone to put the pressure on you if they were going to fire you. Maggie was a support to me, and more — she could tell me to slow down if she thought I was getting swept away.

My old friend Michael Bedford-Jones came out of the bishop's office and greeted me with a concerned look. He had been promoted to the office of executive assistant to the bishop three years earlier, just before I moved to Unionville. The mantle of responsibility was not resting on him easily that morning as he informed me the bishop was almost ready to see me. When I introduced him to Maggie and said that I would like her to come in with me, he disappeared for a few minutes and returned to tell me apologetically that she couldn't join us. I knew then that I was about to be fired.

A few moments later, with Michael taking notes, the bishop began our meeting by asking how things were going in the parish. Candidly, I told him that the enemy had been recruiting others and writing letters. Surprisingly, the bishop said that the only letters he had received so far were supportive and that there had been no communication from the group that had made the initial threat. I assured Finlay that they would have come to see the bishop if I hadn't caught them by surprise by coming first.

"Help me to understand what went through your mind when you came to me, Jim. You knew that I would have no alternative except to ask for your resignation, didn't you?" probed the bishop.

"I didn't know what you would do. I knew the odds were high that you might ask for my resignation, but I hoped you might find a more just and compassionate way of dealing with the situation."

I went on to tell him that I had always believed that the bishop was the first one to talk to if there was trouble brewing. I couldn't live under the threat of blackmail, I told him, and I felt I was being violated. The Church's standard that it's all right to be gay but wrong to love somebody is sheer hypocrisy. People don't choose to be gay and they should be allowed to love, because you can't separate a person's *being* from his or her *doing*. For a few minutes I poured out my pain and frustration with the Church's injustice, and the way it was supporting homophobia. When the bishop tried again to bring me to the point of admitting that I *knew* he'd have no choice but to ask for my resignation, Michael interjected, saying that he didn't think that was quite what I was trying to say. Again I reiterated that I hadn't known what Finlay would do but that I had hoped he would find some just and compassionate way of treating me.

The bishop moved the conversation on to a discussion of how we might handle my resignation, so that some good might come out of it for the parish and the larger church. Perhaps, Finlay suggested, the people of Unionville who were actually wrestling with the issue might have something to say to the House of Bishops in November when it examined the guidelines, so that some good might come out of my leaving. Would I consider drafting a letter outlining my resignation and both the bishop's and my positions, in consultation with the wardens? Then I could read it to the congregation the following Sunday.

In that moment, the bishop caught my imagination. I knew I was being forced to resign. But if my departure could advance the cause of justice for gays in the Church, then it wasn't a total loss, I thought. I would have a dignified departure, with the bishop figuratively standing with me and calling for a re-examination of the guidelines. It was the only straw in sight, so I grasped it, and agreed.

"What about all the other gay clergy in the Church?" I asked as the conversation moved on to other issues. "I've been one of the most discreet gay clergy in the diocese. Won't this put them — "

"You're not kidding, Jim!" interrupted Michael. "You're so discreet I had no idea you were gay until the bishop told me what was happening!"

I felt vindicated by my friend as I continued, "Won't this put other gay clergy in a terrible position?" I knew it was a rhetorical question, but I asked it anyhow. There was no response.

The bishop seemed pleased with my co-operative stance and concerned for the parish, as we talked about the timing of the letter, and when I would get back to him with a draft of it for him to revise. Then it started to dawn on me that we had talked a lot about the parish and the manner of my resignation, but not at all about Jim Ferry and his immediate future. The bishop was closing off the conversation without a word about what was to happen to me.

"Terry, before I go, I have a couple of questions. What happens to me now, in terms of severance or future employment, or what?" I was getting very nervous.

"Well, Jim, I haven't crossed that Rubicon yet," the bishop replied after a brief pause.

"Well, I'm crossing the Rubicon, and I need to know."

"I'll have to get back to you, Jim, after I make some enquiries." I thought I knew what that meant: he would have to consult Chancellor Hemmerick, the bishop's chief legal advisor.

The bishop showed me out of his office, exchanged a few pleasantries with Maggie, who had been waiting nervously in the hallway, and we headed back to Unionville, my anxiety rising.

"Maggie, he hasn't even thought about me, what happens to me! He hasn't 'crossed that Rubicon yet.' I can't believe he hasn't given a thought to my future or well-being when my life is being ruined by these people!"

I telephoned Darrell, who, together with the other churchwardens, was meeting with Finlay that evening, to ask him to push the bishop on the issue.

Later that evening the churchwardens sat in my living-room with long faces. The bishop had crossed the Rubicon, and they were horrified with what he had told them. There was to be no severance pay or offer of alternative employment in a "safe" position because — here Darrell repeated Finlay's words — "the Church cannot be put in the position of appearing to reward Jim for his behaviour."

I was stunned and, with the wardens, sat in a terrible silence for what seemed the longest time.

"What behaviour?" I cried. "Eleven years of faithful service? Daring to speak the truth?"

The churchwardens erupted angrily, shocked by the brutality with which I was being treated. They had argued furiously with the bishop, only to be told that if the parish wanted to do something for me, in terms of severance pay, they were free to do so, but the diocese could do nothing. The churchwardens assured me that they would do everything they could to get the diocese to look after me; after all, it was the diocese and not the parish that was firing me. How could the bishop expect me to resign under these circumstances? I asked.

In the morning I had thought the bishop would at least stand with me through the trauma. Some good could come out of the evil of my forced resignation, and I could accept that. Only a few hours later, bewildered by the bishop's about-face, I felt I was to be punished and humiliated, held up as a public example of the sort of wickedness that deserved the worst kind of punishment. I knew I had done nothing wrong. It was the Church's rules that were wrong. I had been willing to resign, knowing it was unavoidable, as long as the bishop would stand with me. Now he wanted to strip away the only thing I had left: my dignity. I couldn't stand up and resign before my congregation under these circumstances — it would be like telling them I knew I was an evil pervert and that the harsh treatment was what I justly deserved.

When morning came, I called Michael Bedford-Jones at home and asked him to tell the bishop that I could not resign under the circumstances. The bishop would then have the chance to think carefully about what he would say to me before he called, I reasoned.

When Bishop Finlay called Wednesday afternoon, it was to accuse me of breaking my agreement to resign. I responded that he was supposed to get back to me about the terms and conditions of my leaving, and I needed to know what they were. Then he told me all I was to get was a relocation package — counselling — to help me get into secular life. There would be no severance pay; he apologized, but it was the best he could do.

Shaking, I said in little more than a whisper, "After eleven years of faithful service?"

Emotion coloured the bishop's reply. "Jim, the Church can't appear to reward you for your behaviour. I'm sorry."

After a long pause, I found my voice and asked for time, pointing out that the bishop had taken two weeks to pray about this and I needed the same. No, he replied, he didn't have time to give. If I didn't resign he'd have to "inhibit" me — an official edict would be issued, prohibiting me from functioning anywhere in the Anglican Church as a priest. At least if I resigned I wouldn't be inhibited, and then ten or fifteen years down the line, if the rules changed, I could become an active priest again. If I was inhibited I couldn't, he warned. This was no carrot at all to dangle before a hungry man's nose, I thought. It was a lose-lose situation for me, I told him. He responded that it would be a "lose" for me, for the diocese, and for the parish.

The bishop reiterated that he wanted an answer. I begged for time to think and pray and take counsel. This was all happening far too fast.

He gave me until the next morning. When I called at 9:10 a.m. after a sleepless night, it was to confirm that I couldn't resign under the circumstances. Finlay replied that his position hadn't changed either. I asked if I could make a suggestion, and he said he'd welcome anything at this point.

"If I was the bishop of Toronto, caught between a rock and a hard place, one being Jim Ferry and the other the House of Bishops' guidelines, I'd tell Jim Ferry to take a paid sabbatical until the November bishops' meeting, and decide the matter there." After all, the bishops were scheduled to review their guidelines on homosexuality at their next semi-annual meeting.

The bishop laughed nervously. "That's the best suggestion I've had . . . but I'm afraid I can't take it." He shuffled through papers on his desk, saying, "Let me find the right letter," and then started to read a letter of dismissal. It was followed by the inhibition.

> *Pursuant to Canon 22 of the Constitution and Canons of the Diocese of Toronto, I hereby inhibit you from functioning as a Priest in the Church. I do this with regret.*
>
> *The inhibition means that you are not to function in any manner in the worship of the Church as a Priest. It is applicable not only in this Diocese, but anywhere in the Church.*

"I'm sorry, Jim, but I can't let you go back to St. Philip's. Bishop Blackwell will be there on Sunday to take the services."

Two hours later there was a knock at the door. A courier asked me to sign for a special delivery. Opening the envelope, I unfolded a yellow piece of parchment bearing the embossed red seal of the Bishop of Toronto, together with my letter of dismissal. The bishop left for a month's vacation that afternoon.

Devastated, I stumbled through the next few days. I wasn't even allowed to say goodbye to my people — they would arrive at church on Sunday morning to find a stranger in my place, telling them the startling news. I spent that same Sunday morning in the only place where I knew I was fully welcome, the big Metropolitan Community Church in my old neighbourhood, near St. Saviour's. As I returned to my back pew seat after communion, and sat down weeping, I felt a warm arm envelop me from behind. A voice whispered in my ear.

"Jim, this is terrible. I'm so sorry." It was the gay son of a prominent St. Philip's family. We wept together.

Later Sunday afternoon I got a call from a furious Darrell and Louise. Bishop Blackwell had read a letter from Bishop Finlay, telling them that I had been dismissed because of my "decision to remain in a continuing relationship with another man." I was in too much of a state of shock to grasp the significance of the bishop's expression, but it didn't escape Darrell and Louise. The bishop had "outed" me to the entire congregation. There had been an audible gasp as Blackwell read the letter, and a stunned congregation absorbed not only the fact of the sudden loss of their pastor, but the revelation that he was a gay man in a relationship. An angry mob of parishioners had surrounded the bishop after the service, furious with my brutal expulsion.

Slowly it dawned on me that my right to decide who I might come out to, and when and where, had been violated. Shock waves rolled over me for days, as word of my dismissal and outing spread like wildfire through the clergy grapevine, and angry priests tied up my telephone line every morning with messages of support. Devastated parishioners began to call as well, especially after the churchwardens mailed out copies of the bishop's letter to every family on the parish list. Some people wanted me to go to the press. It was going to hit the media anyway, they said, so I might as well take the chance to frame the story first.

I couldn't go to the press. Ahmad was frightened out of his wits. What about my family and the man I loved? he argued. Did I want to make a media circus out of them, and ruin their lives? I didn't know what to do except protect the people I loved from public violence.

For days I hid in my apartment, leaving only occasionally to visit

Ahmad, always in fear that I might be followed. Long ago I had booked a summer vacation in France with my brother Tom, and the departure date was ten days away. If only I could get through the next week and a half, I would be across the Atlantic, far away from any media invasion, and it would give me time and space to think. For ten anxious days after the bishop's public announcement I prayed that the press wouldn't call.

I heaved a sigh of relief when the plane to Paris lifted off the tarmac. I had made my escape.

◆

The still night air of southern France was shattered by the insistent ring of the telephone. I had just fallen asleep when the penetrating ring jarred me awake. Leaping out of bed in the dark, I cursed as I stubbed my toe on the foot of the bed, and limped to the phone. It was Ahmad. Why was he calling? He had called just last night and I hadn't been away a week yet.

"Where did they get that picture, Jim?" he teased. "You know, the one of you with the flowers."

"What are you talking about? Don't you know it's after midnight here and you've just woken up the whole house?"

"You've made the press, my love."

"No!" I gasped. "How can that be?"

"I don't know, but you were on television tonight, and all the papers are full of it. They even have a colour picture of you with some flowers. You're not mad at me, are you? I just thought you should know."

WOULDN'T GIVE UP GAY LOVER, PRIEST FIRED. GAY REV. GIVES UP CHURCH FOR LOVER. I shivered in the darkness as Andy read articles from two Toronto newspapers that recounted in some detail my firing and the bishop's letter to my congregation.

"Isn't that just great!" I fumed. "Here I am in France, as far away from the press as I could possibly be, and they're telling the whole world about me."

My head was reeling as I climbed back into bed. I had done everything in my power to avoid the media, and in spite of it all I was front-page news. My simple visit to the bishop had set off a chain of events that was careening out of control, and I would have to wait until I returned home to see if anything could be done about it.

"If you see any cameras, leave!" I told Ahmad over the phone the day before my return to Toronto. The airport might be full of reporters, and the last thing I wanted was for my mysterious "gay lover" to wind up in the morning paper. I could take a cab home, I said. Fortunately, the press had been told I was returning a week later than was actually the case, so when I arrived home unheralded I discovered I could count on a week's respite. It would give me time to see my lawyer before the media discovered I was back. I had been able to arrange only a quick initial interview with her the day before I left for France.

The fear and anxiety that had become my daily companions deepened in the following weeks. Ahmad was almost frantic, he was so worried that his name would hit the press next. In his Mediterranean culture, family and the family name were sacred. He said many times that it would be better for him to die than to bring shame on his family. Fear ruled his sleep as he tossed and turned at night, but he said he loved me and would do anything for me as long as we could protect his family, and therefore his identity. In the midst of it all, his passion and ever-present concern kept me from despair. I decided I would do everything I could to protect him and to preserve the deepening love that bound us together.

With my return to Toronto came a deluge of newspaper clippings and radio and television tapes. I was infuriated to discover that the diocese had actually taken the initiative, outing me to the Canadian media with a detailed press release. In my absence the diocese had issued a package to the wire services, including, from the diocese's personnel files, a colour photograph I had given them several years earlier when I moved to Unionville. Worse yet, I discovered, the press kit had an embargo date on the cover of July 14, 1991, 11:30 a.m. They had it prepared to give out to the press at the end of the service where Bishop Finlay's letter was read to my shocked congregation.

Had they been expecting the press? I wondered. Had they been afraid that I would show up for my dismissal with media and protestors in tow? The diocese's director of communications, the Reverend Tim Foley, had been there that Sunday, and I could just imagine him armed with a briefcase full of press releases. The chancellor had been there as well — an occasional visitor, two of his daughters were my parishioners, and I had baptized some of his grandchildren. The press release included the bishop's letter to the congregation, Bishop Blackwell's sermon that day, and copies of statements by the Toronto College of Bishops and the National House of Bishops on "human sexuality."

The press had a feeding frenzy. Bishop Blackwell appeared on a television news broadcast, again with my colour photograph. The biggest radio station in the city had two one-hour shows the next day, with Ruth, my assistant curate, appearing on one and Tim Foley on the other. For a week there was daily coverage of the saga. My lawyer responded to the press release by announcing my intention to seek reinstatement. "Group Expresses Outrage Over Firing of Gay Priest" heralded the plans of Integrity to hold a service at the end of August in my support. "Half of Congregation Backs Ousted Priest" was the claim a week later. As I tried to absorb the bewildering array of media stories, one thing became clear: the media were not painting me as a villain, but as a man "attempting to be true to both his faith and the requirements of love."

Confounding it all was misinformation from the diocese's director of communications. One newspaper article reported Foley's statement that "Ferry went to see the bishop and told him he was in a homosexual relationship and did not want to be a hypocrite. After explaining the Church's discipline and law, Finlay told Ferry he had the choice of ending the relationship or resigning. Ferry chose not to resign and was fired." In fact the bishop had given me no choice at all, except to resign, and no instructions about my relationship whatsoever.

The media coverage provoked a deluge of letters and phone calls from a surprisingly broad spectrum of concerned people — gays and straights, clergy, parishioners, Anglicans, and non-Anglicans across the country. It was becoming clear that enormous numbers of people were outraged at my treatment, even those who had misgivings about gays. One senior priest in my area called to say that he was appalled that I should be summarily dismissed without severance pay, when he knew of another married priest who had been carrying on with women in his parish. The bishops had quietly sent him on a six-month sabbatical without a word of explanation to his parish, he said. Another priest wrote about a married priest who had been living with another woman in the rectory and was fired, but received twenty months' severance pay — a month for every year since he'd been ordained.

It was the cards and letters from parishioners that moved me to tears.

> *James: I received my letter [from the wardens] today. I am horrified and ashamed. We used to burn witches too. The more things change, the more things stay the same. Be Strong.*

Besides personal notes, others sent copies of letters they had sent to Bishop Finlay. One mother wrote, referring to the diocese's mission statement "to embody God's reconciling love, justice, compassion and liberation," saying:

> *Where is the justice and compassion for Father Jim? He has been stripped of his dignity, his profession, his right to privacy, even his financial stability. That this sentence has been delivered by a jury of the highest order of the Anglican Church is most disturbing to me as a lifelong Anglican. It makes me question the arrogance of an institution to flout the civil liberties of Canadians as enacted in the Charter of Rights, it makes me question the values of this same institution in following the teachings of Jesus — love and compassion as long as we're all the same? For the two lines in the*

Bible that might support this autocratic and rigid decision against gay priests, surely we have learned of Jesus' love and compassion for all types regardless of anything that makes them different. I'm in a real "pickle," I've learned everything all wrong, and worse than that, I've taught my children the wrong thing too!

Unfortunately, the message that you are demonstrating, especially to the youth of this parish, is that you play by the rules, regardless of their merit, or you don't play at all. I would really appreciate it if you could explain to them, in their terms, the rationale behind this decision. My daughter can't understand it from your letter. At a time when young people are leaving the Church, she actually looked forward to Sunday morning Youth Group with Father Jim. She liked him, she trusted him, she appreciated the ways in which he made religion "real" for her. He was preparing her for confirmation. Does she want to be confirmed in this Church now? Do I want her to? She feels betrayed and indignant, and her friends in the parish are sharing these feelings. . . .

Clergy and laity alike wrote to the bishop to express their sense of betrayal to the man who had been installed as diocesan bishop in a spirit of optimism, joy, and openness only a few years earlier. Another parishioner wrote:

. . . I am offended that no one in the parish was consulted about this decision although we are surely the ones most immediately and profoundly affected. This despite the fact that Jim had the support of his wardens and many parishioners. No consideration was given to the fact that as mentioned we had already begun to look at this issue with the help of the study resource Our Stories/Your Story *which you encouraged parishes to do. Had we been given the opportunity to*

*participate in our own future this whole process could have
been constructive not destructive.*

Chaplains and laity involved in ministry to persons living with AIDS
wrote to the bishop to say that he had raised the specter of homophobia at a time when they were just gaining credibility in the gay
community, and thus he was jeopardizing their work. Outraged parents wrote from P-FLAG (Parents and Friends of Lesbians and Gays)
to ask the bishop if he was aware of the implications of his actions for
all gays and lesbians, and their parents and friends, asking, "What are
you going to do about other 'closeted' ministers in the church?
Who is next on your list?" At Anglican Church House, the national
church headquarters in Toronto, lay staff members started to come
out of the closet to bishops and colleagues, protesting the assault they
were experiencing as Christians and as gay persons.

As dozens of letters formed a mountain on my desk, the magnitude of my situation became apparent. Clearly, what had happened
to me was more than a personal event, it had traumatized countless
people in the Church and beyond. I was seeing only the tip of the
iceberg; for every copy of a letter to the bishop, there must have
been ten more that I never saw.

In consultation with my lawyer I decided that reinstatement should
be my primary objective. Valerie Edwards had been recommended
to me by a gay lawyer friend who had encountered her at the opposite end of the table in a recent litigation. No higher recommendation could I imagine than to refer a potential client to an admired
opponent. A young dynamic lawyer in a law firm renowned for its success in employment cases, Valerie was an engaging contradiction of
no-nonsense legal acumen and genuine concern for the person and
issue at hand.

In short order, she examined the Church's canon laws and it became
apparent that the bishop had breached canon law in firing me. I was
entitled to due process under canon law, which had built-in protec-
tions against summary dismissal. Our reading of canon law indicated

that, when a bishop believes the welfare of the Church is at stake, he may demand the resignation of a parish priest, but it must be done by letter. After thirty days without a reply from the priest, the bishop may notify the priest that he will appoint a commission of enquiry if a resignation has not been tendered in fifteen days. This could lead to charges, and the institution of a Bishop's Court, whose members are appointed by the bishop, to try the priest and give its findings and recommendations to the bishop.

Additionally, canon law states that while a charge is pending against a priest, to avoid great scandal "the Bishop may cause a notice to be served on the person inhibiting such person from performing any service of the church pending investigation, or until the Bishop shall withdraw the inhibition, or until sentence has been given in such case." And further, "No person inhibited . . . shall be deprived, during the continuance of such inhibition, of any of the emoluments of office."

Inhibition was supposed to be nothing more than a temporary suspension with pay while an investigation or hearing was under way. Since no charges had been laid and no sentence given, our strategy would involve a civil lawsuit claiming that the Church had broken its own canon laws.

The primate was furious, too, I was told by several clergy who had had separate conversations with him. Before he fired me, Finlay had called Archbishop Michael Peers, Primate of the Anglican Church of Canada, for advice, and Peers had advised him not to fire me. Finlay shouldn't take action, especially without a single complaint on his desk, but should let the parish handle it. Then, after a while, if the parish situation blew up, he could act to rectify the situation. I was puzzled by Finlay's spurning of the primate's sensible advice. Surely Peers should know how the guidelines were intended to be used, when he was one of only four bishops still in the current House who was actually present during the 1979 debate.

Bishop Finlay and I were both in the midst of a maelstrom of protest over my dismissal when he called to see if we could meet "off the record." In a last-ditch effort to resolve things, I left Finlay with a personal letter asking for three things: the immediate lifting of the inhibition of my priestly functions; an appointment as an assistant priest at a downtown parish; and an apology "in the same forums in which the damage had been done." When I left the bishop's office on Friday, August 23, it was with his promise that he would pray about it and get back to me. Reasoning that it was not practical to return to Unionville after the upheaval, and that there were lots of downtown parishes with gay clergy and parishioners who would welcome me, I thought it seemed like a good compromise to be an assistant priest in a workable environment. As for the apology, I knew it would never be forthcoming, but I hoped the bishop might say something to the effect that although he didn't condone my lifestyle, he was appointing me an assistant priest while the Church continued its ongoing discussions about the reality of homosexual persons in the Church. I hoped the bishop might grasp at such a face-saving alternative.

Preparations began for a big service to be held by Integrity at Church of the Holy Trinity, a church in the heart of the city. It would be my first appearance in public since my firing, and we presumed the press publicity would draw a big crowd. Facing the media was a daunting prospect, and many friends said I should talk to a media consultant to prepare myself. Jaime Watt, a consultant recommended by a friend, had a practice in London, Ontario, and made the two-hour trek on Sunday to meet with me, donating his time. In a brief session he tried to simplify the enormous complexities of dealing with the media. At his suggestion, seconded by Valerie, I began the process of preparing a press statement to be released on Wednesday before the Integrity service. For a month since the diocese's press release outing me to the public, I had kept silent. Now it was time to break the silence.

Monday evening a small group of trusted friends and supporters met with Valerie and me at her office to hear her strategy and respond to it. This group, which included my brother Tom; my long-time clergy friend Brad; Norm from Integrity; Maggie and Louise from St. Philip's; and Dr. Jim Reed, who had chaired the primate's Task Force on Sexuality over a decade earlier and who was now the president of the Toronto School of Theology, were to form my "inner cabinet." Andy and I had met with Valerie an hour beforehand to allay his fears of exposure.

The strategy was simple: we would file a lawsuit in civil court for wrongful dismissal and breach of confidence, claiming that the bishop had broken Church and civil law in dismissing me and that he had broken confidence in revealing the details of my sexual orientation and relationship to my congregation and to the general public in the ensuing press release. We knew the strong card in my hand was the breach of confidence — the sacred duty to keep in confidence what is told a priest or bishop in private had been broken, we would claim, when Finlay revealed publicly, without my knowledge or consent, the details I had told him of my private life. The lawsuit would take many months to proceed through the maze of legal procedures, perhaps not reaching court for a couple of years. With the support of my cabinet, I was committed to the long haul. Still, there was a glimmer of hope that the bishop would be courageous and find a place for me again.

The bishop never called. In fact, our off-the-record conversation would be the last one for many months. Instead, Valerie received a call from Robert Falby, acting as the bishop's lawyer, asking to meet with her on Tuesday. The meeting was ill-fated from the start. I wanted reinstatement, and all Mr. Falby had to offer was a suggestion of a "pastoral grant" to help me make the transition to secular life. Of course, Valerie did not accept the offer.

I was sitting in the law firm's conference room Wednesday afternoon, undergoing a gruelling mock media interview with Jaime to prepare to meet the press in a few hours, when Valerie was called to the phone. A few moments later she returned excitedly with the news that the bishop wanted to offer me a pastoral grant, but this time with no strings attached. "Take the money," she advised, "with the clear understanding that it won't prevent you from pursuing any legal action." God knows I needed food and shelter, so I agreed.

A few minutes later a fax arrived bearing a heading in big bold letters: WITH PREJUDICE. "We have obtained instructions to accept service of a Statement of Claim should Mr. Ferry instruct you to proceed
with an action. Our client continues to be concerned that Mr. Ferry
be in a position to re-establish himself." I was to receive, solely on a
compassionate basis, a pastoral grant for three months equivalent
to my usual salary — conditional on my undertaking in good faith
the services of a vocational counsellor. The paragraph ended by repeat-
ing, "This offer is made on a 'with prejudice' basis." Valerie sent a
fax back accepting the offer and reminding the bishop's lawyer that
in doing so I was not prevented from pursuing legal action. It was
four o'clock — only a few hours until the Integrity service.

◆

Very soon I learned what WITH PREJUDICE meant. By the time the
packed service at Trinity began at seven o'clock, it had become clear
that the bishop's office had been busy phoning around to make sure
the congregation knew about the bishop's act of charity. Not only had
Integrity been phoned in the three hours since the pastoral grant
was offered, but the administration of Holy Trinity Church and the
preacher had been called. When the preacher reported the grant, he
pointed out the only condition: Jim had to get counselling. The
congregation groaned.

Billed in the press as a "service of outrage," Integrity's event was,
instead, a beautiful and moving Service of Hope and of Prayer, for
me, the parish, and the bishop, in the best Anglican tradition. In the
darkened church, a few candles pierced the gloom as the leader proclaimed, "Jesus Christ is the light of the world," and the congregation responded, "A light no darkness can extinguish." As, one by
one, hundreds of candles were lit, the congregation sang "Light of the
Worlds." The mood was set for a service filled with hope in the God
who liberates the weak, the poor, the oppressed, the needy, and the
orphaned. Brad preached of a day to come of justice for gays and lesbians, and four hundred people prayed, sang, and listened through

the sweltering heat of the August evening.

Almost $7,000 was donated that night for my legal costs by clergy and laity, gay and straight, young and old, many of whom I was meeting for the first time. I knew then that I was caught up in a struggle far greater than a personal job loss. I had to fight this battle not just for me, but for all the wounded.

In the ensuing weeks, life was a whirlwind, not least because I had to move out of my apartment and was surrounded by half-packed boxes. Two support groups formed, it seemed out of thin air, one to meet with me biweekly to be a support and strategy body, the other to begin the process of serious fundraising for the months, perhaps years, of legal wrangling ahead. Letters continued to pour in. I could imagine the avalanche of mail on the bishop's desk as public pressure mounted for "justice for Jim," as my support group called it.

The frequency of meetings with my lawyer accelerated until my statement of claim was filed against the bishop in civil court. Up to the last moment we agonized over whether or not to claim significant damages against the bishop and the diocese. One thing we knew for sure: I was being ignored, and the only thing we thought would make the bishop pay notice was a claim for substantial damages. On September 12 the lawsuit was filed in Ontario Court and served on the bishop and diocese, claiming over $500,000 in damages. I worried people might think that all I wanted was money when, in reality, I wanted only justice and my function as a priest reinstated, but we went ahead with the suit. Warned that it might take months before anything happened, I tried to get on with my life.

On Monday, September 24, three days before the diocese's annual synod convened, I received a postal notice of registered mail to be picked up. Believing that at last my pastoral grant had arrived to shore up my rapidly dwindling bank account, I went in the late afternoon to get my mail. Thinking I could take it immediately to the bank machine, I slit it open and discovered only a single yellow sheet of parchment. In horror I read the few words inscribed above the bishop's embossed red seal:

> I, TERENCE, BISHOP OF TORONTO, *by virtue of the authority vested in me and pursuant to Canon 22, hereby pronounce the sentence of Deprivation of Office upon the Reverend James Raymond Ferry and accordingly, the licence of the said James Raymond Ferry is revoked.*
> *Dated at Toronto the 31st day of August, 1991.*

I felt numb as I searched the envelope for a covering letter, hoping for an explanation. The envelope was empty. On examining it closely, I discovered beside the special "registered mail" seal a postmark dated September 18, 1991. The document was dated August 31, the final day of my vacation. Why, I pondered, did I get this sentence by registered mail more than three weeks late, when my letter of dismissal had arrived by courier only two hours after the bishop fired me over the telephone in July? Did my lawsuit, filed six days before the postmark, have anything to do with it?

Back at the apartment, head reeling, I struggled with the fresh violence of the Church's "justice" as I tried to finish packing. The fight was getting dirty, I thought. Then the telephone rang. Two of my support group were members of synod and had tried to get a motion on the agenda to protest my firing. Caught by surprise, the synod agenda committee had called a special meeting, and the chancellor, they said, had refused to allow the motion. Someone on the agenda committee had told my friends they were wasting their time since *I was going to have a hearing in Bishop's Court* anyway. Now my head was really spinning.

"That's impossible!" I said. "Just this moment I've opened a letter with the bishop's sentence in it. I've been deprived of office! They're just trying to put you off. How could they be pronouncing sentence and calling for a hearing at the same time?"

After some negotiation with the agenda committee, my friends watered down their motion censuring the bishop until it was pure "motherhood," a simple request to diocesan synod in light of my firing to find ways of making gays and lesbians welcome in the Church. It was the only way, they said, that they could get something past Chancellor Hemmerick onto the floor of synod on Friday. Better something than nothing.

Packing madly. Radio interview show. Setting up my legal defence fund with a trustee. Getting the keys for my new apartment. A speaking engagement with the women at the Centre for Christian Studies. Just being Jim Ferry was turning out to be a full-time job.

At noon on Wednesday, in the midst of frantic activity, I picked up a cryptic message on my answering machine from my lawyer's secretary: "The bishop has issued a press release and reporters are calling for a response." Valerie was in court all day, so it was late afternoon before I saw Finlay's press release. The bishop had announced that I would have the opportunity to put my case before a Bishop's Court: "Accordingly, I have suspended my Order of Revocation of his licence and deprivation until such time as a Court can be convened to deal with the matter."

I was back on the payroll, but exhausted by the week's roller-coaster ride. I wondered if the boys downtown knew what they were doing, passing sentence on me one day and revoking it the next. Surely, I thought, it was a sign of crisis at headquarters as the public's protest gained momentum.

The media had another feeding frenzy, as the bishop read his press release to a packed cathedral Thursday night at the opening service of synod. Surrounded by a sea of pink ribbons worn by supporters, I sat in a pew near the pulpit, soaked in perspiration, exhausted from the strain of moving that day, and bitter about the high-handed treatment I had received. Why hadn't Finlay at least telephoned to give me the news of Bishop's Court? Why did I have to find out about it from the media? Worse still, how could the bishop stand in the pulpit and say, "It is not and has not been my intention to deprive Mr. Ferry of an opportunity to put his case to [a Bishop's Court] and since it now appears that he wishes such an opportunity it is my intention to submit the question to a Bishop's Court"? I was dumbstruck. Only three days earlier I had received his sentence preventing me from doing just that!

"Gays and lesbians in the life of the Church is a fact," said Finlay to the cathedral throng. "The Church is enriched by their presence, both as laity and clergy." He went on to read the 1979 guidelines condemning homosexual activity while accepting homosexual persons. No mention was made of the more progressive 1978 statement. "I am committed to a continuing dialogue in the Church in an effort to understand how the Church can be inclusive and just both for gay/lesbians and for people who are sceptical about homosexuality. There are some who fear homosexuality and to them I say, I will not tolerate homophobic 'witchhunts', nor 'gay bashing'. . . . I would encourage parishes to provide safe places where people will make time in the next couple of years to listen carefully and try to understand each other. . . . Is it possible for the Church to be a place of reconciliation in this area?"

St. Philip's could have been a safe place, I thought, if the bishop had consulted the congregation. And what was I, if not a victim of a homophobic witchhunt?

As the bishop's procession left the church, he waded past the people sitting next to me with hand extended, saying, "Jim!" I could barely stand to grasp his hand. Could this be a beginning of a real reconciliation, or was it just a dramatic gesture for the crowd? Did the bishop see his Court as a gracious way out of a predicament for both of us?

Would I get justice in a Bishop's Court? If the bishop laid the charges; appointed the prosecutor, judge, and jury; was the chief witness against me; and had already pronounced sentence once, could a Bishop's Court serve up justice by any definition? In the end, according to canon law, the Court would only make findings and recommendations that were not binding, and Bishop Finlay would make the final judgement and sentence. I had already experienced both.

Believing the proceedings would be seriously prejudiced in a Toronto Bishop's Court, I appealed to the primate a few weeks later to have the case heard in the Supreme Court of Appeal of the Anglican Church of Canada. My situation had become a national issue, I reasoned, and should be dealt with at that level. Because of the massive publicity and the bishop's initial sentence, I questioned whether a fair hearing was possible in Toronto.

The reply was disheartening but not unexpected. The primate had no jurisdiction to act on matters of discipline. The buck stopped at the diocesan bishop's desk, although an appeal might be possible to the provincial archbishop.

Weeks passed as I waited to hear the charges against me. Only the fact of Bishop's Court had been announced, not the specific charges. What was taking them so long? Couldn't Chancellor Hemmerick figure out what to charge me with? On November 20, the charges were finally laid, and Valerie called.

"Jim, they don't want to discuss moral issues at court, they just want to nail you for insubordination. You're charged with refusing to give up a homosexual relationship, not with being in one!"

A shift had taken place in the bishop's approach to the moral issue at hand. He did not want the court to discuss homosexuality per se. Rather, he charged that I had "refused to refrain from continuing a homosexual relationship with another man, contrary to my instructions, your vow on ordination to obey your Bishop, the discipline of the Church and the standard stated by the [bishops]." Disobedience, pure and simple. All of this flew in face of the fact that the bishop had never instructed me to give up my relationship with Ahmad!

Together with the charges came a letter announcing that "in order to avoid any appearance of bias, Chancellor Hemmerick asked Bishop Finlay to replace him with someone who has had no involvement in this matter." The bishop announced that he had appointed the former Chief Justice of the Supreme Court of Ontario, the Hon. William D. Parker, to serve in the place of the chancellor. A more conservative figure could not be imagined to preside at Bishop's Court, my friends in the legal profession assured me. Bishop's Court was to be serious business indeed.

Through all of the weeks of lawyers' letters and unpredictable actions from the bishop, Ahmad was smiling less and less. It wasn't that he didn't agree I was making the right decisions. In fact he supported every one of them along the way, after much frank debate. It was just that fear was crushing the life out of both of us. For weeks the laughter that had been the hallmark of our relationship had been getting sparser. Our love was not dying, but the stress was driving us apart. He had seen me lose everything — my job, my future, my privacy — and he had good reason to fear losing the same. But his worst terror was that his family might find out he was gay. He would rather they heard that he was dead.

Finally, the laughter died. It was Hallowe'en, and the gay community had a huge dance at the Masonic Temple, a large public hall, as it did each year. We couldn't get in the door without being noticed. The entire evening seemed to be one long procession of well-wishers and supporters, including the young man at the bar who rushed over as I carried away a couple of drinks and thrust my purchase money back in my hand, saying, "Put this in your defence fund." As the evening wore on, I saw the panic grow in Ahmad's eyes. We left early.

I knew it was over that night when Ahmad tossed and turned until dawn. Panic haunted his eyes in the morning. I had to get away from him before we were both destroyed by the fear. With bitter tears we agreed we could walk together no farther.

♦

The loss of Ahmad was like a blast from hell. I had refused to choose between the two loves of my life — my Church and Ahmad — and now I had lost both. Never had I come closer to complete despair. Weeks of sleepless nights, a constant feeling that my head was going to burst, and a pain in my chest that wouldn't go away — I was close to physical and emotional collapse.

Where was my God of love, and the gentle Christ who offered those comforting words, "Come unto me all who labour and are heavy-laden, and I will give you rest . . . for my burden is easy and my yoke is light"? All images faded, but one from the Bible: Jacob wrestling with the angel of God through the night. A mysterious figure of a man — God in disguise, or his angel? — appears in the night and wrestles with Jacob until daybreak. He dislocates Jacob's hip in the struggle, but Jacob won't let go. Jacob knows that he is wrestling with God, in an ultimate life struggle. Finally, as dawn begins to break, the man says, "Let me go!" but Jacob refuses, saying, "I will not let you go, unless you bless me." The man departs with a blessing, and Jacob, marvelling, remarks, "I have seen God face to face, and yet my life is preserved."

I knew that I was caught up in the struggle of my life. I was wrestling with one mightier than I who had the power to wound or heal me, to destroy my life or restore it, to condemn me or bless me. Like Jacob I could not, would not, let go until I had received a blessing that would restore me. Bishop Finlay and I were locked together in a struggle and neither one of us could afford to let go. I refused to give up the last scrap of dignity that I held to so tightly. Someday, somehow, I hoped my love for a man could be afforded the public dignity and blessing that I was convinced was God's intent.

My deep immobilizing depression began to lift in December with Finlay's announcement that the Bishop's Court trial would be open to the public. For weeks I had agonized over whether or not to dignify the Court; it was my supporters' considered opinion that I would not find impartiality or justice there. But, if it was to be public, I reasoned, then the public, and especially the media, could hold the Church responsible for its behaviour. And perhaps under the watchful public eye, the Church could be forced to deal with the moral issue that it so diligently was trying to avoid — the place of gays and lesbians in the Church family. Against the advice of most of my advisors, I decided to go to Bishop's Court.

Valerie Edwards realistically pointed out that I was not likely to win my case, at least in the traditional sense. But what would a win look like? To raise in the Church's and the public's mind the plight

of gays and lesbians; to powerfully and positively affect people's perceptions and attitudes; to provoke the conscience of a nation — all
by letting them see publicly the prejudice and hatred the Church
was perpetuating against all gays and lesbians. That would make it all
worth while. More than this, I hoped the Church and public would
see that it was the right to love that was on trial, and the Church's
cruel refusal to allow ten percent of the population the possibility of
intimate love that most people simply take for granted as an essential
part of being human.

My decision to go to Bishop's Court marked the beginning of a
period of intense preparation, as Valerie, my inner cabinet, and I
attempted to devise a strategy and a line-up of witnesses for court.
Bishops, theologians, Church historians, Bible scholars, parishioners,
clergy, psychologists, colleagues from the United Church, gay laity
— a long list was developed, letters written, and phone calls made. It
became clear that Dr. Jim Reed would himself be our chief witness.
This priest/psychologist/theologian had been a key player in the
debate on homosexuality in the House of Bishops since 1975, and
knew all their perambulations over the years better than anyone not
of that House. Reed's position was quite clear: the 1979 pastoral
guidelines of the House of Bishops were established to be used by the
bishops in their discernment of a person's call to ordained ministry.
They were guidelines developed by and for bishops exclusively, and
since they did not carry the authority of any general, provincial, or
diocesan synod, they were not rules or guidelines for the Church as
a whole. Since they were guidelines for bishops exclusively, priests
could not break them. As well, no bishop had ever raised the guidelines with me at any time in the ordination process.

Could we find a bishop to confirm Reed's position? Not in Canada,
it seemed. At its November meeting, the national House of Bishops
had issued a press release under the heading: "Bishops uphold
guidelines on homosexual ordination, plan further study of sexuality during next year." In typically contradictory style, the bishops had
both agreed to the need for re-examination of the guidelines and

had reaffirmed them, all the while pointing out, "In the Anglican Church, ordination to the priesthood is solely within the jurisdiction of the diocesan bishops."

There was only one bishop willing to come to court. Author of many books, John Spong, renowned as a champion of gay rights in the Church and often referred to as "the controversial Bishop of Newark," returned my phone call almost immediately. With genuine warmth and concern, the Southern gentleman whom I had never met said he wanted me to know that I was not alone. If there was any way that he could help, he would do it, he assured me. At the same time, he said, he wanted to be a help to my case and not a hindrance. Because of his prophetic stance he had many enemies, and there was a real possibility that his name might not bring credit to my cause; even worse, the prosecution might bring one of his enemies to town to oppose him. I could sense the wounded spirit in this man, and yet he was willing to take another risk for a cause to which he was deeply committed. Eloquent and forthright, the bishop could draw worldwide attention to my plight and, I hoped, open the hearts of what promised to be a very conservative court. We began making arrangements for his one-day trip to town.

Valerie spent her Christmas break undergoing a crash course in Anglicanism, reading a virtual library of books on the subject. When she returned in January, she had a grasp of complex issues of Church and spirituality far beyond that of the average lay person. She had discovered that her non-religious upbringing had nonetheless instilled in her a sound Christian ethic; it needed only the appropriate labels. Throughout January, Valerie and her staff worked constantly, interviewing witnesses and gathering materials for court.

A Church historian, a psychologist, friendly parishioners and clergy colleagues, a gay Anglican layman, even a bishop were found to testify, but could we find even one gay priest who was out of the closet to a Canadian bishop and willing to say so in court? It could be the winning stroke, especially if he was in the Diocese of Toronto. But would anyone want to take the risk of jeopardizing his career? Already in the diocese it was becoming known that at least one of the Toronto bishops was in the process of a witchhunt, calling in gay clergy and interrogating them. Gay and lesbian clergy were diving for cover; some were opting out of parish ministry, and others were taking up separate residence from their partners of many years. Only one man was willing to come forward: Douglas Fox, an honorary assistant at a downtown parish with a sizeable gay component, who had written a letter of protest to Bishop Finlay shortly after I was fired, accusing him of flagrantly violating human rights, on the one hand, while preaching them, on the other. In his letter Fox clearly identified himself as a gay priest, writing, "I am, however, considerably perplexed by the variability in your treatment of us. You have raised no objection whatever to All Saints' clearly gay-positive ministry in the lesbian and gay community, and, unless I have completely misread you, you have also been supportive of myself and the other openly gay leaders there." Doug, whom I barely knew, had taken the trouble of sending me a copy of his letter to the bishop. In the midst of studies in library science at university, Doug was actually under the jurisdiction of the bishop of Qu'Appelle in western Canada, and did not fear losing an unpaid position. Most importantly, in the summer of my dismissal Bishop Finlay had appointed him interim priest-in-charge of the parish where he had been acting on a volunteer basis, until the congregation found a new rector. Six months after writing the letter, Doug Fox was still functioning as a priest in Toronto unscathed.

When Valerie interviewed Fox she quickly realized we had dynamite on our hands. Not only had Fox been out to Finlay for at least six months by then, but when he was ordained ten years earlier he had come out to his bishop, Michael Peers. Peers, Fox said, obviously saw the guidelines as guidelines, and had not required him to make a promise to "abstain from sexual activity with persons of the same gender." In the succeeding ten years Peers had risen to the position of Primate of the Anglican Church of Canada. It would be a bombshell if Fox testified in court, but he was willing to speak in the cause of justice for the oppressed. Reluctant to bring possible embarrassment on the only bishop in Canada who had opened his door to me with real pastoral heart, I asked that we not call on Fox unless we felt it was absolutely necessary.

With only a couple of weeks left before Bishop's Court, the pace of preparation picked up. The Friends of Jim Ferry swung its fundraising activities into full gear. They had been meeting for months under the inspired leadership of Garry Lovatt, assisted by Norah Bolton, both parishioners at the Church of St. Mary Magdalene, a historic Anglo-Catholic parish in the working-class west end of Toronto. Together with a few parishioners from St. Philip's and St. Saviour's and friends new and old, my team committed itself to raising the estimated $60,000 it would cost for my defence at Bishop's Court. The cost of the initial civil action — $15,000 — had long since been raised and paid out. We hoped that the publicity surrounding court would make the fundraising easier. Connections were made with a number of parishes, a schedule of parties and speaking engagements was organized, and I began to tell my story to large and small groups of already well-informed and supportive people.

Startling discoveries were made as I waded through reams of documents in the archives of the Anglican Church of Canada and the Canadian Gay Archives, both in Toronto. It was in the dismal cramped quarters of the Gay Archives that I found the first treasure, buried in a file of old Integrity newsletters. In May 1980, the Archbishop of Toronto, Lewis Garnsworthy, wrote to the premier of Ontario, asking the provincial government to ensure the protection under law of homosexual persons in its review of the Human Rights Code. Building on the 1978 statement of the Canadian House of Bishops, the Ontario House of Bishops and the Provincial Council had unanimously passed a resolution "that all homosexual persons are entitled to equal protection under the law and to equal justice in regard to employment in common with all Ontario citizens."

It seemed likely that the existence of such a letter was not well known, but it might prove to be a key ingredient in the Bishop's Court trial or, later on, in a possible appeal to the Ontario Human Rights Commission. A cruel paradox was, however, apparent: while the Church had asked the civil authorities to protect the human rights of gays and lesbians, it was all the while denying those same rights to one of its own people, claiming that the Church was exempt from the civil code. (Indeed, all churches had fought years earlier for a general exemption from the Human Rights Code, claiming that, as voluntary associations, they had the right to discriminate against those who did not fit into their criteria of membership.)

In the National Church Archives I discovered that the minutes of the meetings of the House of Bishops were available to the public. While the most interesting bishops' discussions were held *in camera* and kept locked in a secret vault, the public minutes grudgingly gave up powerful evidence bearing on my case. Besides tracing the bishops' acrimonious debate on homosexuality over a decade and a half, I discovered that the bishops had decided that the primate's commission's *Study on Homosexuality*, though confidential, was to be carefully circulated by individual bishops to appropriate persons for feedback. Could I find this elusive document through one of them? Mysterious comments in the House minutes indicated that the commission had made recommendations that the bishops were determined to keep quiet. Two of these were the development of sexual standards for ordinands and separate sexual standards for priests. The 1979 guidelines were the public outcome of the first, but, regarding the sexual standards for priests, the bishops decided "to withhold, for the moment, any action in this matter." In fact there was no evidence that the House ever did develop such standards for priests. Did this mean the 1979 guidelines did not apply to priests, in spite of the charges against me to the contrary?

The minutes for November 1990 made my heart sink, however. A motion had been made by Bishop Read (who ordained me as deacon in 1980): "That the House of Bishops reaffirms the [1979] House of Bishops' Statement regarding the ordination of persons of homosexual orientation in relation to the document *Human Rights Principles of the Anglican Church of Canada*, and refers our statement to the NEC." The motion had been seconded by Bishop Finlay. Although the motion had ultimately been withdrawn, the implications were clear. The *Human Rights Principles* included an item prohibiting discrimination on the grounds of sexual orientation. Four months before advocating publicly that clergy and parishioners read *Our Stories/Your Story*, it appeared that Finlay had tried to prevent the inclusion of sexual orientation in the Church's *Human Rights Principles*. This despite the fact that Finlay's wife had been involved in the national Church's Human Rights Unit, which had developed the principles. I was devastated. It looked as if my liberal, gay-positive bishop was really a conservative.

The fourteen-year-old primate's commission's *Study on Homosexuality* fell into my hands more easily than I expected, after a few discreet enquiries. It quickly became apparent why the document was still marked "CONFIDENTIAL — For the House of Bishops only." While the scientific material was outdated after fifteen years, the nine pages of recommendations were remarkably progressive for the day. Indeed, they are still so a decade and a half later. Touching on a wide range of issues within the Church — nurture in the faith, education, clergy training, pastoral care, the welcoming of gays, sexual standards for ordinands and priests, and the blessing of relationships — the study went on to advocate a critique of our whole society, touching on such issues as employment, housing, public services, legal protection, the criminal code, and child custody.

The House of Bishops' 1978 statement picked up some of the issues of inclusivity in the Church and human rights protection in society, producing what was probably, for its day, the most progressive stance on homosexuality in the Christian world. But the central component of the recommendations was omitted, and then, a year later, under considerable public pressure, repudiated. The recommendation read: "We recommend that the House of Bishops accept homosexual men and women for ordination subject to the same ethical criteria for sexual behaviour applied to heterosexual ordinands."

Lest there be any confusion as to the meaning of "same ethical criteria," the commission elucidated three major options for dealing with homosexual ordinands: "(a) complete opposition to ordination for any declared homosexual; (b) ordination on the clear understanding that abstinence from sexual contacts with other people is part of the sacrifice required for ordination; (c) ordination based on the same ethical criteria applied to heterosexual ordinands."

The 1978 Bishops' Statement had made no mention of ordinands, but in 1979 the bishops publicly repudiated the commission's recommendations by opting for (b) instead of (c). Since the document was shrouded in secrecy, no one would ever know that the bishops had acted contrary to their commission's recommendation.

The position of the primate's commission could best be captured in one of the four theological and ethical positions they summarized from current debate: "Homosexual acts are to be evaluated in terms of their relational significance." As they put it: "Recognizing that homosexual acts do not always need to be evaluated in terms of a procreative objective, this position states that the nature and quality of the relationship between two persons are of primary importance. Homosexual acts, neutral in themselves, become moral when they are 'expressions of self-giving love.'"

In other words, there should be no double standard. The same ethical standards applied to heterosexual intimacy should be applied to homosexual intimacy.

An appendix to the report, quoting an article by James Nelson, stated explicitly what the ethical questions were for both heterosexual and homosexual intimacy:

> *What sexual behavior will serve and enhance, rather than inhibit, damage, or destroy, our fuller realization of divinely intended humanity? The appropriate answer is a sexual ethics of love. This means commitment and trust, tenderness, respect for the other, and the desire for ongoing and responsible communion with the other. On its negative side such an*

ethics of love mandates against selfish sexual expression, cruelty, impersonal sex, obsession with sex, and against actions done without willingness to take responsibility for the consequences. . . . It is an ethics equally appropriate for both homosexual and heterosexual Christians. There is no double standard.

Buried for fourteen years, could the secret report of the primate's commission be presented in court, or was it so dangerous to the prosecution's case that they would try to prevent its submission in that public forum? Time would tell, but I believed my case was getting stronger by the day.

One thing was deeply troubling me as February 3, the first day of Bishop's Court, approached: my outstanding lawsuit against Bishop Finlay. Months earlier I had agonized over whether or not to include large punitive damages in that suit, worrying that, without such damages, my suit would be fluffed off and ignored. I had decided that $500,000 in damages would guarantee my case would be taken seriously, knowing that some would think all I really wanted was money. Now, as the court date approached, colleagues and friends told me that the damages were sticking in their craws.

Valerie Edwards warned me that I would be giving up the strongest card in my hand if I dropped my suit against the bishop, but I knew what I had to do. I needed to make it clear to the bishop, the court, the Church, and the public that I was driven by a matter of principle, not money. It would be an act of good faith to drop the suit, and I could only hope that it would be taken as such. Some of my friends thought I was being pretty naïve, but I dropped the lawsuit anyway. With the threat no longer hanging over the bishop's head, I hoped he would begin to ask gospel questions instead of questions of law. *What would Jesus do?* The ultimate question for Christian ethics and action seemed not to have been asked between the day of my firing and the weeks before Bishop's Court. Could I encourage the bishop and his court to ask it now?

Signs of a new media feeding frenzy appeared in the days before court. But, as I sat at home on the Sunday evening before my scheduled appearance in court, and watched my life unfold on the national news on television, another image stirred my mind and my resolve. A week earlier I had spoken during the worship service at Metropolitan Community Church of Toronto, where my friend Pastor Brent Hawkes and hundreds of gay and lesbian Christians had welcomed me with a standing ovation. It was Peter, however, a tall, grey-haired man, who had moved me most deeply. In the church basement afterwards, with an inarticulate groan, he had thrust a crumpled piece of paper at me with one of his unco-operative arms. The note read: *Jim, this isn't just about gay rights, it's about human rights. The disabled are next.* Crumpled inside the note was a hefty donation from a man on a meager disability pension.

CHAPTER 8

WHY THEY PICKED ST. MATTHEW'S as the site for Bishop's Court, I don't know. Situated in the far reaches of Toronto's suburbs, beyond the end of the subway line, the nondescript 1960s red-brick building had only one redeeming feature: a large parking lot. The wide variety of community and church groups that used the complex day and night were turfed out so that the court could have exclusive use of the facilities. With church halls in many parishes in the heart of the city lying unused, it seemed a bizarre administrative decision.

Vehicles spilled out onto the access routes to the jammed parking lot on the morning of Monday, February 3, 1992, the opening day of Bishop's Court. Telescopic towers shot up from television-news vans, bearing microwave dishes that overshadowed the peaked church roof. Media from around the world had gathered for what *The New York Times* described as "an archaic forum used by Anglicans to hunt down Heretics and other miscreants since the time of King Henry VIII."

In the dingy gymnasium, hastily converted into a courtroom, a dais had been installed for the members of the Bishop's Court, the fronts of tables carefully veiled in blue fabric. Facing that long head table, several smaller ones had been set up on the floor below, one each for the prosecution and the defence, and smaller unadorned stacking tables had been positioned at the foot of the main dais to serve as boxes for witnesses, registrar, and court reporter. Behind the defence and prosecution tables was the visitors' gallery — row upon row of ancient stacking chairs for the anticipated standing-room-only crowd. Along the side of the room stretched the press gallery, with room for a dozen reporters on a first-come first-served basis. The overflow would have to make do in the large basement press room, which had been equipped with loudspeakers that piped in sound from the elaborate public-address system installed in the gymnasium above. A sound box with multiple jacks for tape recorders — enough for every reporter in town — was provided in the press room. Father Tim Foley, the diocese's director of communications, had prepared well.

My friend and comrade from the United Church in Unionville, Debbie Savage, had picked me up at my apartment and driven me to the suburban court, as she would every day of the trial, to act as moral support throughout the ordeal. As we pushed through the side door from the parking lot on that cold but bright winter day, past the throng of reporters and spectators, several television reporters who had interviewed me in the preceding weeks railed about the inequity of the diocese allowing full sound recording of the court's proceedings, but prohibiting television cameras in the courtroom. They would have to rely on press scrums in the basement and the hallways in the ensuing days. That would not be difficult, since the site organizers had located the preparation rooms for both prosecution and defence immediately across the hall from the press room, in a couple of smaller Sunday-school rooms.

Valerie and her two female assistants on my defence team were edgy but intent on the proceedings at hand. Weeks of preparation had produced reams of documents, crated in large carrying cases now sitting on our table. Despite the edginess, there was a sense of resolve in both me and my team. The opening day of court would set the tone for the whole proceedings, we knew, and what happened this day could make or break my cause. I was thankful that I was not scheduled to take the stand until mid-week. The interruptions of a stream of photographers seeking a good shot for the next morning's paper provided some necessary relief. It was on the journeys to and from the church's worship space that I discovered the "jury" was comfortably ensconced in the church's lounge.

It was a mob scene when my lawyer and I tried to make our way into court. A dozen television cameras formed a horseshoe around us, lights glaring, as we walked across the lobby to the gymnasium door. It was very disorienting, but only a foretaste of what was to come. The courtroom, overflowing with spectators, did not have enough seating for the press, who spilled out into the hallway. Reporters were gathered from across the country and around the world. Even the English and American press had their reporters placed for first-hand coverage. Sitting along one wall, with paints and sketching pads, were three court artists from various television networks. They might not be able to get their cameras into the courtroom, but they would still get their pictures. In the weeks ahead the media would keep my face and situation before the Canadian public on a daily basis. I was counting on them to keep the Church court honest.

A sea of pink ribbons and friendly faces greeted me as I slipped into the courtroom with Valerie. Months earlier my supporters had taken to wearing the ribbons as a plea for my reinstatement. On the lapel of my tweed jacket I was wearing a small pink triangle like the one the Nazis had forced homosexuals in concentration camps to wear, that now was a symbol of gay liberation.

Amidst the throng of supporters and press were interspersed a few sour faces, as well as the eager ones of the thrill-seekers. Altogether, the media's and the public's attention far exceeded my wildest dreams: I had wanted my battle to be as public as possible, and it would be.

Seated at the gymnasium door was the Reverend Ken Maxted, the court's sergeant-at-arms. A tall, imposing former military man, his red hair and moustache sprinkled with grey, he was famous throughout the diocese for his booming voice and the ceremonial kilt he wore in his capacity as an aide-de-camp of the Lieutenant-Governor of Ontario. Sitting below the Court President's chair at a small table was Ann Wainwright, a diocesan employee commissioned as Registrar and Clerk of the Court. The middle-aged, bespectacled church administrator seemed ill at ease with her prominent new role. Fumbling with the microphone, she asked everyone to rise as the Members of the Bishop's Court filed in. Sitting to one side was the court reporter, speaking into a mouthpiece and fiddling with a tape recorder.

The procession wound into the gymnasium in single file and, one by one, took their seats. Seated to the extreme left, directly in front of me, was Canon Gordon Baker, recently retired as rector of Grace Church-on-the-Hill in affluent Forest Hill. A greying, beard-ed, heavy-set man, formerly the principal of a Western Canadian theological college, in semi-retirement he was working as director of a Church foundation. Seated beside him was Dr. Dorothy Ley, a semi-retired oncologist and haematologist who headed up the AIDS Committee of the diocese. She was well-known to me from the year and a half I had spent as a member of that committee. At the centre of the bench was the president, William Parker, QC, retired chief justice of the Supreme Court of Ontario, an aging man with a slight hearing impairment. To his left was the only member of the court who was not a senior citizen, the Reverend Victoria Matthews, a woman in her forties who was rector of All Souls' Church in a northern Toronto suburb. This priest was known to me chiefly in her role as director of field education for divinity students at Trinity College in Toronto. Sitting beside her, at the far end of the bench nearest the gym door, was John Graham, QC, an elder statesman of the Church. He was a retired lawyer who had served as Registrar of the Synod of the Diocese of Toronto for many years. All in all, this "jury of my peers" was an aging and conservative court and imposing enough to instill a sense of foreboding in all but the coldest of hearts. The Church establish-ment was well represented, indeed.

Sitting to my right, near the gym door, was the prosecutor with his lone female assistant. Robert Falby, QC, had been hired months earlier to defend the bishop in my civil litigation against him, but now, in an ironic role-reversal, was the official prosecutor in the bishop's case against me. The competent white-haired lawyer was a member of St. James' Cathedral, one of the most conservative, reactionary churches in the diocese, where he had served as churchwarden and in other leadership roles.

Most ominously, sitting in the front row of the spectators' gallery, inches behind Mr. Falby, was the chancellor, William Hemmerick, QC. In the days to come I would discover that he was Falby's almost constant companion, and could be frequently seen passing scribbled notes up to the prosecutor during the proceedings. Just a few days ago, I had found in the National Church Archives, in the November 1977 issue of *The Canadian Churchman*, an article entitled "Toronto Passes New Discipline Canon" bearing Hemmerick's photograph. Hemmerick was the author of the diocese's canons on discipline and on procedures for Bishop's Court! The new canons had caused an uproar in the Toronto newspapers, as well as at diocesan synod, where they had been presented for ratification.

Said *The Churchman*:

> *Although he did not quarrel with the need for discipline, Rev. Andrew Hutchison said he opposed the canons because "they cast a veil over the gospel of forgiveness" and therefore were pastorally offensive.*
>
> *Mr. Hemmerick pointed out that the tone of the canons is legal because they are documents of canon law. The place for compassion is in the interpretation of the law, he said. "Either a man is compassionate or he isn't," he said and pointed out that one must trust the bishop to exercise compassionate discretion in his interpretation of the laws.*
>
> *This was the crux of the matter to some who opposed the new canons. "This bishop is all right," one priest said, "but we could get another who isn't, and he could use this pretty powerfully if he took a dislike to you."*
>
> *"The removal of the bishop from the court is meant to benefit both an offender and the bishop," Mr. Hemmerick said. "No bishop should have to be accuser, judge, sentencer, and court of appeal."*

The sour-faced, grey-haired little man's constant presence at Bishop's Court, in spite of his removal as president of that court, meant only one thing to me: the author of canon law, who had been the legal advisor behind my original dismissal by the bishop, was there to ensure my conviction. Terence Finlay was Garnsworthy's successor as Bishop of Toronto, and the first to put the new canons and a Bishop's Court to the test. Under the author's sway, would the new bishop "exercise compassionate discretion in his interpretation of the laws"?

The Members and officials of Bishop's Court were sworn in with proper dignity, and the court declared in session. But there was one thing missing — prayers. In the ensuing days, prayers would neither open nor close the sessions of Bishop's Court, in contradiction to the godly nature of the ecclesiastical proceedings.

The clerk read the charges:

> *A Charge is laid against the Reverend James Ferry pursuant to Canon 22, Section 6, in that the Bishop of Toronto believes on reasonable grounds that you have acted and continued to act in a manner unbecoming a member of the clergy and have committed ecclesiastical offences triable and punishable under the provisions of Canon 22 and in contravention of Canon 22, Section 4, paragraphs (1), (6), (7), and (15), in that you have refused to refrain from continuing a homosexual relationship with another man, contrary to the Bishop's instructions. You have acted contrary to your vow on ordination to obey your Bishop, the discipline of the church, and the standard stated by the National House of Bishops of the Anglican Church of Canada and the College of Bishops of this Diocese.*

In preparation for court several weeks earlier, my lawyer had written Falby, requesting particulars of the charge, since mere subsection numbers were not very explicit. The subsections spoke of wrongdoing and wilful, persistent, or habitual neglect in the discharge of duties (subsection 1); any act which involves a violation of a cleric's oath of canonical obedience (subsection 6); contumacy and disobedient or disrespectful conduct towards the Bishop (subsection 7); criminal, immoral, dishonourable, or disorderly conduct or evil report (subsection 15); and conduct unbecoming a member of the clergy (under no subsection).

Falby's response was illuminating, especially with regard to one point: under subsection 15, I was charged only with dishonourable or disorderly conduct. The words "criminal" and "immoral" had disappeared. The bishop did not want to charge that my gay relationship was immoral in itself. He simply wanted to evade the moral issue by charging me with disobedience, etc., for refusing to give it up.

Before Bishop's Court, Valerie and I had made some strategic decisions. We wanted to shift the focus of the court to the moral issues. The Church was steadfastly refusing to deal with me on moral grounds, preferring instead to focus on technical legalistic matters. Could we force the court to broaden its scope to include the substantial issue: the morality or immorality of gay relationships? If my love for a man was not a moral issue, then why should I be asked to give it up and then be fired for not doing so? The real immorality, it seemed to me, was the Church's refusal to deal with me honestly about that relationship by reducing my love to a matter of mere disobedience. Another decision we made was to concede that the bishop had, indeed, given me an instruction of sorts to give up the relationship. To be sure, it wasn't an explicit verbal order, but one might say that it was implied. We didn't want to argue the case purely at the legalistic level — the Church's level; instead, we wanted to argue that the Church's standard was itself immoral and discriminatory, and could not therefore in good Christian conscience be imposed on anyone.

As Falby began his opening submissions, he strove to ensure that there would be no discussions in court about the morality of homosexual relationships, the morality of the 1979 guidelines, or the morality of the bishop's request. Falby contended that all the court needed to determine was whether there existed a standard of conduct and whether it was properly imposed.

"Some have suggested that homosexuality is on trial here," he remarked. "That is not correct. What is on trial here is the order and discipline of the Church."

He reminded the Court of Bishop Finlay's charge to synod several months earlier: "There are some who fear homosexuality and to them I say, I will not tolerate homophobic witchhunts nor gay bashing." Falby went on to add that the Church was addressing the issue of homosexuality, "but not in this Court. . . . The broader issue and the ultimate position of the Anglican Church with respect to its gay members will be dealt with by others in due course."

Valerie began her submissions by reading from the House of Bishops' statement in 1978: "'We accept all persons, regardless of sexual orientation, as equal before God; our acceptance of persons of homosexual orientation is not an acceptance of homosexual activity.'

"Gay Christians believe that God's love for them is absolute. It is the Church's love and acceptance of gay people that is conditional; conditional on gay people denying who they are, denying who they are by not entering into intimate relationship, by not expressing their sexuality in a healthy, loving partnership, denying who they are by pretending to be heterosexual or pretending to be abstinent and leading secret lives.

"My client, the Reverend Jim Ferry, tried to live in the Church and remain true to himself and to God. He has a deep and abiding faith in Christ and a deep and abiding love for his Church. He also has the capacity and need to enter into a meaningful, enriching and loving relationship with another human being.

"If he were heterosexual, he could marry and receive the Church's blessing. He could have both the Church's love and the love and support of a caring spouse. But he is not heterosexual. He is gay. Because he is gay the Church makes him choose. The Bishop of Toronto asked him to choose. We are here today because Jim Ferry refused to make that choice.

"The Bible says, 'The truth shall set you free.' Jim Ferry told the truth to close and trusted friends, to the Church and to the bishop. He went to the bishop in painful circumstances. He should have been freed for telling the truth. Instead he was fired.

"Now, you may say, wait. If a priest goes to his bishop and tells him he has stolen from someone or raped someone or assaulted someone, he can hardly expect to escape punishment by virtue of his honesty. But this situation is totally different. Jim did not steal, he did not hurt anyone. On the contrary, he loved someone. He told the truth about his love and he was asked to make an impossible choice.

"The charges are before you. They speak of discipline, of oaths, of obedience. Since these are the charges clearly, let's deal with them. But the real issue here, in my opinion, is not discipline, it's discrimination. It's not about oaths, it's about what it means to be a Christian.

"Obedience. You will hear a lot about obedience during the course of this trial, but this is not the Army and this hearing is not a court martial. Obedience must be defined in the context of the canons of the Church against the backdrop of Christian belief.

"Determining these issues will be extremely difficult. At the risk of being bold, I would suggest to you that if, after hearing all the evidence, you find your decision easy, then you have avoided the hard issues. That is what my friend [Mr. Falby] will invite you to do. I will ask you to go deeper, to seek the truth and understanding which will permit Jim Ferry to function once again as a priest within his Church.

"What do we hope to accomplish in this process? I would like to advise the Court on behalf of my client that he does not seek reinstatement to the incumbency at St. Philip's on-the-Hill in Unionville. Too much has happened since last June. It would not be good for either the parish or for Jim for him to go back there.

"We are asking to have Jim appointed as an associate priest in a supportive parish in Toronto. The particular parish would be selected through consultation and negotiation with the incumbent, the congregation and, of course, the Bishop of Toronto.

"Is there a parish that will accept Jim Ferry? We think so. We think there may be a few. Jim has a gift for ministering and with the support of his rector and with God's love he's sure to be rewarded with the love and respect of his congregation."

The battle to introduce the moral issues into Bishop's Court had begun. For six gruelling days spread out over two weeks, a lawyer with no Christian faith would struggle against all odds to introduce issues of Christian ethics, faith, and theology in a Church court where the Bishop of Toronto was trying desperately to avoid those issues. "If the Church can't deal with a moral issue," I asked someone, "then who on earth can?"

The prosecution called its first witness. A friend commented that having Ted Scott on the stand was like having God testify in court, such was the respect universally accorded to the former Primate of the Anglican Church of Canada, who had been moderator of the Central Committee of the World Council of Churches for ten years as well as Canadian Representative of the Commonwealth Group of Eminent Persons, Advisors on South Africa. He had been an outspoken advocate for the abolition of apartheid. I could never forget my first Christmas as a deacon when Art Brown dug his elbow into my ribs as we proceeded into St. Michael and All Angels' Church, and whispered, "Jim, did you see who's here? The primate! You're going to have to preach to the primate." He grinned gleefully and, sure enough, my tongue literally stuck to the roof of my mouth during the sermon, I was so nervous. But "just-call-me-Ted" Scott had been very gracious when the service concluded. He was a man I loved and admired greatly.

The dilemma for the former primate was, I think, painful. I didn't think he really wanted to defend the bishops' guidelines on homosexuality, not in this forum. And I didn't believe that, on a personal level, he hated gays. But as a former primate he had one task in this court: to protect episcopal authority. I was sure he knew that from the Church's point of view, my trial was not about sexuality or morality — the rights or wrongs of my loving a man — but about the authority of bishops. If Bishop Finlay lost this case, it might throw the entire Anglican House of Bishops into disarray.

Archbishop Scott would prove to be the diocese's witness of greatest substance. A thoughtful, articulate, compassionate man, he elucidated the best of Anglican thought, and how the Church's mind is shaped by three things: scripture, tradition, and conscience enlightened by reason. New scientific knowledge affects the mind of the Church through the third element, which was how the Church began to understand that "a person's homosexual orientation ought not be a barrier automatically of itself for ordination," although the Church had not yet agreed about the matter of sexual expression for homosexual persons.

When Scott's testimony moved on to the authority of the bishops, especially in the discipline of clergy and laity, he admitted that, while no one has any doubt that the bishops in fact have authority, "nowhere can you find spelled out explicitly what the powers, jurisdiction and authority inherent in the office [of bishop] are." And so the bishops act collegially, and from time to time pass "guidelines that relate to the areas of authority and responsibilities which the bishops have, which they set for their internal life and operation. They give provision for the collegiality of the House of Bishops so that you don't act as individuals, you have a common context within which you work." The bishops have a primary responsibility to guard the faith, unity and discipline of the Church, "but you don't always do that by coming down with clear-cut, definite positions." He went on to add, "It seems to me that one of the tasks of the bishops is to maintain the Church as a community within which issues can be raised very openly and very directly, differences of opinion can be held and take place, but there will be respect for each other in the struggle to find out how you've moved from one position to where you are at the present time."

Valerie's cross-examination of the archbishop was tough. There is a difference, she pointed out, between the authority of the House of Bishops and the Order of Bishops within General Synod of the Anglican Church of Canada. Bishops have clear legislative authority only when they act in conjunction with the other two "orders" of clergy and laity within General Synod. The House of Bishops, really just a gathering of colleagues, has no independent legislative authority. The authority of bishops in particular areas is clear — for example, only bishops can ordain deacons and priests. Even so, Valerie argued, wasn't it General Synod that passed legislation authorizing the ordination of women? "In that framework," conceded the archbishop, "the bishops could make a lot of the subdecisions."

The cross-examination was long and involved, but several points were scored. Valerie pointed out that the guidelines on ordination of homosexual persons "assume that the candidate for ordination is volunteering the information [that he/she is gay]. There is no obligation in here on the bishop to ask. Is that right?"

"Right" replied the archbishop.

Only under great pressure did the former primate finally admit that the bishops had not gone as far as recommended by the Primate's Commission on Sexuality, that "the House of Bishops accept homosexual men and women for ordination subject to the same ethical criteria for sexual behaviour applied to heterosexual ordinands."

Finally the crunch came. "Is it your position, sir, that the House of Bishops can legally bind, in law — not in conscience, in law — a diocesan bishop on matters of ordination?" asked my lawyer pointedly. We wanted to know if a bishop could use the guidelines according to his own conscience.

"They can set the framework within which the bishop has to operate. They do that," dodged the archbishop.

"Does the bishop have to legally operate within that framework?" she asked.

Mr. Falby jumped in. "Perhaps my friend could define what she means by 'legally'."

"If the bishop does not operate within that framework, there's no legal sanctions which can be brought to bear against that bishop?"

"Essentially," admitted the archbishop, "the Church doesn't see itself primarily as a legal structure. There is the moral issue of the community. . . ."

"I appreciate that, sir, but the oath that my client took spoke of obeying the bishop in all legal and honest demands. I would not be raising the issue if it were not the very oath which has brought us here today. My understanding, sir, and the understanding of the witnesses which I will be bringing forward, is that the House of Bishops does not have the legal authority to tell a diocesan bishop who he should ordain or who he should not ordain, or even the parameters of that."

"I agree," said the archbishop.

The atmosphere in the courtroom was charged. "You, I think, were very instrumental in bringing about the ordination of women . . . and there must have been a time when women that you knew in the Church . . . had no hope that there would ever be a day that one could be ordained, and I imagine there were some women who always had hope that there would be a day that women could be ordained. Is that fair?"

The archbishop nodded in the affirmative.

"Are you prepared to look at my client now and tell him that he has no hope for a day where he can be a priest in this church and continue to be involved in a relationship?"

Speechless, the archbishop shook his head.

Mr. Falby, rising, objected. "How is that relevant to these proceedings?"

Valerie replied, "He answered the question. No, you're not." After a pause she continued, "My client is here today pursuing his rights, defending himself against these charges, and asking this tribunal to say that for him today is the day, and he has every right to be here doing that. Is that true?"

Falby replied, "Well, surely that is not an appropriate question for the witness. My friend can argue that, if she wants to, but it's hardly a fair question."

Judge Parker interjected, "Well, whether the views of this witness — it may be his views, but it's the Court that has to decide, not this witness."

"I appreciate that," answered my lawyer.

"And," continued the judge, "you shouldn't, I don't think, be asking the witness the question that the Court has to decide."

"My concern," pushed the defence counsel, "is that the witness may have inadvertently left the Court with the impression that there is no issue to decide."

Arguments among both lawyers and the judge circled and recircled until at last Falby and Parker had to admit that Archbishop Scott was being presented by the prosecution as an expert witness, and could express an opinion on the question before the court.

Finally, the persistent defence lawyer reiterated, "Archbishop Scott, is my client within his rights under canon law to come to this tribunal and ask this tribunal to say that, for him, today is the day that gay people, or my client in particular, should be allowed to be a priest and remain in a relationship? Is he within his rights?"

"As an individual person and individual priest, I think he has a right to hold that view," conceded the archbishop.

"And if this Court, after hearing all of the evidence, believes in good conscience that they should acquit my client, that's what they should do?"

"Certainly."

The prosecution's next two witnesses, a suffragan (assistant) bishop and the Dean of Toronto, spoke confidently of canon law, order, discipline, and obedience. The only grey areas unearthed emerged during the cross-examination of Bishop Douglas Blackwell.

After some exploration of the 1983 Toronto College of Bishops' statement on sexuality, my lawyer asked the pointed question of whether the bishops believed that the expression of homosexuality is a sin.

"That's a word we try to stay away from," said the bishop, with an amused smile. Groans and applause filled the courtroom. Quickly Blackwell added, "But I guess I would have to say yes."

"Is it a sin regardless of the context — even in the context of a loving, committed, faithful, monogamous relationship?" she pushed.

"For clergy, yes." He paused, searching for words. "Well, I guess until the Church changes its mind, I would have to answer in the affirmative."

"Let's talk about the distinction between being homosexual and expressing homosexuality. How about the feelings that a gay person has, sexual feelings towards a member of their own sex? Is it a sin to have those feelings?" Valerie was really pushing the limits.

"No, I don't believe so."

Tension was building as the media and court spectators began to sense the direction in which the brilliant young lawyer was heading.

She pointed out the fifth paragraph of a 1983 statement from the National House of Bishops and read, "'We recognize that many people, both men and women, need help in learning to accept their sexuality as a gift from a loving Creator, given to enable us to enter into mutually enriching relationships which affirm the intrinsic value of each person involved. Our sexuality permeates every aspect of our being. Its reality is far wider and deeper than physical contact. The mutual attractiveness which flows from it opens the possibility for relationships which express respect and affirm the dignity and value of human beings as persons to be related to, and not things to be manipulated or exploited. Such relationships are enriching and give life one of its highest meanings.' Do you agree with this statement?"

"Yes," replied the bishop.

"It refers to sexuality as being a gift from God." Pausing thoughtfully, Valerie asked, "Is a gay person's sexuality a gift from God?"

"Well, I don't know," shrugged the bishop, to loud peels of laughter and bursts of applause in the courtroom. Parker called for order and scowled the spectators into silence.

"If it isn't a gift from God, and it's not a sin — the feelings — what is it? A disease?"

Falby leapt to his feet. The courtroom was electrified. The moment of truth had come much sooner in the trial than my lawyer had expected. Angrily, Falby argued that the line of questioning was not relevant, and the courtroom fell into silent wide-eyed anticipation as Falby, Edwards, and Parker argued over the admissibility of my lawyer's questions. Could we broaden the scope of the proceedings so that moral issues could at least be debated?

Dramatically, Valerie declared that the court had to permit discussion of the Church's position on homosexuality or "I might as well sit down and rest my case and pack up my bags and go home, because that's what this is about."

"Don't tempt us," grumbled Parker. I thanked God the press corps was listening attentively with eyebrows raised. Could the Court afford to fumble its responsibility to explore the moral issues?

The heated discussion went on like a game of ping-pong when the winning point is at stake. Eventually, the Court agreed to adjourn and deliberate over lunch.

We spent lunch hour in the defence prep room, anxiously munching sandwiches. The entire case was at stake. Would the Court allow us to move to the higher moral ground the prosecution was so assiduously avoiding, and allow the defence attorney more latitude in her line of questions?

When court reconvened an hour later, the retired chief justice conceded the defence's line of questioning was permissible, if Valerie would rephrase her questions to be "more relevant." "We're quite willing to give you wide latitude."

The major hurdle had been cleared, opening the way for my defence to include a variety of witnesses on the moral issues the bishop had tried to suppress. Valerie decided to move onto theological ground with Bishop Blackwell.

"My understanding of sin," she proffered after a brief preamble, "is that sin is something which separates us from our self and from God."

"That's one of the definitions, yes."

"So I take it that the expression of homosexuality is an act which separates that person from himself and from God."

"Yes, in terms of broken covenant."

"Now, you indicated earlier that the feelings that a gay person has are not in themselves sinful. You are not sure whether or not the feelings are a gift, so we won't get into whether or not they're a disease. But if I could establish in this Court that the feelings are natural, and that the expression of those feelings is natural, and that to ask a person to repress those feelings essentially separates them from their selves and from God, would you agree with me, sir, that this Court would have to take very seriously in consideration whether or not homosexuality and the expression of it, is then a sin?"

Falby interjected, in a flustered tone of voice, "I'm sorry, I didn't hear the last part of the question."

"If I can establish through the evidence that's led that the feelings that a gay person has are natural and that the repression of those feelings separates him from himself and from God," Valerie paused, apparently deep in thought, "I will have established that homosexuality is not a sin. Isn't that right?"

"I suppose going by your definition . . . yes," conceded the bishop.

In fact, what every bright mind in the courtroom recognized was that my agnostic lawyer had established that the *repression* of natural homosexual feelings is a sin, and, by implication, the bishops' statements instructing homosexuals to repress their innate feelings are themselves sinful.

♦

Buoyed up by the success of the first day of court, Valerie and I were nonetheless wary of the prosecution's final witness, who appeared on Tuesday. It was my old friend Michael Bedford-Jones, who had left Bishop Finlay's employ as executive assistant shortly after my firing to become the Dean of Ontario and rector of St. George's Cathedral in Kingston. He had been present, taking notes, at my final interview with Finlay on July 9, 1991, seven months earlier. The question burning in my mind was: had my memory served me well in relating to my lawyer the details of that conversation?

He approached me sheepishly moments before the day's proceedings began, and apologized for the role he had to play in the trial of a friend. What else could he do, he said, and expressed the hope that I would understand. As he read back the notes he had taken that fateful July day, I began to relive the interview with Finlay. While he left out some details, such as his own part in the conversation, the story sounded very familiar. After a few minutes, Valerie leaned over and whispered that she was impressed with how well Bedford-Jones's account of what was said jibed with what I had told her weeks earlier. There were no surprises, except for the slight discrepancies that would be natural when two different people tell the same story. Most important, the dean's testimony made it clear that my memory had been correct on one point: at no time had Finlay instructed me to give up my relationship with Ahmad. In fact, he hadn't expressed any concern about me and my partner at all.

Surprisingly, we discovered that Michael B-J, as he was called by one and all, had recorded the bishop's end of my telephone conversation with him the following day. Again, except for minor discrepancies, it rang true to my memory.

Under cross-examination, Valerie established that at no time in the July 9 interview or the telephone conversation had the bishop informed the priest whose resignation he was requesting of his rights under canon law. In fact the canons had never been discussed. The bishop had never mentioned my right to retain a lawyer, or to appear in Bishop's Court.

"It appears that on July 10th [from the memorandum of the telephone conversation] that my client was asking for time to think. . . . The bishop took two weeks to think and pray. . . . Sir, don't you think it's reasonable that my client, when going back to the second meeting and asked to resign, have some length of time to reflect on it, to pray on it, to seek legal counsel if he saw fit, to determine for himself the full ramifications of this decision?"

There followed some discussion about the bishop's need to act because of the perception of a growing scandal in the parish. In fact only a few parishioners knew that I had gone to see the bishop. Not one complaint against me had yet been received.

"The bishop understood my client to have a desire to seek legal advice?"

"Yes," replied the dean.

"But the bishop said he could not wait, he had to proceed, he couldn't let the situation in the parish go on."

"That's what the bishop said."

"Let me quote from the memorandum: 'The bishop asked whether Jim realized the implication of not resigning, since it became a lose-lose situation for everyone. . . because the bishop would have to "inhibit" him. He told Jim if Jim was, in fact, inhibited and in the future should the standard change, the inhibition would not be as favourable to Jim as a resignation.' The bishop was essentially saying to my client that if he resigned, and the standard changed, the bishop would look more favourably on having him back as a priest in the parish."

"The bishop or some other bishop," interjected the dean.

"But, sir, surely the Bishop of Toronto is not suggesting that because my client has exercised due process, and requested the rights that were always his, that he should be prejudiced for that some day if the standard changes?"

"Could you repeat the question again please?"

"I don't need to repeat the question." Turning to the judge, Valerie said, "I have no further questions." With a perplexed expression, the dean left the stand and disappeared from the courtroom. He was the prosecution's final witness.

◆

If the bishop's first line of offence, Archbishop Scott, had seemed like having God in the witness box, then our first witness was revered by all as a Saint of the Church. The white-bearded, portly grandfather who assumed the stand was Dr. Cyril Powles, a soft-spoken retired professor of Church history. He had been my history tutor in my first year of theological studies, and for all his grandfatherly looks had a keen mind and a progressive outlook. With an open expression and a warm smile, he began by telling the court about a course he had taught at Trinity College entitled "Change, Conflict, and Continuity."

"Change," the professor testified, "rarely comes from the top down, but takes place when those on top have to deal with a good deal of evidence of pastoral necessity, of conflict coming up from the bottom, and it is at that point the change is either accepted or rejected at the top."

Beginning with the early Church's first controversy over whether Christians had to be circumcised and obey Jewish laws, Powles laid out before the court the history of the Church's struggles over the ages to break down barriers and become inclusive. The status of women, the abolition of slavery, the remarriage of divorced persons, and the ordination of women were all issues concerning which the Church had had to reverse its previous positions and practices. Pastoral necessity, he said, was the starting point for change, which takes place in the context of the basic principles of love and justice. In implementing those principles, reformers "feel themselves in tune with the mind of Christ." Sometimes brave people take great risks in straying from the received tradition to open up new understandings. That was what had happened in 1974 when three "American bishops got tired of waiting for general convention and went ahead and ordained eleven women in Philadelphia. This put pressure on the church, both in the United States and Canada, to deal with the question."

Powles went on to point out that "controversy is needed in order for truth to be revealed." Certainly the ordination of gay priests in relationships is a parallel issue to the ordination of women. In both cases, church historians have demonstrated that for centuries in the early Church women were ordained, and gay relationships were officially blessed in ancient Latin and Slavonic rites.

The Church, said Powles, is currently struggling with the issue of gays, and "there is a lot of mixed-up thinking and contradiction about this, because bishops recognize the fact that homosexuality is a fact of this present time, and it's something that is already present in the church, and they shouldn't persecute it. Our own bishop [Finlay] has also emphasized that fact, that we shouldn't persecute homosexuality. Yet, when it comes to the clergy, they are moving away from the principle that the Anglican Church established at the reformation, that clergy could exercise their God-given sexuality. And we have set up a double standard where we recognize heterosexual relations but not homosexual ones."

Under Falby's cross-examination the professor became more animated. On the issue of homosexuality, he said, "We have a chance to take the lead."

"You're a liberal in this battle, Professor?" queried the prosecutor.

"Well, maybe a radical," Powles replied, beaming.

"Maybe a radical . . . all right. I notice you're wearing a pink ribbon. Does that make you a radical?"

The professor's only reply was a delighted smile.

"Homosexuality is a very controversial issue in this church and people are trying to work it out, and as yet, the bishops of the Canadian church haven't arrived at an ultimate conclusion. Do you agree with that?" The pitch of Falby's voice was rising.

"I agree with that, but I think the bishops have to be pushed, and I think one of the favourite sports in the Anglican Church is pushing bishops." The historian went on to point out that this was how every major change in the past century had occurred. "This is one reason why I feel the pressure is needed, because in the case of gay clergy honesty is punished. If a person comes out they're punished, but the bishops are exhorted not to search gay people out. So there's a double standard here."

The line of questioning reverted to the legality of "guidelines" and the authority of bishops, and ended abruptly. Our first witness retired from the stand.

We knew the prosecution would see our second witness as the chief enemy. Dr. James Reed had headed the Primate's Commission on Sexuality over a decade earlier, and had been a key player in the bishops' discussions over the years, including their most recent meeting only two months before court. If Falby could shoot him down in flames, it might destroy our whole defence.

The two opponents eyed each other warily as my lawyer began the friendly portion of Reed's testimony. Carefully she led him through his impeccable credentials as psychotherapist, priest, theologian, ethicist, professor, and consultant to numerous national and international commissions on a variety of topics. Painstakingly, like Dr. Powles, Reed elucidated how the Church's understandings of a variety of topics are challenged and changed. He spoke of the times of ambiguity that exist while change from one position to another is accomplished, and how Anglicans hold all of that contradiction and ambiguity together in an inclusive fashion that respects diversity of opinion. One example of that respect was the "conscience clause" that allowed individual bishops to refuse to ordain women for several years after the Church had legislated the inclusion of women. "Unity in diversity, rather than uniformity" is a hallmark of Anglicanism, Reed pointed out.

Somehow, we had managed to get past the obstacle of the "confidential" label on the report of the Primate's Commission on Homosexuality by including it in a much larger bound collection entitled "Respondent's Document Brief." Did the commission come to any conclusions about whether or not homosexual orientation could be changed? Valerie asked. The priest/psychotherapist explained that it is still not clear why people are homo- or heterosexually oriented.

"The issue of cure [of homosexuality] is essentially a misleading one, and the place of psychotherapy, intervention and the healing of the church deals with important issues that surround the life of a gay or lesbian person, but don't alter the fundamental reality of who that person is." In other words, healing the gay person is a matter of relieving the anxiety that comes from the hostility of the world around them.

As the line of questioning moved on to the infamous guidelines and the authority of bishops, the atmosphere in the courtroom became heated. Guidelines were just guidelines, said Reed, not binding on the bishops or on the priests in their charge. One by one, members of the court jumped in — first Dr. Graham, then Judge Parker — until I began to wonder where the line between prosecution and jury lay. It seemed a role-reversal was taking place, as Graham, especially, interrogated the witness.

The courtroom blew up as Valerie attempted to introduce copies of the minutes of a meeting of the House of Bishops, over Falby's objections. Falby wanted Valerie to prove their authenticity and that they were not confidential. Valerie tried to explain that she had sent me to the National Church Archives, and that I had returned with public minutes. She asked if we should summon the archivist to court.

"I'm concerned with whether he stole them or whether he asked for them and got them," fired back Judge Parker. I was stunned.

"I'm sure you're not seriously suggesting that my client stole documents, Mr. President." My lawyer went on to point out that they were pages from the same minutes that Falby had previously submitted to court.

It was only because the assistant to the primate happened to be in court that the issue was resolved over lunch recess, since he could verify the authenticity of the documents.

Quite simply, the minutes pointed out that the primate's commission had distinguished between sexual standards for ordinands and those for priests. The House of Bishops had deliberately not acted on the second recommendation to develop standards for priests, so clearly those for ordinands did not apply to me, a priest, said Dr. Reed.

In the hours of Reed's testimony that followed, Dr. Graham and Judge Parker continued to jump in to shore up the prosecution's cross-examination. The court focused intently on my ordination vows "to follow with a glad heart" my superiors' "godly admonitions" and "to obey my bishop in all legal and honest demands." What was an admonition? What made it godly? What did the word "legal" mean, and how does one decide what is or is not legal, honest, or godly? It was mind-boggling. I knew that when I took the stand I had better have my answers clearly in mind.

Concerning the ordination vow to make my life a wholesome example, Dr. Graham asked, "Do you feel that an open homosexual relationship is a wholesome example to the flock of Christ?"

"I would say," responded Reed, "that if he's acting in relationship to his conscience and in good faith, of course, integrity is always a wholesome example to anyone. The demonstration of integrity, of committed love, and a faithfulness to work at that would in fact be a wholesome example. It would certainly be much more wholesome than, for instance, a lot of the violence that goes on in clergy families."

The tone of the prosecutor's voice became increasingly strident as his worthy opponent resisted the logical traps Falby was laying for him, until things got out of hand. It was over the question of the bishops' statements on homosexuality.

"Are you suggesting that an Anglican priest in Canada who read that would not accept it as a statement of morality?" asked the prosecutor angrily.

"Well, numerous clergy don't," responded Reed matter-of-factly.

"How many? Do you know?"

"I'm not at liberty to tell you that."

"You haven't done a survey, have you?"

"I can tell you the number in this diocese."

"Well, why don't you, then?"

"It would be breaking confidence," said Reed.

Valerie jumped in, saying, "I object. It is highly, highly improper for a lawyer on behalf of the diocese to be asking this witness to talk about numbers of gay clergy in the diocese. We are not here today to expose other gay clergy or make an issue of that."

"My friend misinterprets my question. Let's move on," said Falby, cooling down.

"If he wants to ask it, he can. I don't know why he would want to," remarked my lawyer.

"It's not relevant," said Falby.

"I'm not too sure very much of what we're hearing is relevant," said Judge Parker.

"Well, I'm with you on that one, Mr. President," replied the prosecutor.

When Dr. Reed finally stepped down from the stand after several gruelling hours, the entire court was damp with perspiration.

Our last witness for the day was not an official expert, unlike the previous two witnesses, and so it was anticipated that his examination and cross-examination would be much more easy-going. Brad Lennon, ordained with me in 1980, had been a good friend and stood by me from the beginning.

Brad described briefly his work with the Gay and Lesbian Task Force, of which he was one of the few straight members, and then went on to describe the sexuality discussion that night in Unionville. Gay clergy, he testified, know that they are taking a terrible risk every time they decide to talk with someone honestly about themselves, and so they reveal themselves only to people they really trust.

Under cross-examination, Brad spoke of the issue of gays in the larger Church, and how St. Philip's had indicated a clear commitment to explore it in a dialogue.

"You have a definite point of view concerning the activity of gay priests, as to the sex life of a gay priest," commented Falby.

"I object to the way my friend has phrased that question," interrupted Valerie.

"Let's talk about relationship. You have a point of view about gay priests' relationships."

"Yes."

"And that, I take it, is not something that you found broad acceptance of at St. Philip's."

"Quite the contrary. I found all points of view," corrected Brad. "There would have been a good deal of support within St. Philip's."

"I think you told my friend that you know other priests who are gay and not celibate," probed the prosecutor.

"Yes."

"And I take it that's something they told you, and not something you know on your own account?"

"That's right."

I could hear grumblings from the spectators. Some told me later that they thought it was a crude attempt to out Brad, if he was gay. Of course, few of the spectators knew that he was married and straight.

After a few more brief questions, the court was adjourned for the day.

I tossed and turned all night without sleep. Admonition . . . godly . . . legal . . . honest . . . the words burned through my mind as I tried to anticipate the prosecutor's questions the next day. Only as dawn broke did my weary mind begin to focus clearly. I was prepared.

◆

Once again the media army gathered. They had obviously heard that I was to take the stand Wednesday morning. The constant jostling was getting on my nerves. Fresh photographs, more questions. Finally I took refuge in the Church. I needed to pray, to feel in this dreadful time that God had not deserted me. The irony of the lack of prayers at Bishop's Court accentuated my feelings of isolation from my Church. Where are you in all of this, God? As I prayed for strength and clarity of mind in the solitude, a sense of calm filled me. The whole world would be listening, and I would have the chance to tell them how much my love for Ahmad meant to me. No one could take that away from me. It would always be for me a matter of love, and the cruelty of those who wanted to deny me that love.

The pain in my chest had worsened in the preceding days — the psychiatrist I had started to see to manage the stress assured me it was like a backache, only in the front of my rib cage — so I tried not to cough, as doing so sent out jolts of pain. I took the stand nervously before a crammed courtroom and, under my lawyer's gentle prodding, began to relate the story of my life. The worst moments came when I had to talk about Ahmad and our break-up. The pain was so fresh I almost lost control. The break-up would be new information for most people in the church gymnasium. Last November, I had been sure it would appear in the next day's paper, if not on the television news, if I had mentioned it to anyone, such was the complete loss of privacy I had endured. I had kept my grief to myself for three months — now it was public.

Painfully, I recited the whole story of the developments leading up to my dismissal, and my sense of betrayal by the bishop who had, at first, seemed to deal with me pastorally, but had ended it all abruptly by saying, "The church cannot appear to reward Jim for his behaviour."

I told the court that in my final meeting with the bishop, "I also expressed some concern for the other gay clergy in the diocese and the implications that that would have for them. And I said, 'You know who the gay clergy are. You know that some of them have partners, that they've bought houses together. This is going to be very difficult for them.' And I said, 'And I'm one of the most discreet of the gay clergy.' It was at that point that Michael B-J jumped in, saying, 'You're not kidding, Jim. I had no idea that you were gay until the Bishop told me last week.' The bishop made no reply."

Continuing my testimony, I reported that I had said to the bishop, "The conspiracy of silence in the church was killing people, that everyone knew that there were gay clergy, gay bishops, gay laypeople, but everyone was going around pretending, and that there was an unwritten set of guidelines which say that it's okay to be gay and in a relationship providing you don't offer the information to your bishop. And he, of course, will not ask any embarrassing questions. And everything's fine unless somebody blows the whistle. And then, all of a sudden, it's a setup for blackmail."

"When you went to the bishop," Valerie probed, "you told him the truth, but at that point there were people who were speculating, and they could never have hung you on a rumour. Why did you tell the truth? Why didn't you just lie?"

"Because I couldn't lie. For years I had been discreet, but when push comes to shove, to have to lie about who I am when in the face of God I know that I am fully human, fully accepted in all of my being — I simply could not lie to the bishop."

After I testified about my refusal to resign, Valerie asked, "Is this just a matter of receiving severance pay for you? Was it about money for you?"

"No — for me it was the utter contempt, the brutality of the statement, 'The church must not appear to reward Jim for his behaviour.' In the morning, I had felt like the bishop was going to stand with me, that he would be there to preserve my dignity, and that was all that was left to me. With those words he was stripping the last thing away from me that I had, my dignity. And he was saying that Jim is worthy of punishment, Jim is such a bad person that he deserves to be kicked out of the church without any thought or consideration. I just felt so devalued, so rejected, so unloved by this man that I loved and trusted — and I just kept saying, 'It can't, it can't be, it can't be Terry.'"

You could hear a pin drop in the crowded courtroom as my lawyer pushed on to deeper questions, asking me to reflect on the bishops' statements and guidelines on homosexuality issued over the years. "How do you feel about this statement?" she asked, and read, "'We accept all persons, regardless of sexual orientation, as equal before God; our acceptance of persons with homosexual orientation is not an acceptance of homosexual activity.'"

"I feel that it is terrible hypocrisy," I replied. "How can one say that one accepts persons regardless of sexual orientation and then not allow any possible expression of that sexual orientation? I believe that I'm a whole person. I'm not chopped up into bits and pieces. I don't commit 'homosexual activity'. I'm a loving person. My sexuality is a gift from God as much as anybody else's sexuality, and surely, that gift from God must be honoured within the context of a relationship that is loving, mutual, supportive, caring and faithful. I think it's a terrible assault on the dignity of every human being to deny their essential humanity.

"I think what this [guideline] does is it strips away all of a person's humanity. It trivializes their love, their ability to enter into supportive relationships, all of the good about a person; it strips it all away and reduces them to 'sexual activity' in order to condemn them for it.

"We don't do that to heterosexual people. We don't talk about 'heterosexual activity'. Why is it that when we talk about heterosexual activity we talk about 'delight and tenderness in acts of love'? But when people of the same gender are doing and loving the same way, we talk about 'homosexual activity'. It trivializes ten percent of humanity and it condemns them, condemns them to lives of isolation and loneliness. It denies them the opportunity to know God through the love and support and nurture of one other special human being."

"Did the bishop ever ask you to stop being in a relationship?" asked Valerie, breaking the sermon-flow of a born preacher.

"No, he did not."

"Did you feel that implicitly he was asking you to make a choice between the Church and your relationship?"

"I think that would be a fair statement."

"Why didn't you just choose one or the other?"

"I could no more choose between the two loves of my life than I could choose to chop off my arm. The two most important gifts from God in my life, the person that I love and the Church that I love, are both gifts from God."

Valerie moved on to questions about my ordination vows.

"If Bishop Finlay had actually asked you to stop the relationship, expressly, do you feel that that would have been a godly admonition?"

"No, I do not. For me, I understand the godly admonition to be an advice that is rooted and grounded in God's love. It's something in which there is love for the person involved, where there is a sense of justice, and to tell me that I should stop loving another human being is, I believe, beyond the scope of any other human being, including a bishop."

It was with a tremendous sense of relief that I ended my initial testimony. But the cross-examination by Falby was long and gruelling, an elaborate game of cat and mouse. By mid-afternoon I was exhausted; after all, I wasn't just giving testimony about an issue, this was my own life on the block. It was with even greater relief that I finally heard him say, "No further questions." Under his cross-examination I had openly condemned the actions of Bishop Finlay in firing me, and the Toronto College of Bishops as well as the entire National House of Bishops for their "ungodly" admonitions in the realm of gay sexuality.

We decided to play our trump card — our surprise witness — since it was obvious that the prosecution was playing for keeps. If they wanted to talk about guidelines, discipline, and obedience, Douglas Fox could, we hoped, blow their arguments out of the water. The young gay priest was willing to risk all in the court of the Lord Bishop of Toronto.

A small, slight man whose face bore a gentle open expression, Douglas Fox had probably already been dismissed as unimportant by the time he got to the witness box. But it was a matter of moments before the courtroom was awakened. Even the reporters dozing in the gallery snapped alert as my lawyer quickly moved her questioning to the crunch.

After questions about his education and ordination, she asked, "Are you a gay man?"

"Yes, I am."

"Are you now or have you ever been committed to maintaining a celibate lifestyle?"

"No."

"Prior to your ordination, did you have discussions with your bishop concerning your sexual orientation?"

Falby was beginning to stir. Surely he realized where this line of questioning might be heading.

"Yes," replied Fox, "I discussed it fairly extensively with him."

"Could you tell us what you talked about?"

"We talked about the 1979 guidelines — he gave me a copy of them."

The prosecutor leapt to his feet and said furiously, "Objection! I don't think it's appropriate for a witness to give hearsay evidence about what a bishop said in this court."

"This witness is giving evidence as to his understanding of the guidelines, and the very issue before this court is whether these guidelines set a standard in the Church. Whether or not they are adopted or accepted by other bishops I think is about as pertinent a question as you can ask." Valerie was prepared for a tough fight.

Archbishop Edward Scott, who had been sitting quietly in the spectators' gallery through three days of hearings, fled the courtroom. Clearly he could see that his successor as primate, Archbishop Michael Peers, was implicated in the testimony unfolding before him.

The courtroom was electrified, as judge, jury, and attorneys for prosecution and defence held a heated discussion about the admissibility of Fox's testimony. Some argued that Fox might be misrepresenting the bishop; the bishop should be there to speak for himself.

"I don't want to make all the rulings in this court," said the President. Judge Parker obviously wanted his colleagues on the bench to enter the fray.

"The court should keep in mind in discussing this issue," said Falby forcefully, "that questions of ordination are solely up to diocesan bishops. So, it is also irrelevant as to what another diocesan bishop thinks or does." At this there were gasps from some of the spectators.

Finally the court recessed in disarray. It seemed obvious to me that Falby wanted to block Fox's testimony as "hearsay," but what would that do to the testimony of at least one of the prosecution's own witnesses? Michael B-J had given his accounts of Bishop Finlay's conversations with me, including just one side of an overheard telephone conversation. Would that testimony have to be ruled as "hearsay" too? Would Bishop Finlay himself be forced to come to court "to speak for himself"? The court faced a dilemma.

When court reconvened ten minutes later, it was with the concession that Fox's testimony could continue, although the court reserved its decision on what weight it would give it. Fox went on to describe how his bishop, Michael Peers, had discussed with him on several occasions his sexual orientation, agreeing in the end to ordain him without requiring a promise of celibacy.

"The way he [Archbishop Peers] put it, was that he knew in not requiring me to do that, that some day I would come to him and say, 'Bishop, this is the man I love.' Those were his words."

"And he would have to deal with it at that time," suggested Falby.

"That's right," responded Fox, going on to describe the two relationships he had had, the second one ending with the death of his partner from AIDS. During that time, Peers had become primate, and Eric Bays had become the new Bishop of Qu'Appelle, so Fox had shared with Bays the terrible dilemma of his dying friend and his own family, who weren't taking it well. Bishop Bays's response, Fox testified, had been pastoral — he had simply cared for Doug and helped his family to reconcile with him. Fox's testimony provided a very different story from mine of how two bishops had dealt with a gay priest, neither requiring a promise of celibacy on ordination, nor revoking his licence when he shared the fact of his gay relationship later.

Fox's testimony had been so poignant that even the prosecutor seemed moved, so much so that the President interjected, "You're whispering to each other." After a few more gentle questions, Fox stepped down from the witness box.

Fox's surprise testimony was followed by Dr. Rosemary Barnes's assessment of the psychological damage done to gays and lesbians when they are forced to deny who they are. The professor and chief psychologist at a Toronto teaching hospital was largely ignored, as the prosecution and court worried about Fox's damning testimony. Slouching back in his chair without paying any apparent attention to the only woman to testify at the hearing, Falby announced that he had no questions.

As court adjourned at the end of the day, I discovered that the focus of media attention had shifted to my shy associate. That night his face and voice appeared on national television, apparently accusing the Primate of the Anglican Church of Canada of breaking church rules. LEADER OF ANGLICAN CHURCH ACCUSED OF VIOLATING RULES bannered the newspapers the next morning. The press had missed our point. The primate had not broken any rules, nor was he accused of doing so. He had simply used the guidelines at his discretion, according to the original intent of the 1979 House of Bishops. What we meant to get across was that my bishop, Terence Finlay, had acted entirely at his own discretion as well. No one could force a bishop to interpret the guidelines a particular way, no matter how much he might protest to the contrary. It was the key point to my defence.

♦

Compared with the day before, the court seemed subdued on Thursday. The spectators and media were beginning to show signs of fatigue, as demonstrated by their vastly reduced numbers.

Walter Stewart, an out-of-the-closet gay Anglican and professor of English, spoke of the terrible suffering the gay priests he knew were experiencing at the hands of the Church.

"Many are lonely. Many feel alienated. They have warring calls. God has called them to be gay and to be priests. The calls are genuine and are at war with each other within the Anglican Church. I know many who long for a relationship, who long for openness, who do not like living the lie they have been called upon to live — who see the way they are forced to live that lie as a real impediment to their ministry. It's a bad model. The Church should be in the business of creating wholeness among people. Gay clergy are forced to be less than whole."

Darrell Briggs, the churchwarden who had accompanied me to my first meeting with Bishop Finlay, testified both to the quality of my ministry and to the events surrounding my dismissal. He told the court of the meeting on *Our Stories/Your Story* and how the parish had dealt creatively with the issue, beginning a process of dialogue and study. In his estimation, the parish could have handled their priest's sexuality and relationship well, if they had only been given the chance. When asked how my firing had affected the parish, he testified, "It was almost like a death experience. The suddenness of him being there one day and gone the next. It was very painful. A few of the children from Sunday school thought that Jim had died. Jim was always there for us. He did the job and he was loved in the parish."

Jack Fricker, the sixty-five-year-old parishioner who had initiated the appeal to Finlay before my dismissal, spoke of the friendship that had grown up between his wife and him, and me. Many times they had invited me for dinner in the condominium building we lived in. He spoke in glowing terms about my ministry, but more importantly brought forward the justice and human rights issue that had been raised with the bishop, to no avail.

Our final witness for Thursday I had had flown in from Newark, New Jersey. The Reverend David Norgard was director of The Oasis ministry there, a "Mission and Ministry of the Episcopal Diocese of Newark with gay and lesbian people and their family and friends." The purpose of the ministry, he testified, was to promote reconciliation between the lesbian and gay community and the Church, through evangelical outreach, pastoral care, education, and advocacy. With the blessing and support of Bishop John Spong, the diocese had initiated a unique ministry to break down the prejudices that had historically diminished the Church's gay and lesbian sons and daughters. Norgard, in a twelve-year committed relationship since college days, was to be a public role model of the many gay and lesbian people who were living whole and beautiful lives. In his preaching in churches throughout the diocese he attempted to give a public face to the "unknown" in the hopes of breaking the power of homophobia and the ignorance of most Church people about gays.

The court listened patiently to Norgard, but I wondered if his testimony was simply going in one ear and out the other. I was sure the court would decide his testimony was irrelevant to my situation. The real reason I had brought him in was to provide an example to my bishop of how the Diocese of Toronto could handle the issue of gays and lesbians. But the bishop wasn't there, and the hint might be a little too subtle for him to pick up on. Still, I hoped against hope.

With the conclusion of Norgard's testimony came a three-day recess. I spent the next day, Friday, showing him and his partner, Joseph, around Toronto. As it turned out, Joseph was the livewire of the two, David being a very modest, conservative man. If it weren't for the fact that he was gay, I knew the young priest would reach the heights in the Episcopal church. But then, his branch of the Anglican Church was far ahead of ours on the issue, so who knew?

Monday, February 10, was the day the media had been waiting for. The controversial Bishop of Newark had gotten off the plane Sunday night, waving *The New York Times*. "Jim, you've made the third page of *The New York Times*. Do you know what that means? You're international news! I'm really proud to be here with you." He was accompanied by his delightful wife, Chris, a pretty, grey-haired Englishwoman whom the middle-aged widower had married a few years earlier. It was my first face-to-face encounter with the bishop who had come all the way to Canada for a young priest he had never met, but for whom he cared in a time of tribulation. Spong, I discovered, always had a loving, encouraging word — a real father-in-God, I thought.

Spong would be a key witness, a real live bishop who was willing to break the silence and speak the truth about homosexuality and the Church. In frequently moving testimony, he spoke of the integrity of the lives of the gay and lesbian priests in his diocese who had had the courage to come out to their once homophobic bishop, changing his life. He spoke of their sacrificial ministries in difficult urban parishes that other, straight clergy had declined to serve, and of the love of their congregations for them.

"Have you always been of the opinion that gay people in relationships should be permitted to be ordained as priests in the Episcopal church?" asked Valerie.

"Absolutely not," responded the bishop with disarming honesty. "I'm as homophobic as anybody in this room. It's been a struggle for me to deal with that level of prejudice. I grew up in the South. I'm quite sure that I was a racist. The Civil Rights Movement helped me to confront that aspect of my prejudice.

"I'm quite sure that I am a male chauvinist, but I have three wonderful modern daughters who have confronted me and dragged me screaming and kicking into the twentieth century.

"I am quite sure that I am homophobic, and it has been the witness of beautiful homosexual lives to me that has challenged that prejudice. I believe deeply in the principle of incarnation. The only way that I think I could know the meaning of the love of God was because

I had seen it incarnate in the life of Jesus of Nazareth. The only way that I came to know and to trust gay and lesbian people was to see gay and lesbian people incarnate as real people, as gentle people, as loving people."

"Why is this issue important for the Church?" asked the defence attorney.

"If the work that I am privy to is accurate — and I'm convinced of it, though it is still being debated in scientific circles — then homosexual people are born with their orientation. It is not abnormal. It is just different — so is red hair, so is left-handedness. There are all sorts of differences in the human family. What we have tended to do is ascribe moral value to differences, and somebody that is different from the majority is devalued. I think we have just got to break that. I like to remind people that the word 'faggot' comes from the name of the sticks used to burn homosexual persons at the stake.

"If the only crime of gay and lesbian people is that they were born with their brains sexed differently from the majority through a biochemical process, then the Church has got to face the fact that out of its ignorance we have murdered, burned at the stake, run out of town, fired, demoralized, and discriminated against these people.

"Prejudice is a pernicious evil, and it's one that I think has got to be rooted out. I have a hard time imagining the love of Christ having limits.

"Sometimes I try to picture Christ on the cross, with his arms outstretched in a universal sign of welcome, and I try to listen to him saying words that Matthew's gospel quotes him as saying — not on the cross, but in the course of his life: 'Come unto me all ye that travail and are heavy laden.'

"Then I try to imagine Christ having mental reservations. I try to imagine him saying: 'Come unto me all ye that travail and are heavy laden, unless you are gay, or unless you are black, or unless you have had a divorce, or unless you might commit suicide, or unless you are left-handed,' or any of the other things that we have used as barriers of discrimination throughout our history."

Spong had cast a spell over the courtroom. Judge Parker was listening with a thoughtful expression, and Dr. Dorothy Ley, rapt in attention, broke into a smile.

"For the life of me, I cannot imagine Christ having mental reservations. I cannot imagine boundaries on the love of Christ. If I cannot imagine boundaries on the love of Christ, then I cannot imagine boundaries being exercised by an institution that dares to call itself the body of Christ."

The overflowing courtroom congregation burst into applause. Even members of the court were caught up in the moving testimony of the great man of God. Suddenly, as if awaking from a trance, the President scowled. He looked sharply at the sergeant-at-arms, who had also been caught up in the spirit of the moment.

"This is a court, not a circus!" cried Judge Parker. Spitting out his words, he continued. "If people don't want to behave in here, they can leave." After calm was restored he said, "Carry on, please."

Bishop Spong went on to speak of his advocacy in standing up for blacks in the desegregation movement in the South, and the threats and violence his family endured.

"Sure it disturbed the Church. The Church is an institution. Institutions think that their own survival is what is most important. I happen to think the truth of God is far more important than the survival of an institution called the Church. I'm not even sure I want an institution that's not faithful to the truth of God to survive. We could have had a peaceful Church in the South, if we had just kept blacks out, but it wouldn't have been the body of Christ. It would have been an ecclesiastical club."

The same was true of the issue of women and gays, the bishop assured the court.

"We hang signs in front of our churches saying 'The Episcopal Church welcomes you' but do we really mean it?

"I hold before this court, and before the world at large, that image. Does the Church welcome? Is the Church the body of Christ? I'm not interested in being part of a church that is just an ecclesiastical club of like-minded people. I'm interested in being a part of a Christian community that dares to love as God in Christ loved us all — unconditionally, while we were yet sinners, to quote St. Paul."

Spong was the final witness for the defence. After the prosecution called a couple of rebuttal witnesses, who spoke briefly about discipline and obedience, the court was adjourned until the following Saturday. That would give both prosecution and defence lawyers four days to prepare their final submissions.

Monday evening a reception was held for Bishop Spong at the Rosedale home of Nancy Jackman, a well-known feminist and benefactor. It was there that the bishop pointed out, "It is not Jim Ferry who is on trial today, but the integrity of the Church's message that God's love is for every human being." Later in the evening Spong addressed a packed house at the Metropolitan Community Church of Toronto. Both events had been organized by my small fundraising committee to help defray the costs of my defence.

◆

The final submissions on Saturday in Bishop's Court were long and detailed. The prosector opened.

"There are those who suggested here in their evidence that the tradition, order, and discipline of the Church should give way in a conflict with what they perceive to be individual rights. That position, of course, assumes the propriety of the individual right.

"It's our submission that that assertion in these circumstances is a grave error, because what is central to this case is no less than preservation of the order and discipline and unity of the Anglican Church of Canada, so that we have the freedom to enter into an important debate. It is a challenge to the rules of order flowing from the Episcopacy.

"At the outset of this case, we submitted to you that homosexuality is not an issue here but that what was on trial is the order and discipline of the Church. That continues to be the case, and it is, in our submission, grave unfairness to suggest some element of homophobia in attempting to preserve the order and unity of the Church.

"There are only, in our submission, two basic issues for this court to address. The first is, is there a rule of conduct, and the second is, did Mr. Ferry breach the rule. The wider issue as to whether or not the rule of conduct should be changed will remain before the Church, and ought to remain before the Church.

"You have heard a great deal of evidence which may be useful in that debate, and it's to be hoped that that evidence, on the wider issue, will assist in the debate, much as Bishop Finlay hoped would happen with Mr. Ferry's co-operation, that co-operation which Mr. Ferry ultimately denied him.

"But this court, if it finds there was a rule, has no jurisdiction to change it. The bishop's commission to the court is to try the matter and report to the bishop on its findings and its recommendations as to sanction. That's what the court is to do. The role of the court is judicial, not political. The court is not being asked the wisdom of the rule, only whether there is one."

Law, authority, vows, discipline, obedience, legality — arguments were traced through references to witnesses' testimony, and appeals to other ecclesiastical tribunals in England and the United States. In the end the prosecutor asked for a guilty verdict and called for a sentence somewhere in the middle of the range between the least drastic, a private reprimand, and the most severe, a stripping of the holy orders of a priest, commonly known as "defrocking."

"In our submission," said Falby, "that's not to be invoked unless the court is of the view that Mr. Ferry has no place in the Church. It is a severe penalty, but because there is some potential, and we ought not to prejudge it, that the Church might change its position, that is not the appropriate penalty." Instead, he called for the withdrawal of licence, otherwise known as "deprivation of office." That would leave me still a priest, but unable to function as one in any way. The effect would be much the same as defrocking, I thought, in terms of employment in the Church.

"Why is it," I asked my lawyer after Falby finished his summations, "that the Church can only talk about rules and legalities instead of grace? Why hasn't anyone asked the simple question, 'What would Jesus do?'"

"Unfortunately, Jim," she replied, picking up her binder to begin her own summation, "we have to win this case on legal grounds." She took the podium, and set out her notes.

"The Diocese of Toronto," she began, "has argued that this trial is not about discrimination and prejudice against gay people. You are invited to draw a distinction, as reflected in the House of Bishops' statement, between accepting gay people on the one hand and condemning the expression of gay sexuality on the other. You are implicitly asked to accept the proposition that you can distinguish between one's being and one's doing, between one's being and expressing one's being.

"Let me give you just two examples of this distinction between being and doing and ask yourself whether or not these examples constitute discrimination. Imagine that a French Canadian is a candidate for ordination. He's told that he can be ordained, that the fact of his being French Canadian is not a barrier to ordination, but under no circumstances may he ever speak French, not in church, not at home, not to his family, not to his friends. Is this discrimination? Would that French Canadian feel accepted by the Church under those circumstances?

"Take a second example. Imagine that we live in a totalitarian country where there is no Charter of Rights. Imagine the government of that country saying to Anglicans: It's okay to be Anglican, it's okay to call yourself Anglican, but it is against the law to gather with other Anglicans in churches to worship. It's against the law to read the Book of Common Prayer, even in the privacy of your own home. Under those circumstances would you feel accepted in that society as Anglicans? Would that not be discrimination against you?

"I could give you a hundred similar examples involving both genders, every ethnic minority, every race, young people and old people, and in every case, after due consideration, I have no doubt that you would conclude that decision-making based on the distinction between one's being and expressing one's being is ultimately discriminatory.

"The official House of Bishops' position on gay men and lesbians is no different. The feelings, said Bishop Blackwell, are not a sin. But expression of those feelings is sinful and can never be accepted or condoned under any circumstances. This, in my submission, is an extraordinary statement.

"One of the basic purposes of human sexuality is procreation, but it is not the only purpose. We have seen the passages in the House of Bishops' statements on human sexuality, which speak of sexuality as a gift from God given to us for the purpose of entering into mutually enriching relationships which affirm our intrinsic dignity and value.

"It is this second purpose of marriage, the receipt and giving of love, support and companionship, that permits the Church to bless marriages where the couple practises birth control, where the couple has made a decision never to have children, or where the couple, for health reasons, simply cannot have children.

"For heterosexuals, individual exceptions are permitted to the general rule. Individuality is recognized and honoured. For gay people, however, the House of Bishops says that there can be no exceptions. There can be no situation where their sexuality can be expressed in intimate, loving and faithful partnership.

"Individuality and individual circumstances are lost in a sweeping generalization. Making generalizations about a group of people and ignoring individual personalities and circumstances diminishes every individual in that group as a human being. Is prejudice at work here? Of course it is.

"The official statements speak of homosexual activity. Who would ever look at a newly married couple, in love, happy, looking forward to a life together, and reduce the intimate and tender expression of their sexuality to mere 'heterosexual activity'? It is debasing and demeaning to reduce the loving expression of human sexuality to a simple sexual act. But this is what the official House of Bishops' statement does to gay couples. It trivializes their love and reduces their deepest sexual feelings and capacity for intimacy to simple 'sexual acts'.

"Do gay couples make love? Not according to this statement.

Gay couples simply engage in 'homosexual activity'. The very words strip gay people of their humanity, their dignity and their intrinsic value as human beings. It makes the expression of gay sexuality something less than human. Is there prejudice at work here? Of course there is.

"Gay Christians in the Anglican Church are asked to repress their sexuality. Why? Because to express their sexuality is sinful, according to Bishop Blackwell. You have heard evidence about the impact that this condemnation has on gay Christians who are asked to choose between their love of church and God and their love of self and partner.

"Dr. Reed gave evidence about the sense of powerlessness, anxiety and depression in gay Christians engendered by the Church's condemnation of them. Dr. Barnes talked about the damage that these attitudes do to gay people, destroying their self-esteem and making meaningful and healthy relationships with family, friends and partners difficult, if not impossible.

"The uncontradicted evidence before this court is that the attitude reflected by the official statement actually hurts gay people, causes them emotional damage. You may conclude, however, that an inquiry into the psychological harm caused by the Church's official attitude towards gay people is beyond the scope of this inquiry. But it *is* within the mandate and jurisdiction of this court to consider and measure the impact of prejudice and discrimination on the capacity of gay Christians to develop spiritually, to come to know God's love, and to find their love for God. . . .

"The treatment of gays within the Anglican Church is not a trivial matter. We are dealing with a fundamental, human, psychological and spiritual question affecting a tremendous number of people within the Church. There is one issue that this court must decide and one issue only: Is there within the Anglican Church of Canada a law clear enough or authority weighty enough to permit discrimination of this severity and magnitude? If there is more than one legitimate perspective, if there is ambiguity, if there is doubt, then, in my submission, you must in good Christian conscience acquit Jim Ferry."

For the next two hours Valerie Edwards went on to weave a rich tapestry of arguments from canon law, church writings, and case histories, as well as Christian theology and ethics. The structure of the Church, the meaning and exercise of canon law, issues of obedience, the nature of "legal and honest demands," the jurisdiction of bishops, the nature of authority in the Church, what it means to be a "wholesome example to the flock" — all were eloquently argued in compelling detail. The entire court panel seemed spellbound — Judge Parker was nodding his head and taking copious notes.

A pregnant silence filled the courtroom as the defence lawyer finished and sat down. It was broken finally by a noticeably agitated prosecutor. Perhaps he had been expecting a simple harangue on issues of discrimination, and not the compelling legal and theological arguments that had so obviously captured the jury's imagination.

Apparently taken aback, the prosecutor began to speak in increasingly strained tones as he attempted to counter the points scored by Valerie.

"My friend goes on and says, the Canons are silent, they don't give prescriptions on this [homosexuality]. Well, the Canons, as I said earlier, don't say anything about wife beating. They don't say anything about child abuse! . . ."

Shocked gasps filled the courtroom; I held my head in my hands and cringed. I hadn't expected the prosecution to make such cruel comparisons. Neither, perhaps, did the Reverend Victoria Matthews, who looked at me with an expression of deep pain and shock. My love compared to wife beating and child abuse. Falby went on slowly and tensely to attempt to rebut his opponent's compelling arguments.

"I want to say something about the conflict in the parish. My friend suggested that the conflict in the parish only arose after the bishop issued his Notice of Inhibition, and that things could have worked out and so on." Falby's tone became more piercing. "Well, with great respect to my friend, that's like saying Saddam Hussein wasn't responsible for the Gulf War by invading Kuwait!"

A wave of quiet cries swelled through the gymnasium. A few minutes later that wave swelled again when Falby accused me of refusing the bishop's pastoral advice for the sake of money. The tone of my trial in Bishop's Court had plummeted to a new low.

A few minutes later Mr. Falby was telling the television news teams that the Church is like any organization. It has rules. If you don't like the rules, you get out. So much for Bishop Spong's testimony that the Church is not an ecclesiastical club of like-minded individuals.

I went home exhausted, and waited for the verdict.

Chapter 9

VALERIE WAS FURIOUS. Two weeks of grinding anxiety dragged by before the bishop finally sent us the decision of Bishop's Court. It had taken the court only four days from final submissions to make their decision, write it up, sign it, and deliver it to the bishop, and over a week for him to pass it on to me. We were invited to make submissions as to sentence, if we so desired. Strangely, one thing was noticeably absent from the bishop's office: the recommendations of the court.

"That's one of the laziest pieces of work I've seen from any court!" Valerie fumed over dinner one night. "It's completely contradictory, even on the face of it!"

She was right. Of course the court had found me guilty; it had to back up the bishop, I knew. But it had found me not guilty of the central point in the charges against me: disobedience. Of the five charges against me, the one on which the other four hinged was "any act which involves a violation of any cleric's oath of canonical obedience."

"It is the finding of the Court that as no evidence was offered either orally or in writing to demonstrate a non-compliance by the Respondent with any order or direction given by the Bishop of Toronto that this charge is not proven."

At the same time, on the charge of "wrongdoing" the court found "that the Respondent was guilty of wrong-doing by refusing to refrain from continuing a homosexual relationship, contrary to the Bishop's instructions, the Respondent's vows on Ordination, and the discipline of the Church."

It didn't take a brilliant legal mind to see the clear contradiction; at one and the same time I was found guilty of refusing the bishop's instructions and not guilty because he had never given any instructions in the first place.

The court document went on to find me not guilty of the charge of "any criminal, immoral, dishonourable or disorderly conduct" because of lack of evidence and the removal of the words "criminal" and "immoral" from the charge. I understood this to be a slap on the bishop's wrist for refusing to deal with my relationship and my alleged disobedience as moral issues. "It cannot find the conduct of the Respondent to be dishonourable or disorderly. To find otherwise, the Court would need to substitute its own subjective judgement of the conduct of the Respondent, which it is not prepared to do."

In another contradictory twist, the court found on the charge of "contumacy or disobedience or disrespectful conduct towards the Bishop of the Diocese" that my conduct had been contumate and disrespectful, but not disobedient. And yet the dictionary definition the prosecutor had given in court of "contumacy" was "wilful disobedience."

To compound the court's muddled findings, the fifth charge, "conduct unbecoming a member of the clergy," was simply overlooked. Nowhere in its decision did the court give any findings or even comment on that charge.

Most disappointing of all was the court's decision regarding what every observer knew was the real issue in my trial: the Church's treatment of homosexuals. We had tried to concede that the bishop had given me an *implicit* instruction to give up the man I loved, in order to move the court's considerations to the real issues surrounding homosexuality and discrimination. But the court had steadfastly refused, and ruled that it "could not express its views as to whether the order and discipline of the Church should be amended, or whether other matters affecting the lives of Priests of the Church with respect to their personal homosexual orientation should be examined by the appropriate bodies of the Church." I could just picture Pilate washing his hands of Jesus' blood, as the court refused even to suggest that the Church needed to look at the moral issues at stake.

My loving relationship had been reduced once again to a matter of mere legalities, and even then the court could not find that I had disobeyed my bishop. I had pretty much expected that the court would find me guilty one way or another, but I still found it hard to believe that a court presided over by a former chief justice and lawyer could so thoroughly contradict itself and condemn me at the same time.

Why hadn't Bishop Finlay forwarded to us the court's recommendations? we wondered. Was there something to hide? The recommendations might well be the key needed to unlock the court's confused findings. Valerie resolved to request a copy of the recommendations first thing the next morning.

"Jim, don't you see?" she said brightly, two days later. She had received the recommendations quickly. "You've won!"

It didn't look like a win to me. It looked as if I was about to be fired again. But, as she went over the recommendations with me, I began to see her point: the court had made clear, not in its findings but in its recommendations, that Bishop Finlay was not legally bound by the guidelines but was free to act on his conscience.

"The unanimous recommendation of the Bishop's Court," wrote Finlay, "is 'that you remove Mr. Ferry from his charge at Unionville, that he be reprimanded, in private, and that he be advised that he will be considered for other employment within the Diocese PROVIDED that he will undertake to you to refrain from homosexual relationships with another man. Should he not concur in this package, it is the recommendation of the Court that you remove him from his charge, that he be reprimanded (in private), that you withdraw his licence and that he be continued on the clergy list of the Diocese of Toronto until either the discipline of the Church changes or some other Bishop is prepared to accept him, in which event you would furnish to him Letters Bene Decessit.'"

It seemed the court was giving both Finlay and me a slap on the wrist. After all that had happened, and all the upheaval in the Church and the massive publicity, I need only cross my fingers behind my back and say that I wouldn't have sex with another man, and I would be rewarded with a private dressing-down and a new parish. Of course, it was a ridiculous suggestion after what I had been through.

The whole point of my actions in the past year was that I refused to lie about who I was and who I loved. Surely the court knew that I wasn't about to start lying now. Perhaps it was more a slap on the bishop's wrist — "You didn't even ask him the question in the first place, now do it right this time."

The most stunning cryptic message, however, was contained in the second half of the recommendation: I should be kept unemployed on the clergy list until either the discipline of the Church changed or another bishop accepted me. With one stroke of the pen the court acknowledged both that the Church's stance on gay clergy was in the process of changing and that the guidelines were not legally binding on bishops. If, as the court admitted, other bishops were free to exercise their conscience and employ me, then so must the Bishop of Toronto. To drive the point home, the court had added "in which latter event you would furnish to [Ferry] Letters Bene Decessit." These "Letters" are the standard form of transfer from one diocese to another in which a bishop bears witness that a priest is "in good standing." The implication was amazing: the court apparently considered me, in spite of all that had transpired, a "priest in good standing."

Now I could clearly see that the court was not only washing its hands of responsibility in my case, but deliberately throwing the hot potato right back at the bishop. It was like saying, "Jim's a good priest, and you can deal with him according to your conscience." Of course, there was a downside to this: the court was acknowledging that the bishop had power to do whatever he wanted with me — he could fire me again or he could act on the implicit message they were sending him. Either way, the court had kept him covered.

It was disheartening, knowing that I had essentially won the case in court but would still be unemployed. What could I reasonably expect when, through the events of the preceding nine months, I had been treated at every possible opportunity not with graciousness but with disdain? At any moment along the way, I believed, the bishop could have stopped the spiral of events that compounded his bad initial decision, simply by finding some face-saving way of keeping me in the Church as a priest.

Suddenly an opportunity for face-saving presented itself. The congregation of Church of the Holy Trinity in downtown Toronto, the same church where Integrity regularly met, held a special vestry meeting. They offered a compromise to the bishop "in the hope that taking [their suggested] actions will allow healing to take place after the events that have caused such pain in the Diocese of Toronto over the past few months." They asked that the inhibition of my priestly orders be lifted, and that the diocese establish a ministry similar to The Oasis in Newark to promote healing and reconciliation for gays and the Church, and said that the Parish of Holy Trinity would welcome me as a member of their staff if the financial arrangements could be worked out. It was a gift to both the bishop and me, a face-saving way out of a polarized situation. The bishop could acknowledge the conflicting views on gays in the Church, and also point the way forward through concrete action.

Unfortunately, with the copy of Holy Trinity's letter to the bishop came a copy of another letter that filled me with foreboding. Shortly after summations at Bishop's Court, the two churchwardens from Holy Trinity had written to Bishop Finlay complaining of Falby's personal aspersions on my character, especially the inference that my behaviour could be compared with wife assault or child abuse, and the comparison of my actions to those of Saddam Hussein. Bishop Finlay had given the letter to Chancellor Hemmerick, who had been in court every day, passing notes to the prosecutor. Hemmerick had fired off a five-page reply on March 2, defending Mr. Falby and making extensive reference to court transcripts. All this had transpired before I even heard the court's decision, and before final submissions as to sentence or the bishop's final judgement. It sounded to me as if another worst-case scenario was in the offing.

Together, my lawyer and I agonized over what we could reasonably expect from the bishop, especially with Hemmerick advising him. In the end, we decided to make submissions to the bishop, offering a range of possible actions that Finlay could take, making it clear that I was not prepared to give the undertaking referred to in the recommendations from Bishop's Court. The first alternative we offered was to consider licensing me as an assistant priest to a parish such as Holy Trinity, which would welcome me as a gay man. The second was to consider licensing me as priest-missioner of a special ministry like The Oasis, which the diocese would establish to promote reconciliation between the lesbian and gay community and the Church through evangelical outreach, pastoral care, education, and advocacy. The third was to consider appointing me as an unpaid honorary assistant to a parish willing to welcome me as a gay man. Valerie and I were not too optimistic. The best we thought we could realistically expect would be unemployment, but permission to function as a priest in a voluntary capacity. It seemed a reasonable compromise in the spirit of the court's recommendations, although it was far less than I had hoped for.

We also suggested that the bishop and I meet privately without lawyers. It was not to be.

The day of "Submissions as to Sentence," March 10, was cold and drizzly. As we made the short trek along Adelaide Street from Valerie's office to the Diocesan Centre, we overtook a woman dragging a strange wheeled suitcase, shielding herself and the baggage with a big umbrella. It was the court reporter. My heart sank — this looked very official. When we arrived at Synod Office, it was to discover Chancellor Hemmerick, Bishop Taylor Pryce — my area bishop — and Bob Falby and his assistant waiting. We made our brief submissions to Terence Finlay surrounded by them, the court reporter talking into her special device.

We knew I was doomed when we left the bishop's office. With Hemmerick simmering at Finlay's right hand, and Falby arguing that to allow me to function even as a volunteer priest would be to give away everything, I knew I could expect nothing but the worst.

For ten long days I waited for the bishop to speak. Finally, on Thursday, March 19, Valerie was called and asked to summon me to the bishop's office on the following morning at nine o'clock. Bishop

Finlay would be holding a news conference immediately following. Valerie complained that surely her client was entitled to at least hear his sentence privately more than a few minutes before the press heard it. And so it was settled that I would meet with the bishop late that afternoon, but only if we gave our word that we would keep the sentence secret until the bishop's press conference the next morning. We agreed.

Only an hour or two before my meeting with the bishop, the press started to call. They had received notice of the press conference the next morning. When was I meeting with the bishop? Could I tell them what the outcome was? I declined, saying I was sworn to secrecy. *The Toronto Star* wanted to catch the news for the final Friday edition. Wasn't there something I could say? Their deadline was shortly after noon. And so I agreed to send them some comments during the bishop's press conference, when the verdict would already be out. They would send a photographer to take a picture of me at home. Would I hold a press conference? The time was fixed for one o'clock Friday afternoon, three hours after the bishop's press conference.

Once again, when we arrived at the bishop's office, we were greeted by Chancellor Hemmerick and Bishop Pryce. After Valerie and I promised to keep the sentence confidential until ten o'clock the next morning, the bishop told us nervously that he had prepared a pastoral letter to be read to all congregations in the diocese. Why didn't he just read it to me, he suggested. And that's how he pronounced his sentence.

> *I, Terence, Bishop of Toronto, by virtue of the authority vested in me, hereby pronounce the sentence that Mr. Ferry is hereby removed from his pastoral charge and his licence for St. Philip's on-the-hill, Unionville, is withdrawn. Without a licence Mr. Ferry may not exercise the duties of a priest.*

My worst fear had come true.

After he finished reading the three-page letter, Finlay handed me a sealed envelope that he said contained the sentence. The chancellor responded tersely to a few questions my lawyer had directed to the bishop. Then we shook hands, and Valerie and I trekked off through the drizzle, hearts downcast.

◆

Show time: the press conferences the next day made the lead story on the evening news on both national television networks, as well as coverage in every newspaper and radio and television station in the country, *The New York Times*, and the front page of *The Toronto Star*. Even the primate managed to squeeze a press release into the noon hour between the press conferences the bishop and I held. His was an olive branch to both sides, saying that Terry Finlay had "shown sensitivity and care" and that he had "exercised discipline with wisdom," while noting that "Mr. Ferry has acted with courage during a difficult public ordeal." He went on to add, "I know his willingness to appear before a public court was not simply for his own vindication, but to raise up the predicament of all gays and lesbians within the Church. I hope he will not be seen simply as an offender, but as a person who has acted out of a deep commitment to the faith we share as Christians." There was a breath of vindication in his words, but I was nonetheless a public outcast, unemployed and unable to function even as a volunteer priest in the Church I loved.

At his press conference, the bishop admitted the reality of gay clergy. "A very difficult, difficult situation. There are clergy who are gay or lesbian, who are living in a committed relationship. I have some understanding of that." Pressed by a reporter about the possibility of threats to expose other gay clergy, Finlay responded, "I don't go around with flashlights, investigating another person's situation. One hears all sorts of rumours. I don't have time to deal with rumours. I'm not about to go out investigating rumours or possible slurs that people may want to make."

All I had to do was lie, it seemed. Apparently, it wasn't that the bishop objected to my loving another man, he just didn't want to hear about it. The message to gay clergy was clear: keep the conspiracy of silence going and the bishop will hold up his end of the bargain.

On Sunday morning I sat in a pew at the Redeemer, where I had been welcomed in the months since I left Unionville, listening painfully to the bishop's pastoral being read. At that very moment in three hundred churches throughout the vast Diocese of Toronto the bishop was passing sentence on me anew. Dozens of gay clergy I knew had to read the sentence condemning one of their gay clergy brothers for his love, and then go home to their own gay partners. My shirt was damp and my head aching from the searing irony. The only difference between them and me was that, in a moment of pain, confusion, and need, I had been honest.

◆

It is time the Church got honest. A wink and a nod and "I'll look the other way" is simply morally bankrupt. For centuries, the Church has maintained a conspiracy of silence, forcing gays and lesbians to lead secret lives; it has used them, rewarded them, perhaps even loved them, and then acted violently against those whose secret was exposed. Is gay love a sin only if and when it becomes known to the public?

Some say that science needs to point the way to acceptance of gays. If it can be proven that sexual orientation is biologically determined, they say, then the Church must accept gays. I say that it will be a tragedy if the Church has to wait for science to prove gay orientation is innate. Surely the Church should be leading the way purely on the basis of its own ethical teachings and its message of inclusive love. The Church didn't have to wait for science to advocate the abolition of slavery. Nor did it take a new scientific discovery to end discrimination against women. What will it take to end discrimination against gays and lesbians?

It is a case of prejudice, ancient and modern. The Bible, to which appeals are so often made, is a book filled with the prejudices and limited understandings of an ancient world. Women were property. So were children. The world was flat. Slavery was condoned. Even genocide was advocated as the Israelites displaced the ancient people of

Canaan. The Church has recognized that these ancient prejudices have obscured the Bible's central message of the equal dignity of every human being, rooted in a love that knows no barriers.

These are dangerous times for gays and lesbians, in society and in the Church. Ironically, this is not because there is more prejudice than ever, but because there is less. Society has already begun to change its fundamental rules on gays, paradoxically at the Church's behest, among others. The mind of the Church has already changed to include gays, if the outrage in Unionville and beyond at my firing is any indicator. It is precisely because we are nearing the end of that process of change in the Church that things are so dangerous. Those few who are locked into old prejudice and hatred are rising up in arms to prevent that change in mind and practice. Tragically, the bishops' fear of the angry, prejudiced few who would exclude many of God's children is more powerful than their love for gospel virtues of honesty, truth, inclusion, justice, and love for all.

I am still puzzled by the bishop's contradictory treatment of another gay priest. A month after my dismissal from Unionville, Douglas Fox wrote a letter to Terry Finlay accusing him of supporting his ministry as a gay priest while firing me at the same time. Six months later, Fox came out publicly at Bishop's Court and made it clear that he was not celibate. Six months after Finlay fired me a second time, Fox not only continued to function with the permission of the Bishop of Toronto, but acted as Finlay's chaplain at the induction of the new rector at All Saints' Church. He stood beside the bishop, holding his pastoral staff and wearing the Integrity rainbow stole. Fox's presence there was living testimony to the arbitrary ways in which bishops and the entire church system treat gays, and to the continuing courage he demonstrated when he came out in Bishop's Court in an effort to end oppression.

♦

As I write this in November 1992, my life is in limbo. The diocese stopped paying me at the end of July, and has not offered me any form of employment. While I am no longer inhibited (prohibited from functioning) as a priest, neither am I licensed to function anywhere. The effect is the same, as no bishop in Canada has come forward to offer me a position, and none is likely to do so for the foreseeable future. I continue to attend Church of the Redeemer in downtown Toronto as a lay person, and I have recently joined the choir there after a year sitting in the pews. Twice now I have been allowed to take turns with other laypeople, reading a scripture passage during Sunday worship. The congregation is welcoming, with many gays in the pews and in leadership roles.

Soon I will begin looking for other work. The vocational counsellor the diocese provided doesn't think it's going to be easy to find an employer for whom my notoriety will be an asset rather than a liability. But even though I don't know what shape my future will take, I still have faith that somehow it will work out.

For the time being I am burdened with the outstanding legal bills for Bishop's Court: more than six hundred donors from across Canada and the United States have been generous in their support, but almost $35,000 remains of the $85,000 it cost to defend myself in court. The diocese has acknowledged its costs for Bishop's Court at well over $100,000, a small portion of its multimillion-dollar budget. Chancellor Hemmerick has retired and Bishop Finlay has replaced him with Bob Falby, some say as a reward for his performance in court.

My life has changed profoundly. I have in fact become the very thing I was trying to avoid: a professional victim, the Church's official faggot, a newsworthy item because I am a gay who happens to be a minister. Newspapers, magazines, and television talk shows continue to seek me out. My privacy is gone, and for many, I am just a one-dimensional character — a gay priest. I long to return to the richness of parish life and ministry that I so enjoyed, to be valued as a good minister who just happens to be gay.

The look of fear mingled with love in the eyes of the man I loved still haunts me. All I ever wanted was to live without fear. Now, at last, I do — but it has involved losing both the man and the vocation I loved. I talk with Ahmad from time to time, and see some signs of growing self-acceptance as he recovers from the pain and loss of the past year and a half. Perhaps some day he will be able to break through the tyranny of fears within and without.

Meanwhile, I intend to continue the struggle to hold the Church accountable to its own message of inclusive love. I refuse to be silenced. Church and society will open up to gays and lesbians only as we stand up and become known as people of love and dignity.

Ultimately, I believe that the Church will drop all its barriers, including its prejudice against gays. In the meantime, it can take some practical steps. It can get to know the many beautiful gay people who already offer so much to the life of the Church. The roots of ignorance and fear can be challenged. And the Church can officially recognize the reality of our lives, by admitting that we are already in her midst, loving and giving; acknowledge that good Christian people disagree about the ethics of the expression of gay sexuality; allow for an official period of ambiguity, so that parishes that would welcome gay clergy are free to do so openly; and then move on to full inclusion, full acceptance, by admitting that a gay person's sexuality is a gift from God. Finally, the Church should affirm and support gay and lesbian couples by officially acknowledging and blessing our relationships, and providing the support we deserve. The General Synod of the Anglican Church of Canada should pass a resolution to hold up one standard of faithful love for all Christian people, regardless of sexual orientation.

There are promising signs that the process is beginning. After Bishop's Court, General Synod added to its triennial meeting agenda in June 1992 a forum on homosexuality. For the first time in a public Anglican forum, the stories of gay Christians were deeply and sensitively heard, and bishops openly presented opposing points of view, ending their pretense of unanimity. An important hurdle has been cleared, allowing good Christian people to openly disagree and dialogue. At General Synod, a serious three-year study and dialogue program for the whole church was approved, the results to be heard at the next General Synod. The issue has been wrestled out of the exclusive hands of the House of Bishops, into the public forum. Several parishes in Toronto have already begun this process of study. And a few brave gay clergy and laypeople across the country have started coming out to their bishops. It is a good beginning.

In the end, of course, legislation will not win the day. A resolution gathering dust in the national archives won't do much to change people's perceptions, attitudes, and behaviours towards gay people. Such change will occur only as Christian people take to heart the mission they proclaim: "to embody — in word and action — God's reconciling love, justice, compassion, and liberation."